ASTROLOGY FOR REAL RELATIONSHIPS

ASTROLOGY FOR REAL RELATIONSHIPS

Understanding You, Me, And How We All Get Along

Jessica Lanyadoo and T. Greenaway

Illustrations by Joel Burden

TEN SPEED PRESS
California | New York

To everyone fighting for dignity, equality, and love—especially in these uncertain times.

CONT

ENTS

INTRODUCTION

I'm going to let you in on a little secret. This book isn't just about relationships. Yes, that's how I've lured you in, but this book is actually about you.

Astrology offers you a great way to learn about the people in your lives. But, more important, it also provides you with useful tools you can use to get to know yourself. Once you understand all the pieces of your own personal puzzle—who you really are and what you really want—you can become an actualized and an empowered participant in each and every relationship you decide to pursue.

Astrology is a vast and amazing system for understanding your insides and your outsides, and how to bridge the gap between the two. And when I talk about relationships and intimacy, I'm really talking about your mental, emotional, and spiritual health. How you feel in your own skin is directly related to how close you are willing to get to other people. And for those of us who have been discouraged from having agency around our feelings and our bodies, letting people in can be especially hard.

I hope you use this book as a resource for understanding how the placement of the planets in your birth chart relates to your intimacy issues with friends, lovers, and romantic partners. Astrology is complicated! So, let's start at the beginning.

WHAT IS ASTROLOGY?

Astrology is a system of divination. It's the study of the movements of celestial objects that has been used throughout cultures and time. Astrologers look at where the planets are in the sky and in relationship to one another to determine cycles and trends of experience.

Astrology isn't a belief system; it's a tool for understanding that has been associated with a wide range of belief systems for thousands of years. There are agnostic astrologers, Buddhist astrologers, anticapitalist Radical Fairy astrologers, and Christian astrologers. There are those who believe everything is light and love, and others who believe we're all doomed. You can apply any spiritual or philosophical viewpoint to the stars.

ARE YOU GOING TO TELL ME ABOUT MY SIGN?

Most popular astrology reduces a super complex, multi-planet system down to your Sun sign. Because of this, people have a tendency to categorize and pathologize individuals based on their Sun signs. That is not only narrow-minded, it's also a missed opportunity. The Sun governs your identity and your sense of self—it's important, yes, but it's just one part of who you are. For instance, the placement of the Moon tells you about your emotions, the placement of Neptune tells you about your ideals, and where Mercury falls in your chart offers insight about your mind and your thoughts.

WHAT IS MY BIRTH CHART?

Your birth chart is a visual representation of the night sky at the moment and location of your birth. In Western astrology, a birth chart is always a circle. It provides you with information about your nature in the past, present, and future. This book won't teach you to thoroughly read birth charts; these charts are a tool for astrology students and professionals alike to more deeply understand the relationship implications of planetary placement by sign and house.

In order to find out in which house a planet is found, you need to know your time of birth and to plug it into a chart-drawing tool along with your birth date and place. You can find one on my website, LoveLanyadoo.com. Your ascendant (also called your Rising Sign) is a key part of your identity and relationships, but this book will not cover the four major angles, the Ascendant (ASC), the Descendant (DEC), the Midheaven (MC), and the Imum Coeli (IC).

Like a pizza with twelve slices, a birth chart is a wheel divided into twelve parts; one for each zodiac sign. These pieces of the pie are called houses (see the list on page 4), and each house governs a part of your nature that gets expressed in different parts of your life. Each sign is governed by a planet and has a house that it calls home (see chart, opposite). All of these layers of information make up your nature.

HOUSES, PLANETS, AND SIGNS

THE HOUSES

FIRST HOUSE: Your personality on the surface and how you present to others

SECOND HOUSE: Your personal values and what you own (your finances)

THIRD HOUSE: Friendship, your neighborhood, and your immediate environment

FOURTH HOUSE: Family of origin and chosen home life; also "mommy issues"*

FIFTH HOUSE: Creativity (including babies and art), play, and dynamic sex

SIXTH HOUSE: Your habits, day-to-day life, work, and your body

SEVENTH HOUSE: Partnership and long-term relationships (your BFFs, your significant other, your active frenemies)

EIGHTH HOUSE: Your sexual drives, deep emotions, and shared resources

NINTH HOUSE: Your philosophies, spiritual beliefs, and attitudes toward religion

TENTH HOUSE: Your conscious life objectives and career; also "daddy issues"*

ELEVENTH HOUSE: Your social life and humanitarian inclinations

TWELFTH HOUSE: Your subconscious, mental health, and very early development/childhood

*I'm referring to archetypes here, not gender roles.

THE SIGNS AND THEIR ELEMENTS AND QUALITIES

All twelve signs are broken down by elements: earth, air, water, and fire. Earth signs set down roots and are concerned with the material world; air signs are motivated by inspiration, freedom, and ideas; fire signs are about excitement, creation, and change; and water signs are responsive, emotional, and deep.

Each of the signs is also associated with a quality: Cardinal, Mutable, or Fixed. These are related to the seasons, and all four elements are represented in each quality. Cardinal signs initiate a season, Fixed signs maintain that season, and Mutable signs mark a time of transition.

ARIES: Cardinal, fire, Mars, first house

TAURUS: Fixed, earth, Venus, second house

GEMINI: Mutable, air, Mercury, third house

CANCER: Cardinal, water, Moon, fourth house

LEO: Fixed, fire, Sun, fifth house

VIRGO: Mutable, earth, Mercury, sixth house

LIBRA: Cardinal, air, Venus, seventh house

SCORPIO: Fixed, water, Pluto, eighth house

SAGITTARIUS: Mutable, fire, Jupiter, ninth house

CAPRICORN: Cardinal, earth, Saturn, tenth house

AQUARIUS: Fixed, air, Uranus, eleventh house

PISCES: Mutable, water, Neptune, twelfth house

MORE ABOUT THE PLANETS

The planets are telling the story of who you are. Here's your quickie cheat sheet:

⊙ **The Sun is your identity.**

☽ **The Moon is your feelings.**

☿ **How you think and communicate is Mercury.**

♀ **How you romantically express yourself is Venus.**

♂ **What you do is Mars.**

♃ **How you intend to grow is Jupiter.**

♄ **What you think is possible or realistic is Saturn.**

♅ **How you seek to break away and be free is Uranus.**

♆ **Neptune is where you're escapist or idealistic.**

♇ **Your relationship to trauma, healing, destruction, and rebirth is Pluto.**

WHY I LOVE THE OUTER PLANETS (AND YOU SHOULD, TOO)

Of the ten planets we use in astrology, five are referred to as the "personal planets." Those are the fast-moving babies: the Sun, Moon, Mercury, Venus, and Mars. Then there are the social planets (Saturn and Jupiter) and the outer or "generational" planets (Uranus, Neptune, and Pluto), which move slower, reveal inherited conditions, and shape the values and experiences of entire generations. The slower-moving planets can seem less personal because so many of us have them in the same places. But what they reveal in your birth chart is deeply personal. You are part of your generation and a product of your ancestry. The generational planets represent the issues that are handed down through our families; they speak to our compulsions, our deepest hopes and fears, and the issues that really drive us. Learning about these planets can serve up truths about us and our intimacy issues that—when revealed—can feel like getting hit by a truck. The inner planets relate to our moods, and the outer planets can unlock our triggers and the keys to our mental health.

The house placements and aspects of the outer planets describe how you are likely to participate in the times in which you live. For the outer planets through the signs, some of the information repeats through the sections, and I've included interpretations specific to friendship, dating, and long-term relationships.

WHEN YOUR STARS DON'T ALIGN

If you read something in this book that doesn't resonate with you, that may be because you have aspects or placements in your chart that shift the context and therefore change the big picture of your experience. Nothing exists in isolation. Your nature is most accurately described with astrology by the synthesis of your planetary placements and aspects.

For example, you may have your Sun in Leo, which is typically a showboaty, "extra" sign. But if you have strong aspects from Saturn—that could be from Saturn sitting on an angle, or being conjunct, square, or opposite two or more planets—it will make you less likely to be stereotypically outgoing. Or you may be a Pisces—traditionally a sensitive and retiring Sun sign—but if you have strong aspects from Jupiter, you will likely be more outgoing, dynamic, and talkative than other people with your Sun sign.

WHAT ARE ASPECTS?

The angular distance between two or more planets (or points) is called an aspect. Different aspects indicate what kind of conversation the planets are having: Are they yelling at each other? Are they snuggling? Are they frenemies?

The major angles that astrologers consider are:

 0 degrees = conjunction = intensity and emphasis, as the planets involved are inseparable

 60 degrees = sextile = creativity and self-expression

 90 degrees = square = challenge and tension

 120 degrees = trine = harmonious flow and opportunity

 180 degrees = opposition = tension and projection

Don't freak out if you see a lot of difficult aspects (squares, oppositions, or even conjunctions) in your birth chart, because, as all astrologers know, tension is directly linked to creativity, and many of the most interesting, dynamic, and successful people have conflicting aspects in life. The key is to make use of your struggles—astrology gives you the tools to do that.

WHY IS THERE SO MUCH CONTRADICTORY INFORMATION IN MY BIRTH CHART?

You'll notice that I often describe binaries when discussing the planets through the houses, using sentences like, "these people either are obsessed with worldly possessions or reject them completely." That's because when I'm talking about astrology in general terms, and when I'm not reading an individual's unique birth chart, there are certain themes that function like coins. We're looking at either its head or its tail, but it's still a nickel. The theme is the same, but its expression may be very different. This doesn't mean that astrology is imprecise or general; it means that no piece of your chart exists in a vacuum. The details of your chart are essential to learn, but their synthesis reveals who you truly are. One planet's placement might indicate that you're suited for casual sex while another will tell you the opposite. In other words, you're a complicated person with mixed feelings and competing needs. Ideally, astrology can help you articulate which part of yourself needs what, so you can live your happiest, most fulfilling life.

You also, of course, have free will, so the choices you've made, and will continue to make, play an important role in shaping how each planetary placement functions for you.

ARE WOMEN REALLY FROM VENUS AND MEN FROM MARS?

Absolutely not. Women, men, and those who live outside the gender binary all have Venus and Mars in their birth charts. In spite of what some people would have you believe, all women are not destined to be nurturers, and all men are not meant to be warriors. People of all genders deserve to have space to be vulnerable and to experience love, connection, weakness, and ambiguity. Everyone deserves to have great sex and cum. Competition, ambition, and anger are not gendered impulses.

The idea of binary genders and rigid roles comes from centuries of male thought, male writing, and male sovereignty over what we collectively agree as true. Men have had the power in publishing, finance, and other influential industries. Women and genderqueer people have often lacked freedom of movement and agency within our economy and the ability to take an active role in society. Men have been telling women what we are for so many centuries that it only makes sense that astrology would reflect the same limited understanding of what gender is/was. Let's not use astrology to pathologize people based on gender, their Sun sign, or anything else. Your birth chart describes your nature, but within your birth chart you have agency, regardless of your gender.

SELF-LOVE AT THE CENTER

This book is meant to be a resource for understanding and coping with whatever comes up in your relationships—but relationships are an inside job. Astrology is an invaluable tool for learning to love yourself, which is an essential part of all your relationships. In order to achieve true intimacy, you must be willing to be loved, liked, and desired—even if it hurts, you fail, or you have to cut your losses, and mourn. We *fall* in love; we don't step intentionally or gracefully into love—and sometimes it's painful.

You don't have to love yourself perfectly in order to have good sex, beautiful friendships, or healthy love relationships. But no matter how many great people you surround yourself with and how wonderful your relationships are, if you're not a good friend and lover to yourself, none of those things will feel like enough.

The goal of relating to others shouldn't be perfection or even permanence. Relationships ebb and flow, and they may end altogether or they may be excellent at times and awful at other times—but none of those things make them failures. Learning not to abandon yourself when the going gets rough is essential. If you're willing to show up and be your best self, you can determine what's healthy for you to do in any given relationship instead of worrying about what other people want or what you "should" do.

Throughout this book, we will look at different forms of loving and relating to others. Self-love is the connective tissue that holds the whole game together. If you don't take care of yourself, you're essentially asking others to take care of you. Finding a healthy balance between caring for yourself, caring for others, and letting yourself be cared for is essential for all relationships to thrive.

Love,
Lanyadoo

ONE

FRIENDS AND CHOSEN FAMILY

Friendship in the modern world is hard. While it's arguably more important than ever, it's also harder than ever to establish and maintain IRL. Astrology isn't just a tool to help you figure out how to date or keep a relationship strong; it also helps you find your true partners in crime, your chosen family, and the people that you can build your best life with. Friends are a resource for understanding yourself and your other relationships; they offer a sounding board and much-needed reality checks, and they love you through your least glamorous moments.

CONNECTING IN REAL LIFE

Understanding your friendships is a powerful way to understand yourself. How you choose to participate in friendship is a reflection of your own nature, aka your birth chart. Your choices, your actions, your feelings—and what you consent to—are all about you.

The planet Mercury is responsible for all collegiate and platonic connections in our lives, including our friends, pals, acquaintances, neighbors, and siblings. Texting, DMing, and talking on the phone are all also ruled by Mercury, because it's the planet of communication, ideas, and plans. Mercury's influence plays an important role in the formation of relationships, but it's only one piece of the puzzle. While it's the main planet we look to for friendship, the more emo connections are ruled by the Moon and

Venus; the way we need to get our identities validated is ruled by the Sun; and the activities we pursue and the pace at which we pursue them are ruled by Mars.

Technology is interwoven in all of our lives and most of us have meaningful online friendships, but when these connections aren't somehow rooted in physical presence and time spent together, the level of trust just isn't the same. (Anyone who has shared secrets over text with someone who may be DMing three other people at the same time knows exactly what I'm talking about.)

We don't need all friendships to hit all the bases, but we do need at least some friendships that *do*—and finding them isn't always easy. Developing connections that encompass more than just our Mercury is important. Availing ourselves of the world, opening ourselves up to interactive experiences IRL, and trying new things, even when it's so much easier to stay home with our screens, is key to developing deeper, more satisfying friendships.

CHOSEN FAMILY

Family isn't just about our long-term relationships and our children—human or fur babies. For those of us who have lost members of our families of origin or don't have great relationships with them, our community of friends serves an essential purpose. But fostering long-term platonic relationships takes effort, care, and a willingness to change over time. Friendships that span ten or more years and involve sharing our seminal life experiences can bring about a form of closeness that we might not be able to find any other way.

When the foundation of love or closeness is there, friendship can take any number of forms. More and more people are opting out of one-on-one romantic partnerships, in favor of polyamorous or less-structured relationships. Cultivating friendships or platonic loves with whom you can grow old (and even cohabitate) is important. As with dating, compatibility in friendship isn't just checking boxes. Ultimately, it's about chemistry, trust, and shared values.

There is no prescription for growing and maintaining friendships because it involves all of the planets in your chart and in the other person's chart. Look to the Moon for how you emotionally avail yourself, Mercury for how you communicate, Venus for how you relate, Mars for the pace you adopt, and the Sun for the style in which you present yourself. Once you tap into your planetary placements, you still have to act.

FRIENDSHIP PRO TIPS

1. Show up. You can't have real intimacy when you're not really there for yourself or the other person.

2. Try. Sometimes friendship is about meeting at carnivals, petting ponies, and holding hands under a rainbow. And sometimes shit gets real. You may have to see your friends make stupid choices, or deal with how someone hurts your feelings. In all these scenarios, friendship requires effort.

3. Listen. It's not just about hearing the words others say. People are always revealing themselves to you, and it's your job to listen—when you get important information and ignore it, you're being a bad friend.

4. Discern. This is different from judging. Discernment means allowing your critical faculties to help you determine what your felt experience is, the information you're being given, and how to apply that to the context of your relationships.

5. Repeat.

Platonic connections either flow or don't. Astrology teaches us that everywhere you go, there you are. In that way, the friendships we get involved in, the people we choose as family, and what we consent to participate in are reflections of our own birth charts.

Planets in the seventh house give you great information about your close one-on-one relationships, platonic or romantic. The eleventh house is where we learn about your approach to groups of friends and group activities. If you don't have planets in either of these houses, you can always look to the planets that rule the sign on the house cusp, which are there to tell you what you need to know.

Draw a diagram of all your connections (circles are cute, but do whatever feels right). Put your bestie in the center, then move outward. It should go from people you hang out with a lot to your work wife, your favorite housemate, the people you like going to movies or shows with but don't trust deeply to friendships that only exist online—from work friends to peers to frenemies, and finally to enemies.

By filling people in to the diagram, you may begin to feel grateful for what you have and more mindful of what you need to cultivate. Friends and enemies exist on the same continuum—people whom you're indifferent to are in their own category.

CONFLICT WITH FRIENDS (MOVE ON OR STICK IT OUT?)

People often come to me for advice at times when they have realized that they're outgrowing many of their friendships. This is especially common between the ages of twenty-six and twenty-nine. (This is a time when we all go through a transit called the Saturn Return, which means that Saturn has cycled through all the signs to return to the exact location it was in when you were born.) There are also other individual transits and cycles that occur when a planet in the sky forms a specific mathematical angle to a planet or point in your birth chart in real time and they can tell you what you're going through, for how long, and what you're meant to get out of it. Many transits and cycles trigger friendship issues, including some associated with middle age. During these periods, people often find themselves longing for their true people.

Astrology describes cycles of development that every human is going to go through, where we question or outgrow our friendships. Of course, this type of questioning doesn't always mean that all your friendships are meant to end. But it can help you get more comfortable doing work within your friendships, and it can also make you more likely to recognize when a relationship is reaching its end. Some people are not meant to be in your life, and some connections can be explosive or destructive, and turn people into your enemies. How someone else feels about you is not in your control, and

it's often just as much about them as it is about you. What you *do* is on you.

There are also times when the people you love do things that annoy, unnerve, or hurt you. In those cases, engaging in conflict with them is a way to invest in the friendship. Processing with people you don't trust is unwise, but when you choose to unpack or process something with a friend, it can be an affirmation of your willingness to work on the friendship.

If you're truly invested in a friendship and you don't communicate what's wrong, you're not giving the person a chance to show up. Most of us don't communicate what's wrong because we want to take care of ourselves by avoiding conflict. Or we overcommunicate problems and we yield a similar result: a lack of intimacy and collaboration, which is the centerpiece of friendship. Similarly, being able to listen without defending yourself is an essential part of what it takes to build friendship and closeness.

There is an abundance of cultural messages to make us think that all conflict is bad. But in order to have true closeness, you'll need to be able to tolerate the hard parts. It's also important to remember what you love about people when you're dealing with what you don't like. Friendship is meant to make you feel at home, so make sure that your friends—and the ways that you show up as a friend—are supportive.

SUN ☉

Time it takes to traverse the zodiac: Approximately 1 year

Sign it rules: Leo

House it governs: Fifth

FRIENDSHIP: THE SUN

The Sun governs your identity and your will. In friendship, that's a huge component of showing up and being your real self. A lot of popular astrology only addresses the Sun's placement in your birth chart, so some of what you're going to see in this section will probably be familiar to you. But it's important to remember that the Sun is only one piece of the puzzle. While there are millions of Geminis or Leos out there, your heart, your soul, and your unique experiences belong to you alone.

The Sun can play an important role in friendship because it rules how we see ourselves—and how we want to be seen and validated by others. And unless a friendship is intimate (and involves the Moon), the way you connect with others platonically can stay fixated on the part of yourself you hope to project. This may look like having all your friends share similar identities, but not necessarily the same Sun sign. In other words, you will likely gravitate toward people whose identities you recognize as similar to your own.

The Sun isn't about appearances; it's about how you feel yourself to be at a core level. It's a very me-focused planet, similar to Mars, and its placement in your chart describes how you relate to others and how they relate to you. It's important that your friends see you in the same ways that you see yourself, even if that means they can see the dark or difficult parts of you. We want our friends to know us. And getting validation from others—of our experience of ourselves—is an essential part of a real friendship.

When we try to hide our true selves from our friends, it's like trying to put the Sun in a dark corner; limiting your own light is a tricky enterprise. While it can be necessary in some situations, it doesn't lead to feeling good over the long haul.

A NOTE ABOUT SUN SIGN ASTROLOGY

When you read your horoscope, you're reading about your Sun sign. Why is modern popular astrology so fixated on the Sun—and on the idea that we all have "a sign," or that we *are* one specific sign? This is largely because the Sun is consistent. It generally moves one degree a day and never retrogrades (that is, it never moves backward in its orbit). There are 30 degrees to each sign, which makes it really easy to know where the Sun was when someone was born, and easy to find out your Sun sign without doing a lot of math. That simplicity has translated brilliantly to mass publication and made it easy to put general information out there that resonates with lots of people.

When astrologers in most Western cultures speak to the general population, as in horoscopes published in newspapers and magazines, identity and will are the focus. They are what people assert themselves with, how they wish to be perceived. The Sun is also a source of our sense of vitality. It's the energy we draw on to shine. These things are incredibly important, though I would argue that there are other, equally important parts of the self. And that's why it's important to develop a holistic understanding of how all the planets function in our charts.

WHAT DOES IT MEAN TO BE "ON THE CUSP"?

Astrology is math! Every zodiac sign is one twelfth of a 360-degree wheel, or 30 degrees, and based on that math, you're either one sign or another. My experience has shown that most people who feel "cuspy" do so because they tend to have planets in two adjacent signs.

HOW TO WORK WITH THIS PLANET

When you shape yourself into what you think others want, you risk dimming your own light. Pay special attention to the people you are comfortable being yourself with and seek more of those types of relationships. A big part of being yourself is listening, so pay attention—with healthy discretion—to what others are reflecting back to you about yourself.

THE SUN THROUGH THE SIGNS

SUN IN ARIES

These people can be supportive, dynamic, and fun. Having them on your side is like befriending a personal cheerleader. On the other hand, they're not the greatest listeners of the zodiac. They can rush to fix problems you didn't ask for help with or get bored by things they think have nothing to do with them. People with the Sun in Aries tend to be quick to get mad, and quick to get over it. They also enjoy having activity partners, especially those who are willing to take physical adventures with them.

SUN IN TAURUS

No one likes pleasure more than a Taurus. These people make loyal and considerate friends, when they're not totally distracted by their own needs and desires. Their support is very valuable because they're good at expressing their love through actions. Problems can arise when there's a conflict because they have a tendency to favor diplomacy over honesty. They're also not the most flexible sign in the zodiac; they tend to be rigid about their perspective, and have a hard time seeing things from others' points of view, which can create problems in friendships.

SUN IN GEMINI

Talkative and easily distracted, Twin Stars have a reputation for being duplicitous. In truth, they can usually see all angles of a thing, and whatever truth they're looking at in the moment can seem like the most important one. They are really fun and willing to do all kinds of activities with friends, including going to the far corners of the Earth when needed. Smart and odd, Geminis are always interesting, if you can maintain their interest. They can be vague, so you may have to press them to commit to plans. But don't worry; that doesn't mean they don't like you.

SUN IN CANCER

Ruled by the Moon, Cancers tend to be quite emotional. They're tender-hearted; once you become part of their friendship circle, you're also part of their family. Cancers are not always great at expressing their feelings and tend to over-articulate or underexpress what's going on for them (after all, the crab comes at things sideways). They are loyal and supportive, and can be defensive when their feelings are hurt or when they feel left out. When a Cancer invites you over to their house, that means you're in. Their ability to make others feel loved is a thing to be cherished, and their sensitivity to others can make them lovely friends.

SUN IN LEO

Leos love to be the center of attention. They are fun, affectionate, and support-ive, and know how to make others shine, but those good feelings can go away if they don't feel properly appreciated and adored. This placement inclines people to be leaders, and they can be quite asser-tive. Leo is a very "extra" sign, and they have a flair for drama, for better or worse. They respond well to flattery, they're creative, and they're usually up for playful adventures. They love to express care for people in grand and sweeping gestures and don't suffer fools. If you've offended a Leo friend, you'll probably hear about it.

SUN IN VIRGO

Thoughtful and often inclined to be introverted, Virgos are the kinds of friends you can talk to about real things. They're down to help you make sense of your world and figure things out. Virgos are generally quite articulate and can be really great listeners. Best of luck getting them out of their routines or convinc-ing them to have dinner somewhere new if they don't want to, though. Once you make it to their inner circle, their loyalty or love is expressed through considerate acts of service.

SUN IN LIBRA

Libras are chill, supportive, and com-promising. This placement makes them naturally good friends, unless they get distracted by other relationships or obli-gations, in which case they can drop the ball. It can be hard for them to express their critical thoughts or their dissent in a clear way, which can mean you don't always know where you stand with them. Or they hold back their frustration with you and don't share it. They can main-tain friendships over the course of time because they honestly care and they're usually willing and able to let things go when need be.

SUN IN SCORPIO

Scorpios are deep, intense, contemplative, and passionate. Once you have earned their respect or captured their interest, they are loyal and steadfast friends. But if you disrespect or insult them, watch out; they don't let it go easily. They are also persistent and can be quite possessive. These people have a depth to them that many other Sun signs are uncomfortable being around. But that depth allows them to show up when things get real and to be a friend when the chips are down. They are not quick to give their word, but when they give it, it's gold.

SUN IN SAGITTARIUS

Sagittarians can be gregarious and open-minded. This placement makes them enthusiastic, supportive, and generous friends. But that enthusiasm can make them likely to encourage people to do things they themselves don't want to do. Sagittarians need to practice listening as much as they speak. They tend to be extroverted and are very capable of growth and change. The archer's arrow is always pointed toward what's just out of reach—and that can be inspiring, or it can give them a sense of futility.

SUN IN CAPRICORN

Capricorns are serious, ambitious, and very hard on themselves. As friends, in youth, they can either be quite wild or very conservative, and there tends to be a flip in their 30s. They can also be very paternalistic friends if they're not careful. They're not the most flexible people; they like to know their place in a relationship and once that has been established they're very dedicated friends. They can be quite reserved until they're comfortable, but once Capricorns are close to you, you'll get to see their goofy sides.

SUN IN AQUARIUS

Aquarians are weird and super fun to be around, but they're not as motivated by intimacy as people born under other signs. If you appeal to their intelligence and are interesting to them, you'll win their favor. This Sun placement gives them really strong opinions about people and the world around them; they're flexible about everything they're not totally rigid about. Their reputation for being aloof is only partially accurate—they can just get really caught up in their own thoughts.

SUN IN PISCES

Pisces are compassionate, empathetic, creative, and open to joining you on your adventures. This can make them really good friends to have—but their self-care is not always on point. And when they don't take good care of themselves, they have a hard time showing up for others. They will show up for you when you ask them to. They can often come across as nonthreatening and need a fair amount of peace and space to recover from the pressures of the world.

THE SUN THROUGH THE HOUSES

SUN IN THE FIRST HOUSE

These people have a tendency to shine. They attract a lot of attention, and people can't help but notice them. They come across as confident, self-possessed, and extroverted. They can also be quite assertive. Feeling seen by others and getting to be their authentic selves is incredibly important to them. They can feel themselves at the center of things, which can incline them to be quite gracious with their friends or a bit demanding of attention, depending on the rest of their charts.

SUN IN THE SECOND HOUSE

What these people value is incredibly important to their sense of self, and they crave friendships where those things are aligned. This placement can be related to having influential or generous friends—or to being influential and generous with other people. They're likely to be quite aware of money and class, and how that breaks down within friendships is dependent on the rest of their charts. These people enjoy indulging in the finer things of life such as shopping, eating out, and seeing art with others. They are likely to be material girls living in a material world.

SUN IN THE THIRD HOUSE

These people make great friends as they really value friendship and prioritize having different people in their lives for different reasons. They tend to be very inquisitive, interested in the world around them, and capable of multitasking. In regard to friendship, they connect with people for different parts of themselves. This placement can incline them to be distractible or, with difficult aspects, it can make them prone to forgetting what they've said after the fact.

SUN IN THE FOURTH HOUSE

These people are inclined to be a bit shy or reserved. They have a need for downtime, and their closest friends can be like a sanctuary to them. This placement can cause them to be loyal friends, but it can also incline them to be a bit needy. Once someone makes it into the inner circle of someone with the Sun in the fourth house, a lot of expectations and needs around security will emerge.

SUN IN THE FIFTH HOUSE

This placement indicates people who are creative and have a strong sense of self. Self-expression is incredibly important to them; they can be charming, charismatic, and super fun to be around—or, conversely, really good at icing a binch. This placement inclines people to need to have fun, and play is a meaningful part of how they connect; it also influences who they connect with.

SUN IN THE SIXTH HOUSE

These people are dutiful, faithful friends. They have the capacity to be very consistent. But with difficult aspects, they can also get caught up in navel-gazing. They will sometimes forget to value friendship, but they are quite reliable when it comes to showing up for people. The sixth house is a service-oriented house where reciprocity does not always come naturally, so they need to make an effort to allow others to show up for them.

SUN IN THE SEVENTH HOUSE

Partnership is incredibly important to these people. They need to have besties and work wives. They are really fixated on having close relationships and will often prioritize them over other parts of their lives (such as professional obligations, self-care, and so on). They have a tendency to be great at compromising and are easy to get along with. With difficult aspects, they can be kind of superficial and pretty bad at listening.

SUN IN THE EIGHTH HOUSE

These people are intense and private and have the tendency to either intensely avoid or intensely confront important things. As friends, they may disappear or ghost from time to time. With difficult aspects, they have to be wary of addiction and the tendency to hide from others. Having friends in their lives with whom they can be their messy, intense selves is essential for their self-acceptance and happiness.

SUN IN THE NINTH HOUSE

This placement inclines people to have idealistic natures. They're authentically interested in their friends and the world around them. Exploration is a huge part of how they relate to others and it's really good for them to have diverse friendships. If they're not careful, they can be prone to interrupting others.

SUN IN THE TENTH HOUSE

These people often feel a need to prove themselves or to get validation for who and what they are. This placement makes them ambitious and responsible; but when things get rough, they can be a bit controlling. They can often forget to prioritize their personal lives, and so friendships can fall to the wayside. They're loyal to their friends and willing to show up for them in practical terms and do whatever work the relationship requires over the long haul.

SUN IN THE ELEVENTH HOUSE

People with this placement do well in social circles and are often involved with organizations or group efforts. They can also be a bit rigid about their beliefs, while simultaneously being curious and willing to see things from many angles. They need variety and mental stimulation in friendships. This placement tends to concern people with the world around them (such as social issues), or it can incline them to have lots of online friendships rather than IRL.

SUN IN THE TWELFTH HOUSE

These people have a deep need to spend time alone recovering from other people because they are sensitive to external energies. They can be giving and supportive friends, but they're not naturally good at clear boundaries. Easily influenced by those around them, it's important they choose friends who inspire and support them. Remembering to be honest about where they're at is an essential part of having true intimacy with platonic loves.

MOON ☽

Time it takes to traverse the zodiac: Approximately 29.5 days

Sign it rules: Cancer

House it governs: Fourth

FRIENDSHIP: THE MOON

The Moon governs your feelings, your past, your feelings *about* the past, and your sensory impressions of events. How safe and wanted you feel is wrapped up in your Moon.

Friendships that are more about socializing and engaging in activities don't necessarily involve the Moon. But true friendship and chosen family are deeply lunar because whenever you trust and rely on somebody, you are dealing with your Moon.

The people we attract into our lives offer us opportunities to show up and be there for them, as well as a chance to allow ourselves to trust, be cared for, and to intentionally build the kind of family, community, and kinship that we seek. But in order to get true support from others, we must let them know us. And the ways that we reveal ourselves to others and the ways we respond to other people's nakedness and vulnerability are all under the jurisdiction of the Moon.

EVERYTHING IS CONNECTED

The Moon also governs our childhood and our memories. It's important to note that our feelings at any given time aren't just about that moment. They're also about our memories—particularly the ones from childhood.

The Moon governs our style of emotional connection and our desire for that connection. It's ultimately a very private planet; we see its light at night and for this reason, it tends to be related to our private lives and to our subconscious selves. We process and digest information through our feelings. A really common mistake we make in the modern world is to try to process feelings analytically as a way to take charge of them. The trouble with this is if your emotional nature is to be suspicious, you'll interpret all incoming data—including kindness and generosity—through that suspicion. The more emotional self-awareness and self-acceptance you have, the greater your ability to relate to others with your whole heart. This allows you to make healthy choices around whom to trust and when, as well as how deeply you decide to trust them over time.

SHOWING UP

A good way to leverage your Moon in friendship is to cultivate presence. Sometimes the best way to be a friend is to simply show up and bear witness with compassion, but we're not always able to show up for our friends. We may be excited or spun out about a new lover or we might be experiencing major career growth or challenges. That's okay, but don't expect other people to fold in and around your needs and then show up when you need them. Remember to prioritize your friends and to maintain a back and forth with them. It is also a perfectly fair thing for you to expect from others.

With love relationships, there's an expectation that you'll break up, fight, and struggle—that's just part of it. But we tend to expect our friendships to be perfect, lasting, and without conflict. In real life, people change, grow, and evolve— and the Moon plays an important role in all of it. You struggle, you work on it, hopefully you grow together, but sometimes you outgrow each other.

HOW TO WORK WITH THIS PLANET

Have you asked your friends how they're feeling and practiced really listening? Have you shared with the people you are close with what's actually going on for you? Practice not offering advice, fixes, or edits—just listen and be present for whatever is real.

THE MOON RULES YOUR EMOTIONS

The Moon governs your emotions, your childhood memories, and the assumptions that you make based on your past experiences.

You may think all kinds of complicated things, but the range of options for how you feel is simpler than you may realize:

Do you feel s ad, angry, happy, afraid?

When you are able to sit with your emotions, you can identify the motional bedrock beneath what's happening in your life.

THE MOON THROUGH THE SIGNS

MOON IN ARIES

Adventurous, bold, quick to get annoyed, and quick to get over it, people with the Moon in Aries are so independent, they may need to make an extra effort to make the people in their lives feel wanted and valued. Asking for help is not always easy for them, and they can take risks (and take too much on by themselves), whether or not it's necessary. They're more comfortable leading than following. With difficult aspects they may also find themselves irritable and overly concerned with how much space they're taking up.

MOON IN TAURUS

People with this placement are sensual and highly prize their friendships. They feel things viscerally and need validation from their friends (food is a great gift for them). Their sensory impressions are strong, and it's not always easy for them to change their opinions of others once they've made up their minds. While they may be drawn to groups of friends, they're likely to do best in one-on-one connections, so they can give and receive the kind of attention they prefer.

MOON IN GEMINI

People with the Moon in Gemini have emotional versatility and flexibility in how they relate, how they show up, and who they show up with. They are genuinely interested in other people, even if sometimes that interest is a little heady. Easily distracted, they need a lot of different friends for different parts of themselves. Active friendships are the most satisfying, whether that means riding bikes together, taking a class together, or just meeting up to gossip.

MOON IN CANCER

These people are emo (with a side of extra emo). Their emotional responses can be consuming, and they can get overwhelmed by all that they feel and experience. They have a strong need to be needed and want to feel like they can contribute to their friends' lives. It's important that these people make sure that they're clearly communicating their needs before they decide to confront their friends about an issue in the relationship. What may seem obvious to them, may not be obvious to their friends.

MOON IN LEO

People with the Moon in Leo are magnetic, self-reliant, and warm. They can be very generous with their time and their possessions. They really like when people appreciate what they've brought to the table, and when they don't feel appreciated, they can take it extra hard. They have huge hearts, but they're not always very patient about other people's perspectives. They need friends who they can have fun with and who share their creative, artistic sensibilities and preferences.

MOON IN VIRGO

Discerning, contemplative, and introspective, these people can be a bit directive within their friendships as they have strong preferences around how to spend their time and what works for them. They also have strong minds and retentive memories, which means they can have a hard time letting things go; even things that are not actually very important to them in the big picture. They need downtime to support the needs of their hearts, and they usually find one-on-one friendships the most enriching and satisfying.

MOON IN LIBRA

People with this placement care a lot about their friends and can be quite gracious, charming, and chill. They are also diplomatic and not super decisive. They favor partnership-style friendships, and this placement can lend itself toward codependency. They have a hard time engaging in difficult conversations, but they benefit from learning to initiate challenging exchanges and cultivating radical honesty with their friends.

MOON IN SCORPIO

These people are loyal, willing to stick around through difficult times, and not easily scared off by the intensity of others. They're the ones you want around in a crisis. They have deep and powerful emotions, and it can be hard for them to let go of negative experiences. They need a fair amount of space and time away from humans. They are intuitive—and may even have psychic tendencies—but they need to pair their intuition with evidence (luckily, Moon-in-Scorpio people are willing to sleuth the evidence out). These people hate being talked about, but they

are also likely to indulge in gossip. And with difficult aspects, they can be reclusive or paranoid.

MOON IN SAGITTARIUS

People with this placement are so optimistic that they may be foolhardy and jump into situations they technically shouldn't be involved with—but it usually tends to work out well anyway. They may believe that anything is possible and therefore they can see and relate to a wide range of perspectives. While they are very independent, they can have one-track minds, and they love nothing more than partners in adventure and people with whom they can have great experiences. But sometimes they also need to go their own way and might have a tendency to suffer from depression. Honesty is incredibly important to them, even though they're prone to exaggeration.

MOON IN CAPRICORN

The Moon is the least comfortable in this sign. These people are emotionally reserved, sensitive to criticism, and uncomfortable with vulnerability. This position tends to cause people to be critical and brooding, but that energy can also help them develop humility and ownership for their feelings and their needs. In turn, these people often develop a pragmatic approach to relationships. Friendship is rarely easy for them, but they are steadfast and willing to put in the work to make their true relationships stand the test of time.

MOON IN AQUARIUS

These people are interesting friends who are likely to bring surprises to the table. Their relationships and communities need to reflect their unconventional, independent beliefs and values, and they can be friendly and good at talking to different kinds of people. They can also come across as a bit cold, as they're prone to processing their emotions in their minds. Once you get on their bad side, they can be quite dismissive. They are more concerned with what's next than what's behind them. There's often a need for these people to pace themselves in their friendships so that they don't overextend themselves and blow out their nervous systems.

MOON IN PISCES

People with this placement are compassionate, supportive, empathetic, and sympathetic. They're deeply influenced and impacted emotionally by the people around them. Their emotional style of supporting others is devotional, so they have to be careful not to get involved in martyred dynamics, where they repeatedly show up for friends who aren't willing or able to do so in return. They need to establish boundaries and take time to recover from the world, so their closest friends are often the people with whom they can share their sanctuary time. They can be quite optimistic, but that optimism can also be rooted in disassociation if they're not careful.

THE MOON THROUGH THE HOUSES

MOON IN THE FIRST HOUSE

People with this placement wear their hearts on their sleeves. Their emotions often play on their faces, and they may be quick to tears. They have a tendency either to be really warm and close with people or to try to hold others at arms' length in an effort to protect themselves. It's important that they always have one or two trustworthy friends who really get them and let them show up authentically.

MOON IN THE SECOND HOUSE

These people have a great need for stability and prefer their friends to be affirming, validating forces in their lives, rather than sources of drama. They express friendship through their actions and are generally affirming and loyal friends themselves, even if they're not the most flexible people in the world. They also like cute things and cute people, and they like being cute with them.

MOON IN THE THIRD HOUSE

People with the Moon in the third house are capable of having many friends, but the magic number for them is three. While they can get enveloped by their emotions, they can also be quite distracted because they're a little restless. They may come across as fickle, but they earnestly change their mind and opinions often. Their friends are an important part of their lives and their ability to meet new people is strong, unless they have other aspects in their chart that say otherwise.

MOON IN THE FOURTH HOUSE

This placement makes people intensely security-oriented. Their feelings and needs are foundational to their wellness, and they have much less energy for casual pals than they do for real, meaningful connections. Their intense emotionality can also cause them to act in self-centered ways at times, so it's important for them to remember to check in with other people about how they are feeling.

MOON IN THE FIFTH HOUSE

Creative, playful, and imaginative, these people can be easily distracted by flirting and romantic entanglements. For this reason, they do well when they remember to make dates with friends and with the people they want to invest in and maintain strong platonic connections with. Pleasure is really important to them, and they're inclined to make decisions based on what will bring them the most joy.

MOON IN THE SIXTH HOUSE

The Moon in the sixth house inclines people to be methodical about what works for them and how they want to live. They tend to be attached to the way they schedule their lives and so they can vacillate between being very accommodating or being quite rigid about making plans. They enjoy service-based projects or any activities that help build the world they want to be living in. Their bodies often tell them when it's time to leave the party even if their minds would rather stay.

MOON IN THE SEVENTH HOUSE

People are drawn to these folks but they can be approval-oriented, may overextend themselves, or may highly prioritize their relationships. They really value having a best friend. It's important that their relationships with themselves don't suffer for all the energy they give to others. They risk idealizing others and can also find it hard to see faults in their friends.

MOON IN THE EIGHTH HOUSE

Super sensitive and intense, these people are inclined to periods of brooding and need to hide away from the needs and prying eyes of others. Their intensity lends itself toward fierce loyalty and protectiveness of the people they love; conversely, it can make them evasive and hard to get to know. With challenging aspects they may even have paranoid or vengeful ways.

MOON IN THE NINTH HOUSE

These people are really open-minded and enjoy having various kinds of friends, ideally all over the world. Their hearts are capable of holding many kinds of intimacies, and they may also experience multiple layers of friendship. They're idealistic and a bit restless, and have periods where they're in frequent contact with friends and then go quiet at other times. But their hearts remain faithful, even when they're less in touch with those they care about.

MOON IN THE TENTH HOUSE

Their reputation is important to these people, and they need their friendships to feel like they're in some way connected to their larger life goals. They're able to connect with colleagues and peers with grace. They can also be a bit domineering or patronizing with hard aspects in their charts. Their sense of belonging in the world is terribly important to them, but they may also be inconsistent in how they place value on it.

MOON IN THE ELEVENTH HOUSE

People with this placement have an expansive attitude toward others and place value on their friends' uniqueness or individuality. They do well when they feel they're part of a community. Group activities and being part of a crew of friends can be really satisfying for them. Having a sense of connection goes a long way toward personal satisfaction in general and, in turn, it can feed their friendships.

MOON IN THE TWELFTH HOUSE

These people need time where they're not being productive to recharge their batteries, and their most healthy friendships will take that into consideration. This placement can make people a bit shy or retiring, but when they've let others in, they'll drop everything and show up for them because they're emotionally generous with their fam. Learning to check in with themselves effectively enables them to set healthy limits with their friends so they don't overextend and create problems as a result.

MERCURY ☿

Time it takes to traverse the zodiac: Approximately 1 year

Signs it rules: Gemini, Virgo

Houses it governs: Third, sixth

FRIENDSHIP: MERCURY

Mercury governs friendship and other platonic bonds, like the ones we have with our neighbors, siblings, cousins, aunts, and uncles. It's the planet that governs our thoughts and attitudes, as well as how we process information. Mercury is important because it rules our style of understanding information and how we communicate, including how we use social media, and text, email, or DM our friends.

MENTAL HEALTH AND MERCURY

Mercury has a lot of sway in our culture. In the Western world, we often lump mental and emotional health together. And while they're definitely interconnected, they're not the same thing. Information is processed through the mind and digested through the heart. As a culture, we prioritize our thoughts over feelings. We prize intellect and external verbal forms of communication, instead of leaving the space to process emotionally.

I like to think of Mercury as the big-ass disembodied head in *The Wizard of Oz* . . . which is really just a scared little man hiding behind a curtain. When there's too much Mercury in your life, you can hide behind your thoughts and ideas as a way to disconnect from your feelings.

Mercury is also one of the two planets (along with the Moon) that rules subjectivity. It's the force behind the (very human) tendency to generate narratives and experiences that match what we're hoping to see. So, it's essential to look at where you have Mercury in your chart to understand how you communicate and also how you listen. Mercury's placement also has everything to do with how you relate to people and how deep you tend to want your friendships to be. If you want true intimacy with friends, it's important to pay attention to the actual words you're saying and home in on how they impact others—as well as what your friends are trying to tell you about their experiences.

ON BEING RIGHT

We can't achieve or maintain true intimacy if we always insist we're in the right. We may have self-reinforcing ideas about our self-worth (good and bad) or about the value of what we offer our friends—for instance you might think you've been generous with others who feel they haven't gotten enough from you. But what matters is that you're willing to hear what your friends have to say, without planning your response, without defending yourself. You don't need to agree with others in order to really hear them.

Mercury is a fast-moving planet that can incline us to want to rush from idea to idea. Being able to sit with challenging information about yourself or someone you care about—and build mutual understanding—is a skill worth cultivating. And it will bring you closer to your friends. Mercury also governs your mental wellness (not illness) and your ability to recognize when you need to take care of yourself, as well as your capacity for self-care. People often ghost their friends when they're unsure of how to handle uncomfortable situations, or when they get so overwhelmed they absolve themselves of communicating what's going on. When you completely disappear on people for periods of time, it inevitably prompts them to come up with their own stories about why. As a result, you can create fissures in the relationships.

HOW TO WORK WITH THIS PLANET

Remember to listen to others and what they tell you about themselves in equal parts to what you share about your own experience. Friendship is meant to be a two-way street. Take a few minutes to look back at past texts with friends; have you expressed interest in their lives? Have they expressed genuine concern about you?

MERCURY THROUGH THE SIGNS

MERCURY IN ARIES

People with Mercury in Aries are playful and forward-thinking. They're often focused on where things are going and how to get there. Beginnings are really fun for them, and they love situations in which they can shine. They can also be headstrong and have a hard time moving on once they get stuck on an idea. They have to be careful to not steamroll their friends. They're good judges of character who can be really warm or ice-cold when they want to be.

MERCURY IN TAURUS

These people are loyal, considerate, and protective of their friends. This placement also inclines them to be stubborn. They tend to be cautious because they like to feel secure. With refined senses, they're uncomfortable with a lot of change, as well as unpleasant smells or noises. They know what they like, but they may not always be forthcoming about their preferences out of a drive to be diplomatic—sometimes to the point of being disingenuous when there are challenging aspects in play.

MERCURY IN GEMINI

People with this placement are quick-witted and very adept at communication. They enjoy engaging with new ideas, meeting new people, and having new experiences. They're likely to be smart, chatty, and charming, and often talk with their hands. They can sometimes stay on the surface as a way to keep things moving. When they get caught up in a story, they often embellish and add details to make things more exciting.

MERCURY IN CANCER

These people are fantastic friends. They're clannish and have a tendency to turn their friends into family. They can be overly concerned about whether or not people like them, but they're also very dedicated to those they care about. Often secretive or private, they have a tendency to come at things indirectly or sideways, instead of saying them straight out. They are emotional processors and can hold back a fair amount. They're also sensitive and have strong sense impressions that incline them toward having strong opinions about people.

MERCURY IN LEO

When Mercury is in the sign of Leo, you'll find people who are dynamic and fiery and take up a lot of space. These people are also playful and have a tendency to want to keep things light. They're generally not shy and are good at making friends and cheering people up. They're loyal, but easily irritated with others when it feels like their friends are dragging them down or dimming their lights in any way. They like to be respected as a force within their circle of friends. Depending on the placement in the chart, people with this placement can also have warm, rich voices.

MERCURY IN VIRGO

Critical, discerning, and pragmatic, these people are really thoughtful friends who can help others unpack their problems, and they're good at showing up for people if they decide to do so. They are critical but also super insightful. This placement inclines people toward introversion, and they often need time to process their thoughts and feelings away from others. They tend to take in so much data and notice so much that it can be overwhelming. With difficult aspects, these people can be reclusive and have a hard time opening up to others.

MERCURY IN LIBRA

People with Mercury in Libra are dedicated friends and their besties (they may have several) are especially important to them. They place a high value on fairness and look at situations from all angles, which can make them indecisive; the upside is that it can inspire them to be quite agreeable. They prefer to avoid conflict, and they treat others well whenever they can. With difficult aspects they may be straight-up superficial—or find that they tend to surround themselves with frenemies. Like Mercury in Taurus, people with this placement are sensitive to smells and sounds.

MERCURY IN SCORPIO

These people will climb any mountain and swim any sea for the people they care about. They are steadfast friends, but they also need their space and privacy. They have deep and penetrating minds and can be private and secretive, with a tendency to develop paranoia. They're also very sensitive to power dynamics and, with difficult aspects, can become consumed by power struggles. It's important that they have healthy boundaries and self-care around their dealings with others. This is a very psychic or intuitive placement.

MERCURY IN SAGITTARIUS

People with this placement are fun, inspiring, and really great at supporting those they care about. They enjoy engaging in projects with friends, exchanging ideas, and making intricate plans. They also have a tendency to be so enthusiastic about what they think that they say it before they consider the consequences (this placement governs foot-in-mouth syndrome). They're great at seeing the big picture and often overlook details. With difficult aspects they can also lecture from a soapbox and may not be the best listeners.

MERCURY IN CAPRICORN

People with Mercury in Capricorn have great common sense and are willing to do the real-life work involved in friendship. They are cautious, are very concerned with right and wrong, and process life methodically. They often make friends through their work lives and tend to gravitate toward people who share their practical concerns and lifestyle choices. With difficult aspects they may decide that most people just aren't worth it— because of how little sense others make

to them. Their tone can be a little heavy, and they have to be careful not to come across as judgmental or condescending.

MERCURY IN AQUARIUS

People with this placement are witty, are quick at processing information, and tend to be chatty; they may speak fast and have to be careful not to interrupt or finish other people's sentences. This placement inclines them to be a bit eccentric or at least to be perceived as eccentric in their circle of friends. They are great at seeing the symbolism in things and good at reading people. They're very tolerant and open-minded about everything they're not totally pigheaded about.

MERCURY IN PISCES

These folks make tender and considerate friends, but they can get into trouble when they say *yes* to people or situations that aren't right for them. Developing boundaries is important for people with this placement. They are sensitive, empathetic, and creative and can have a hard time in discordant environments. They can also be a bit anxious, and it's important they have emotionally generous people surrounding them. They can vacillate on decisions or change their minds easily and often; this can make it hard for them to make plans with friends.

MERCURY THROUGH THE HOUSES

MERCURY IN THE FIRST HOUSE

These people are chatty, restless, and easily distractible. When thoughts occur to them, you can see it on their faces. Unless there are hard aspects, this is an excellent placement for making friends, fostering contacts, and keeping in touch. They are naturally good at verbally expressing themselves and may have a tendency to bring conversations back to themselves or filter data through their own experiences, so they may need to train themselves to be better listeners and remember that it's valuable to consider other people's points of view.

MERCURY IN THE SECOND HOUSE

This placement can yield a methodical yet diplomatic processing style. These people can be security-oriented; they want things to be stable and have a hard time speaking out if they think it will shake things up. Their friends are really important to them, and they love having someone to be in constant contact with. They can be very persuasive and with difficult aspects they may be stubborn or act like braggarts.

MERCURY IN THE THIRD HOUSE

People with Mercury in the third house tend to be quick and blessed with versatile thinking. They are flexible, fun, and just weird enough to be interesting in lots of environments. They make great writers, although they don't always have the impulse or patience to write. They also want to be really good neighbors—they want to connect with the people around them, make small talk, and do what's needed to build up personal connections. Their siblings may be important to them. They're curious and restless and may have the tendency to fly too close to the Sun. This placement can incline people to be prone to gossip.

MERCURY IN THE FOURTH HOUSE

Memories and the past are important reference points by which people with this placement evaluate the present. This may cause them to have either terrible memories or fantastic, deep memories. They tend to feel the happiest when their friends feel like family to them. But they can be private and, while they're a little quick to develop surface trust, it takes them some time to develop authentic trust. They're capable of being true friends 'til the end—and not always in the best way. They can be clannish and hesitant to change their friendships or end connections that are clearly no longer working for them.

MERCURY IN THE FIFTH HOUSE

These people are playful and enjoy shooting the shit. Laughter is really important to them, and the friends who share their sense of humor are their faves. They may have a tendency to jump to conclusions and a flair for drama. They are creative, pleasure-seeking, and great entertainers. While they can be fierce or dramatic, they also really want people to like them and can feel quite hurt if it seems they don't. They also need to watch out for gossip, especially if it's malicious.

MERCURY IN THE SIXTH HOUSE

This placement can give people reflective and practical dispositions. They have their own ways of doing things, thinking about things, and showing up with people. Unless aspects in their chart say otherwise, they don't take kindly to challenges to their habits. It's really important for them to have healthy habits, especially around food and fitness, so friends who like eating what they do and value exercise in the same ways they do help them feel comfortable in their own skins.

MERCURY IN THE SEVENTH HOUSE

Partnership and friendship are super important to these people. They need BFFs and can even treat their regular Fs as BFFs. Depending on other aspects in their birth charts, they are inclined to debate as a way of connecting or, at the other side of the extreme, keep the peace at all costs. They may need to work to balance the amount of energy and attention they give and receive because their friendships can incline them to err on the side of giving either too much or too little.

MERCURY IN THE EIGHTH HOUSE

These people tend to have deep, penetrating insights and the ability to see what's inside a situation. This placement makes them intuitive, loyal, and willing to do the work of keeping things real. It can also make them sarcastic, paranoid, or possessive. They prefer one-on-one friendships and tend to share different truths with different friends (they can be like emotional squirrels hiding nuts in the yards of many different people). They also definitely need downtime to decompress from other people's energies.

MERCURY IN THE NINTH HOUSE

Learning, culture, and travel are all interesting to these people and are important factors in how they relate. This placement inclines people to seek the truth, but it can have them so caught up in the search that they don't always stop and integrate the data. Education is very important to them, and many of their friendships may originate in school or from their travels.

They can have inspired bolts of insight, which can be a great asset within their friendships. If they're not great listeners, this placement can have them interrupting or talking over people in their enthusiasm.

MERCURY IN THE TENTH HOUSE

Ideas and communication are incredibly important to these people, and their friendships can be big parts of their identities. They tend to impress others—one way or another—with what they have to say. Career is very important to them and can take up a distracting amount of their time. Having work wives and peers with whom they can have collegiate relationships is very satisfying and engaging for them. They should also be extra careful not to engage in dogma or black-and-white thinking.

MERCURY IN THE ELEVENTH HOUSE

This placement gives people a quick and inventive processing style, and they can be idealistic, fickle, or simply of many minds. They have varied interests, and are likely to have many kinds of friendships with different kinds of people. Being parts of groups or organizations is an excellent way for them to meet and connect with people. This placement makes them social, tolerant, and low-key weird. Even though they're distractible, collaboration and skill-sharing is their happy place.

MERCURY IN THE TWELFTH HOUSE

This placement can make people quite suggestible, and they prefer not to be too assertive or aggressive with others, though they do crave attention. It's important that they have alone time and space to figure out what they think in their own terms. If not, they may face challenges with their self-esteem. They are sympathetic, generous with their time and energy, and either genuinely curious about other people or completely turned off to them. They are intuitive, creative, and adept at seeing the interconnectedness of things.

VENUS ♀

Time it takes to traverse the zodiac:
Approximately 1 year

Signs it rules: Taurus, Libra

Houses it governs: Second, seventh

FRIENDSHIP: VENUS

Venus is an important planet for friendship; it governs our social urges—who we like, what we like, how we like, and even social media "likes." Venus makes us feel loved, desired, chosen, and safe in those connections. Where we have Venus in the chart, we don't want to be simply tolerated, we want to be embraced. It rules our impulses to hang out with other people and what we like to do with them, as well as how we make others feel cared for and how we metabolize other people's friendship and love. Although Venus can get a bad reputation for keeping things on the surface, it also enables people to be true lovers, attentive hosts, and a nurturing force.

VENUS AND YOUR SENSES

Venus is also a planet of the arts, in a similar but different way than Neptune is (Neptune is high art; Venus is more about things such as clothing, aesthetics, and design). Shopping and other self-indulgent or pleasure-seeking behaviors are also ruled by this planet, as are our personal finances and possessions. When you make friends with people who like the same music, wear the same clothes, and follow the same social media accounts, that's your Venus responding to their Venus. The planet governs sensuality and brings people together, but it's not what keeps them close—that's more likely to be the Moon (see pages 23 to 29). Venus rules the style of connection we enjoy. The way we present ourselves is related to what we value and what we want others to think we value, as well as the signals we send and the way we curate our external selves for others. The placement of Venus in our charts dictates things such as the volume of sound we can tolerate in a bar, the types of food we like to share, and whether or not we actually care about the strength of our coffee. It's also the reason people from similar class backgrounds tend to flock together. For some people that doesn't mean much and for others it means everything, whether they embrace capitalism and are ruled by their aesthetic values, or because they don't care about those things and need the people around them not to care either.

The energies of Venus are diplomatic and agreeable, often to a fault. It's not healthy or kind to pretend to like something you don't or to consent to something that you don't want to do. In friendship it's really important to be seen for who and what you are. When people like you for something that's not authentic to who you are—for reasons that are curated instead of heartfelt—it can feel pretty bad.

HOW TO WORK WITH THIS PLANET

The key to working with Venus is to figure out how to be real *and* diplomatic at the same time, and to prioritize authenticity over accommodation. When we misrepresent ourselves in efforts to be diplomatic, it can actually have a pretty negative effect on our self-esteem. The way out of situations where we feel liked for inauthentic reasons is always to be more ourselves and to be willing not to be liked sometimes. When we are ourselves and people don't like us for it, it doesn't mean we're not likable—it means we're not compatible with them.

VENUS THROUGH THE SIGNS

VENUS IN ARIES

People with Venus in Aries like to initiate connection. This placement makes them outgoing, enthusiastic, supportive of others, and great at being the ringleader. They have a tendency to act before they consider the consequences. They may be quick to take offense but also quick to get over it. They're really good at drumming up energy and enthusiasm and making people feel welcome (or unwelcome) when they want to.

VENUS IN TAURUS

These people are sensual; they appreciate beauty, food, clothing, and music— anything that speaks to their senses. They pretty much want to be adored and can also be quite stuck in their ways; they value consistency and have somewhat fixed ideas about how people should act with one another. It's a sociable placement, but true, deep, and lasting friendship is reserved for a lucky few. Appearances can matter too much, and it's important for them to remember that the people around them are not commodities. They're also loving and sensitive to the needs and desires of others and make loyal friends for those they deem worthy.

VENUS IN GEMINI

People with this placement tend to have lots of friends because they are flexible and have versatile natures. They love quick wit. They are curious, restless, and love having fun; they're also interested in many things, but few of them hold their interest for very long. They need different kinds of friends for different parts of themselves; it's important that they have both casual connections and deep friendships.

VENUS IN CANCER

This is the "smother-love" placement. It gets that reputation because these people can be focused on giving and getting validation for the bonds they share with others. They hope to have family and friends be more or less the same thing. Because they're so emotionally sensitive, they can be easily hurt. It can be hard for them to tell someone directly when they feel upset, which can get them into trouble if they let things fester. Their desire to feel at home with others makes them great hosts and conscientious friends, as well as being willing to do the work of maintaining relationships.

VENUS IN LEO

People with Venus in Leo enjoy playing, partying, and spending time with their friends. They love being the center of attention, because it makes them feel valued and seen, but this comes with a danger that they'll be too reliant on attention. They are likely to be very creative and knowing what's cool is important to them. Their social capital is often wrapped up in their ability to get along well with others or to be recognized as powerful, valuable, or important. While they can be very warm, loyal, and effusive with the people they care about, they can be equally sharp and dismissive with those they don't.

VENUS IN VIRGO

People with Venus in Virgo have analytic natures, which is really helpful for dissecting a friend's crush but can be low-key annoying when it's time to spontaneously change plans or support someone who is making bad choices. Because this placement inclines people to be introverted, they may come across as quite shy or reserved; it's often associated with people who either really hate socializing with people at work or people who have lots of work wives. Ultimately, they care about humanity, even if humans bug them. And they need friends who are contemplative and reliable when it counts.

VENUS IN LIBRA

These people just want to get along and don't see the need for drama, even though they love gossiping. They would rather tell an untrue nicety than upset someone with an uncomfortable truth. They like to keep things light and need to have friends who are lovely to be around, which is great, until they need people who will stick around for the rough stuff. Their closest friends may be people who they don't hang out with frequently but are important to them; their need for meaningful relationships runs deep. They are creative, insightful, and not great at standing up for themselves, so they should be careful not to align themselves with bullies.

VENUS IN SCORPIO

People with this placement are passionate and intense about those they care for, even if they can be paranoid and defensive, too. Sensitive to the fear of being rejected, they can be a little reserved, even though they love getting attention for the parts of themselves that they like. They need to make sure they don't disappear or isolate themselves from friends without letting them know why. Their nature is to have close, one-on-one friendships, but it's important for them to have casual friends, too, because sometimes they just need to keep it on the surface.

VENUS IN SAGITTARIUS

The life of the party, these people are friendly, warm, and outgoing. They tend to be demonstrative, put themselves out there, and have a diverse set of friends. Because they're easily distracted, they're not always fantastic listeners. Sagittarius is the placement of the eternal student, so the friendships they make through courses or workshops, or while traveling, have extra sparkle for them. They have to watch out for their tendency to steamroll people when trying to help them, as their help isn't always wanted; that said, they love collaborating and inspiring others.

VENUS IN CAPRICORN

These people are reliable, serious about their friendships, and willing to go the extra mile for those they truly let in. They can be either really bad at social nice-ties or excellent at networking. Once a connection is created, they are great at maintaining it—whether it's a friend-ship or a collegiate connection. They may appear snobby and cold, when in fact they're shy. Friendship is based in reciprocity for them; if a friend scratches their back, they'll want to scratch theirs in return. They enjoy seeing how others grow and develop, and they're often really great at having friends of different ages.

VENUS IN AQUARIUS

People with Venus in Aquarius are often the social butterflies of the zodiac. This is not the warmest placement for Venus, but it causes folks to be super chatty. They don't want to have to be any one way socially, so by popping in to different groups, they get to be the full range of themselves. They may have to be care-ful that they don't overemphasize digital friendships as a way to avoid dealing with the messiness of friendships that happen in real time. This placement can also make people progressive, eccentric, and really interested in humanitarianism in a variety of ways.

VENUS IN PISCES

This is an incredibly sensitive placement, indicating that these people are compas-sionate, easily influenced, tender-hearted, romantic, and devotional in nature. They can be quite self-sacrificing, which can get them into trouble if they choose to be friends with takers. Their love for the underdog can also get them into impossi-ble situations, and it's important for them to remember that friendship is a two-way street. They're intuitive, idealistic, and kind—unless they feel that they've been unduly hurt or mistreated by others, in which case they may become bitter. It's important that they choose the people they associate with wisely.

VENUS THROUGH THE HOUSES

VENUS IN THE FIRST HOUSE

These people come across as friendly and warm and have great social skills, making others feel at ease in their presence. They're often perceived as attractive, and they have a natural aptitude for making new friends. The downside is that this can also make them come across as insincere. It can incline them to want everything to be fine, even when they know damn well that it isn't. They might say yes to things that they actually don't want to do because they want people to like them—that said, they're good at making the best of things. They're gracious, sympathetic, and adept at negotiation and diplomacy when it's necessary.

VENUS IN THE SECOND HOUSE

Money, possessions, and status are all pretty important to these people. They're happiest surrounded by beauty. This can be quite a social placement; they need an inner circle of really tight friends who they are quite loyal to, and they like having a few meaningful friendships. While socializing may not always be their top priority, it provides great solace for them. They're loyal, compassionate, accommodating, and generous with their time—if not always with their money.

VENUS IN THE THIRD HOUSE

These people are smart, charming, and chatty. When a compromise seems reasonable to them, they are super down to make one. They're willing to see other people's perspectives and let it change theirs when it seems right to them. This placement can make them fickle or changeable, and they're not shy about changing plans at the last minute. These folks are great at first impressions. While they might get bored with people, they prefer to have multiple friends to turn to for connection, and they're likely to be texting with three people at a time.

VENUS IN THE FOURTH HOUSE

People with this placement can be homebodies, and they love to entertain at home. They want their friends to be family, and the parts of friendship that make them feel rooted and secure in the world are really important to them. Sensitive to their social surrounding, they will opt not to stay at clubs or restaurants that don't have the right ambience. They can be very self-protective, and those feelings can incline them to ice people without saying why; giving people second chances is not their forte. Their sense of right and wrong is really close to their hearts; they love to find people who share their values.

VENUS IN THE FIFTH HOUSE

This placement inclines people to prioritize romantic and sexual relationships over friendship, and they are fierce protectors of their friends and fun to be around. However, they need to remember to ask questions about how others are doing, even when it's not exciting. This is an especially good placement for creative pursuits—whether its dance, painting, or poetry. People can be quite drawn to them, which can make them a bit self-indulgent or lazy with their friendships. This is overall a fun and playful placement for Venus.

VENUS IN THE SIXTH HOUSE

This placement inclines people to be methodical in how they approach their friendships. They need a fair amount of time alone, and it's important that they have downtime with their friends. They can be a little self-indulgent, especially if they feel that they're working hard in other areas of their lives, so surrounding themselves with people who have healthy habits is really important. They can be service-oriented and willing to do things for others. Making your way into their routines is a great way to get close to them.

VENUS IN THE SEVENTH HOUSE

These people are incredibly motivated to have close friendships. The trouble is that this placement can make them a bit passive, so they may expect the right friendships to just come to them or that others will do all the heavy lifting. As friends, they are fun and committed, and love having activity partners (and partners in general). They may have several besties and, if they don't, their sense of loneliness might be hard for them to bear. Remembering that life and love are co-creations will help them get the most out of this really lovely placement.

VENUS IN THE EIGHTH HOUSE

People with Venus in the eighth house care deeply for their friends, and they're great at showing up over time. They're intense, and they like to go deep with people, but that doesn't mean they always want to be around them. Chunks of time alone are really important, and forthcoming communication is something they really have to cultivate. Knowing their role is important to them, and that can be trickier in friendships than in other intimate relationships. The sooner they define their terms and boundaries around friendship, the more successful those relationships will be.

VENUS IN THE NINTH HOUSE

These people have adventurous approaches to friendship; it's one of the ways they enjoy engaging with the world around them. They're always learning, searching for something more. Their values and philosophies and the projects they're engaged in are really motivating to them, and they seek people they can share their interests with. Honesty is really important to them but, paradoxically, they may skim over uncomfortable parts of the truth. They love to learn through experience, and friendships and socializing are important parts of that.

VENUS IN THE TENTH HOUSE

This is the position of the born mayor, kissing babies and shaking hands. These people want to be liked, and they're lucky enough that they usually are. They may find that their social skills land them in a place of power, and they're good at being diplomatic. There's a risk that they may be social climbers, but if they can remember that a rising tide lifts all boats, that's much less likely. They are steadfast, consistent, and funny to be around. Very little goes unnoticed by them.

VENUS IN THE ELEVENTH HOUSE

People with this placement are likely to have lots of different friends in different groups and they can bro down with the best of them. They have a tendency to jump into friendships quickly and form ideas about who people are right off the bat. They may have more acquaintances than deep friendships, and they prefer to do something they see as creative or progressive with their friends. They thrive in clubs, on committees, and in groups, as they enjoy being part of something larger than themselves.

VENUS IN THE TWELFTH HOUSE

Friends can help these people remember who they are, especially when they're in marriages and other long-term relationships. They need alone time to decompress from the world and to separate themselves from other people's opinions. Having friendships wherein they can be open about their spirituality, their feelings about the world, and how safe they feel in it is really important to them. Because they're so sensitive, they're easily hurt and can feel scared that people don't like them (even when they clearly do). Or conversely, they may be convinced that people are in love with them when they're actually being ghosted.

MARS ♂

Time it takes to traverse the zodiac:
Approximately 2 years

Sign it rules: Aries

House it governs: First

FRIENDSHIP: MARS

Mars is the planet of conflict, anger, and war. In the context of friendship, its influence is not just about how you fight with your friends, but also how willing and capable you are of standing up and fighting for what you believe in, how forthcoming you are about your needs and preferences, and how you show up or fall apart when things get confrontational. Mars is also the source of your passion. Where you find this planet in your chart describes where and how you expend your energy. Pouring your whole self into a project, going out dancing, wrestling, competitive sports, screaming and yelling, and driving fast—all those activities are governed by Mars.

MARS, YOUR EGO, AND YOU

Mars's placement in the birth chart describes how and why we want to get our way. Its ego-filled energies are insistent and driving. People tend to be either very comfortable with their Mars energy or very uncomfortable with it. But even when we have a hard time taking ownership of those parts of ourselves, we will still experience their lessons one way or another. When we're unwilling or unable to own or express the energies of our Mars, we'll often find ourselves attracted to people and situations that force us to express it. We may feel backed into a corner and as though we have to come out swinging, or we may simply be attracted to people who express Mars for us, which keeps us in a state of reaction . . . or provocation.

OWNING IT

If you find yourself frequently attracted to aggressive, violent people, take a close look at your Mars and see if it's possible that you're attracting people who are expressing something you're not comfortable saying or doing yourself. If that's the case, it may be time to practice embodying more of your own Martian intensity in a new way. Try doing anything that gets you sweating from exertion (and creating endorphins). Remember: Anger, irritation, annoyance, and frustration are unpleasant feelings, but they're not *bad*. We all have Mars in our birth chart, and we're all bothered by other humans sometimes. You're entitled to the full breadth of emotional and physical responses, and it's only when you actively repress or over-express those feelings that they can get you into trouble.

Mars's energies demand to be expressed viscerally. For this reason, it can be a more active planet in family and romantic relationships than in friendship. But when your friends are acting bitter, resentful, and irritated by everything, and looking to fight, you're experiencing their Mars. This planet also rules your frenemy relationships and casual friendships, especially those that involve doing something together. Having a fully embodied Mars can allow you to fully enjoy going out to "the clurb," joining teams, and yelling your head off in a sports bar. In closer friendships, it shows up in the (inevitable) conflicts. We can't have close friends without sometimes wanting to cut them, fight them, or leave them on the side of the road; that's just friendship.

HOW TO WORK WITH THIS PLANET

What you *do* with your anger and how you *feel* about your anger are two different things. Mars allows feelings that can be demanding and insistent to surface; responding to those demands requires you to be able to tolerate them in the first place. Start by being present with what you're actually feeling. Exercise, healthy competition, and long drives (away from traffic) can shake off your excess natal Martian energy.

MARS THROUGH THE SIGNS

MARS IN ARIES

These people are assertive and independent. Sometimes their assertiveness is an effort to support people, but they can forget to ask friends what they actually want. They make great leaders because they're enthusiastic and don't require a great deal of ego-stroking. But in the context of friendship this can go either way because they cannot always see their effect on others—even with direct feedback. They can often benefit from learning how to soften their approach when expressing frustration and/or support.

MARS IN TAURUS

People with Mars in Taurus tend to be uncompromising, obstinate, and dogmatic while also being loyal and tender friends. "If you mess with a bull, you get the horns" sums it up well. They can show up and be present and connected and then just disappear; sometimes their need for self-care overwhelms them, and they need to go do their thing. These people are loving, sensual, and willing to go the extra mile. They also often express and share friendship through indulgence. Pro tip: If your friends with Mars in Taurus get cranky, feed them!

MARS IN GEMINI

People with this placement are distractible, curious, versatile, and willing to try out new things. On the flip side, they can be easily bored. Their friends are really important to them but they don't always prioritize them. Distractions are a really fun part of their friendships, but are also the very things that can keep them from getting closer to other people. They need to have some superficial friendships in addition to the deeper ones. They're observant and perceptive but can get easily irritated or overwhelmed by everything they pick up on, and they tend to express this irritation before they've had a chance to process it.

MARS IN CANCER

These people can be moody, emo, and irritable, which wouldn't be so bad if they weren't also a little defensive because they really want to be liked. This placement is good for bringing people together, but not so much for compromising. They have a strong sense of the best way to do things, which can be really nurturing for their friends—or they can end up pushing people away because they don't feel listened to. They have to be careful to not act like martyrs when they don't get their way. Cultivating confidence about their value as people helps them truly receive the affection and love of others.

MARS IN LEO

Dynamic, generous, and courageous, these people are fun to be around, but a strong sense of self can also make them the most loving pains in the ass. They want things to go well, and they know exactly how to make that happen, so woe to those who disagree. This is not the humblest placement, and when these people's egos get bruised, they don't take it well. They can fight with their friends, but they're fighting *for* the friendship just as often as they're fighting against it. They're demonstrative and really good at easing social situations and making people feel welcome.

MARS IN VIRGO

People with this placement are methodical and have a discerning and process-oriented nature. They may not be spontaneous, but they're willing to show up and do the damn work when a friend is in need. Those with this placement have specific interests and need their friendships to contain their own distinct interests. This placement can incline people to be judgmental or rigid with their boundaries, so when they can cultivate a willingness to tolerate differences they will make others feel supported rather than judged. Mars in Virgo people need both a healthy dose of time alone and one-on-one time with their friends in order to feel connected.

MARS IN LIBRA

People with Mars in Libra are diplomatic and easy to be around, but they are not always very decisive or forthcoming. There's a danger here of their keeping friendship on the surface and opting for diplomacy over potential conflict. While they are sensitive to injustice, they're not always comfortable standing up for what they believe is right. It's important that they allow friends to support them instead of enabling them, because cultivating self-reliance is a huge part of their growth process. Mars in Libra people have a hard time being alone, but they should be careful not to use friends as placeholders. Libra is the sign of partnership, and these people treat their close friends like partners.

MARS IN SCORPIO

These are intense, sexual, brooding people who can also get super resentful and moody. They are not known for being direct or diplomatic when they feel hurt. Intense feelings can lead to confrontation when a gentle nudge may do. Friends that support them in figuring out how to relax and be adaptable are really important. They can be loyal through thick, thin, and thick again and can take a secret to the grave. They tend to give all or nothing, so long-term friendships may include periods of time where they're not in touch but that doesn't mean they're not still there.

MARS IN SAGITTARIUS

People with Mars in Sagittarius are all about beginnings and enthusiastic bursts of energy—but they can struggle to sustain their energy over time. They're generally pretty mobile and like to travel, experiment, and try new things. They are also supportive, inspiring, and always willing to collaborate on projects and have adventures. They can get easily distracted and, before you know it, they're off to the next project or venture. They also tend to get annoyed easily but get over it quickly. There's an extravagance to this placement that makes it easy for them to make new friends and facilitate social interactions, but it's not always comfortable for them to go deep or get too touchy-feely.

MARS IN CAPRICORN

Once people with Mars in Capricorn have decided they're your friends, they are yours for life. They are diligent, consistent, and motivated. They're often working on something—whether it's an internal or external goal—and want their friends to be along for the ride. They can be very aware of rejection and will barter for affection by showing up and offering gifts or doing things; they're very aware of what their friends can do for them, too. These people are great at networking, and tend to need a few deep, true friends they can count on until the end.

MARS IN AQUARIUS

People with Mars in Aquarius are often more motivated by the idea of friendship than the reality. They need bigger reasons to be in social situations, whether that means a social cause or a shared project. This placement can make people obstinate and stubborn, but they are also convinced that they're open-minded and tolerant, which they totally are—except when they're obstinate and stubborn. They can have many friends from different walks of life, and they don't need everyone to be connected in order to feel at home. They thrive off differences and love being stimulated, especially mentally.

MARS IN PISCES

People with this placement are really sensitive and can be easily overwhelmed. They don't like conflict and have a tendency to want to disassociate and play hard, or they can crave friend time that is protective, nurturing, and fortifying. They use friendship as a sounding board and have tireless energy for listening to the ins and outs of your drama or your sad story. There's a need here to develop confidence, so that healthy boundaries can be assessed and maintained. They are often restless and need quality friendships that help them nurture their creative processes and inspire them to new heights.

MARS THROUGH THE HOUSES

MARS IN THE FIRST HOUSE
These people often act first and think later, and when they're annoyed, it shows on their face. They tend to barrel through interactions and can come across as more aggressive and domineering than they often think they are. They're great at getting the party started and initiating plans. While they might not enjoy small talk, they often have the energy to make things happen and move social interactions along.

MARS IN THE SECOND HOUSE
People with this placement are loyal, steadfast, and willing to fight for what and whom they love. They like shared projects that signify shared interests and values, but they can keep friendship on the surface and may be preoccupied with coolness. Small compromises can feel large to them. This is a very acquisition-oriented placement, so these folks either spend time collecting the right kind of people, clothes, and so on, or, on the other end of the spectrum, doing things with others that reflect their goals and values.

MARS IN THE THIRD HOUSE
These people can be impulsive, fun, and great at reaching out and making new friends. At the same time, they may get irritated by people and are quick to take offense when others don't communicate in the ways they prefer. This placement signifies having varied interests and a willingness to do lots of really dynamic things with friends, but if they're not paying attention, friendship can fall off their list of priorities.

MARS IN THE FOURTH HOUSE
People with Mars in the fourth house can be serious homebodies, which can translate to them wanting to entertain and bring people together in their homes—or use their homes as sanctuaries. They can be a little impatient and critical, but it comes from an honest place. The drive for security and stability can make them low-key insatiable. This placement can also be associated with folks feeling self-protective in regard to whether or not other people like them. Chosen family is incredibly important to them, but with difficult aspects they may inadvertently push people away.

MARS IN THE FIFTH HOUSE
Play is super important to these people, so having friends to do things that involve physical expression—like sports or improv—is really important to them.

They're flirty, can forget to prioritize platonic friendships in favor of sexual or romantic relationships, and often have friend crushes. This placement is a glutton for punishment and a glutton for a good time; they're fiercely loyal friends who may burn bridges by being too self-centered or self-indulgent.

MARS IN THE SIXTH HOUSE

These folks are always on the go. It's common for them to have work friends and frenemies, and having a sense of shared goals or shared ambitions is a big part of how they relate. Their emotions are felt viscerally, especially annoyance and passion, and when people bother them, they get quite agitated. Health is a big part of their life, and it's important that they have friends with whom they can share healthy habits. They're incredibly hard-working and need to be warned against burnout.

MARS IN THE SEVENTH HOUSE

People with Mars in the seventh house tend to be confrontational or find themselves in relationships with people who are. If they find themselves attracted to people who bring conflict into their lives, they'll benefit from being direct and forthright. They may often feel like they're being pushed to stand up for themselves or perform. This placement can incline people to have either many friends they don't go too deep with or just a few people they only connect with when there's a real reason to.

MARS IN THE EIGHTH HOUSE

These people are intense and secretive and it's not always obvious what's going on with them; they need to be warned against becoming paranoid or defensive. They benefit from having someone in their life they can get real with about real things. It's easy for them to share only parts and versions of the truth, which is ironic because of how intensely they value other people's honesty. They're willing to go to great lengths for the people they love and expect a similar kind of loyalty. They often try to collect power through friendship, but their efforts can backfire spectacularly if they misuse that power.

MARS IN THE NINTH HOUSE

People with this placement are down for whatever. They're adventurous, explorative, and not likely to volunteer to take the smallest piece of the pie. They have strong feelings about what's fair, and no problem speaking their minds, but the risk is that their friends may end up feeling lectured. Travel—whether it's actual, physical travel or moving through ideas, philosophy, and education—is their favorite way to engage. Conversely, if they feel stuck or frustrated in their lives, they may end up acting weird, dogmatic, and judgy. They're happiest when they have friends around the globe to visit.

MARS IN THE TENTH HOUSE

Mars in the tenth house can generate such a strong concern for goals and responsibility that people with this placement don't prioritize friendship. Or they may require friends to be involved in whatever effort or project they're moving toward. They're motivated, ambitious, and persistent, but they can also get overly concerned with their reputations. As a result, they may come across as bullies if they're not careful. They're great to have as activity partners and can be incredibly willing to do all kinds of heavy lifting within their friendships.

MARS IN THE ELEVENTH HOUSE

These people are motivated to function in groups, whether it's groups of friends, organizations, or teams. They feel most satisfied when they're getting to assert themselves alongside other people. They are energetic, social, and capable of striving toward shared goals, whether that's humanitarian or competitive; they want to get it done and they're willing to do the work. That said, they can also get irritated if their plans are interrupted, or if other people's egos conflict with their own.

MARS IN THE TWELFTH HOUSE

Highly sensitive, these people would rather spend one-on-one time deeply connecting with friends than hanging out in groups. They need to be careful around social substance use because escaping social anxiety is so appealing to them. They can be private, need to be drawn out, and tend to display their care for others through acts instead of words. People with this placement are often conflict-averse, but they will step out of their comfort zone to protect the people they love.

JUPITER ♃

Time it takes to traverse the zodiac:
Approximately 12 years

Sign it rules: Sagittarius

House it governs: Ninth

FRIENDSHIP: JUPITER

Jupiter wants to go big or go home. It rules storytelling and the desire we have to get on a soapbox and proselytize—whether that's about the reason we should all go to the water park next week, or grander ideas. Storytelling is a wonderful and important part of platonic love. Sharing your stories and your perspective on the world; talking about your day, your past, your future—these are all related to Jupiter. But trouble comes in when we lean too hard on Jupiter, when our stories become more colorful than the experiences we're trying to describe. People under the influence of Jupiter may tell a story for effect instead of for accuracy. And, in community, when stories become more important than felt experiences, relationships may become disingenuous or remain superficial.

PUTTING THE "I" IN BELIEVE

Jupiter can make us open-minded, restless, and distractible. It governs our beliefs and convictions, as well as higher learning and institutionalized religion. This planet is associated with the friendships we make within institutions, shared philosophies, and the times in our lives when we form bonds based on growth, expansion, and truth seeking. It rules things such as meeting in a church basement to talk about God, canvassing for a political candidate together, or bonding while working on a cruise ship or in the cast of a musical.

THE POWER OF TRUTH

Jupiter is said to bring luck, and that's because it's a planet of optimism, openness, and resilience. And while it can bring luck at times, what it always brings is more of something. More isn't necessarily better, however. More is just more, and better is better. In fact, sometimes we can be plagued by the desire for something more or different, instead of inspired. In that case, Jupiter can lead to dissatisfaction and depression. Fortunately, Jupiter also gives us the tools we need—if we're interested and motivated to use them—for uncovering the truth, and for having the best growth experiences possible.

SAUCY

This planet also governs alcohol, excess, and the struggles that arise when we face limitations. Many adult friendships happen over drinks; it's a huge part of how we socialize. If an activity is fun when we're twenty-five, Jupiter says it will also be fun when we're fifty-five, but that's not always the case. If the only way you know how to connect is through drinking, you may have a hard time relaxing and having fun with people on your own. Look to Jupiter through the signs to gain a better sense of who you are without the sauce, so you can expand on the best parts of your nature.

HOW TO WORK WITH THIS PLANET

Take a look at the things you do with your friends for fun. Ask yourself: Am I really having fun? Actively pursue growth experiences, whether that's seeing live music, having deep conversations, or walking in new neighborhoods with your friends. Make that type of activity a regular practice and check in with yourself to make sure your social life is helping you to grow.

JUPITER THROUGH THE SIGNS

JUPITER IN ARIES

These people tend to prioritize themselves and see their own needs first and foremost. On the plus side, they're resilient, willing to take initiative, and willing to take a stand. The downside is they can be selfish, arrogant, and poor listeners. This is an impulsive and willful placement—but those things are only negative when out of balance. Being brave is wonderful, but running blindly into the future is risky. These folks are fierce protectors of their friends and willing to stand up for others.

JUPITER IN TAURUS

This placement inclines people to be indulgent and sensual; they love the finer things when it comes to food and possessions. They're also good at remembering to take the time to enjoy their friends. They really care about being nice and diplomatic with others, but they can also be self-indulgent and forget the implications of their actions—especially if those actions feel good to them. They have staying power for the things and people they care about.

JUPITER IN GEMINI

These people tend to be open-minded and interested in lots of different things, people, and activities, as well as the world around them. They may love gossip and get locked in on certain ideas about others or opinions that can make them come across as a little smug. They're the youth pastors of the zodiac. This placement can incline people to have lots friendships that are fun for all, but it doesn't necessarily incline them to go super deep. They are funny, witty, and quick—but easily distracted. Lots of things capture their interest, but far fewer things can hold it. They often need to be reminded to look up from their phones.

JUPITER IN CANCER

People with Jupiter in Cancer are sympathetic, concerned about the welfare of those they're closest to, and willing to do emotional labor. It's important that they don't become overly dependent or meddle too much with the people they care about. It can be easy for them to see the best in other people. They may find it hard to separate from their families of origin, or they may have been separated from their families too young, but they are excellent at creating community wherever they go.

JUPITER IN LEO

This placement inclines people to be warm, gregarious, and playful. They're ambitious and want to be the best at whatever they do, which can give them a flair for drama or it can make them seem arrogant. They're great at entertaining people and finding ways of enjoying others, but when they're not in the mood to be social, they're *really* not in the mood, and they can find everyone annoying. People with Jupiter in Leo are enthusiastic and demonstrative, and they're exciting friends to have around.

JUPITER IN VIRGO

People with Jupiter in Virgo are inclined to be organized and analytical, and they have great powers of discernment—when they remember to prioritize using them. Because they're so tuned in to the details, they may focus on completely different things than what their friends see and end up feeling out of step. They're considerate and willing to show up and do what needs to be done, including having difficult conversations. They are concerned with the purity of ideas in friendship and are determined to find the best possible way to go about a task, even if it's only setting up their bedroom to create the most chill way to watch a movie.

JUPITER IN LIBRA

These people are good at compromise and highly prize niceness and getting along. This can make them either insincere in the effort to be accommodating and likable—or kind, diplomatic, and balance-seeking. It's important that they don't hold double standards, as they have a tendency to be generous with their besties and hold other people to much higher standards. They have to be careful not to gossip too much.

JUPITER IN SCORPIO

This placement can incline people to be very self-indulgent, as their capacity to experience both pleasure and pain is very deep. They may be quite attached and loyal to those who make it to their inner circle, while not caring very deeply for anyone else, and are likely to either be very judgmental or incredibly tolerant. They can be quite magnetic and mischievous. This is a deeply spiritual and sexual placement, so friendships that are spacious enough to hold those themes are the ones they'll feel the most fulfilled by.

JUPITER IN SAGITTARIUS

Freedom-loving, lucky, optimistic, and resilient, these people are great at bringing out the best in others and inspiring them to do more. They can also be quite impulsive and speculative and hate nothing more than feeling limited or trapped; they can be easily frustrated when others don't see the same potential they see in a situation. They enjoy collaborative projects and love to have activity partners. They're especially interested in travel, whether through the world or through the realm of ideas and philosophy; sharing ideas and concepts are meaningful ways for them to connect.

JUPITER IN CAPRICORN

These people are fantastic builders; they have a capacity to look at something big and then create it, step-by-step. They're impatient until they can align themselves with what they're trying to achieve. They can be rigid or self-righteous when some-body acts in a way they find out of turn or morally wrong. They may also sometimes cling to their ideas of right and wrong in ways that can make them dogmatic. These people have the kind of friends who mobi-lize around their goals, and they're also great at mobilizing others.

JUPITER IN AQUARIUS

This placement can make people idealistic—they're capable of seeing the potential in people and situations in a way that motivates them to move toward the future. However, they can also get bored by the present. They tend to be quite intelligent and often have an interest in politics, social justice, and their com-munities. They're original and innovative, but they can overexplain things they are passionate about. Feeling bored, trapped, or caged is their kryptonite.

JUPITER IN PISCES

Generous, spiritual, and not material-istic, these people are inclined to show up for others through service, empathy, and compassion. They're good to have around when the chips are down. There's

a risk of getting into situations where they have a martyr dynamic or giving without pausing to receive. They're inclined to want to champion the underdog and to connect via the high arts or spirituality. They need a fair amount of time alone recovering from people, even though they're also quite fulfilled by them. With negative aspects they may find themselves in friendships that are based on glamour and illusion, instead of real intimacy.

JUPITER THROUGH THE HOUSES

JUPITER IN THE FIRST HOUSE

These people are talkative, friendly, and broad-minded. They like to be the life of the party, and they're likely to have great sense of humor and the ability to connect with many kinds of people. They may also tend to interrupt others. People with Jupiter in the first house may feel inspired and optimistic or restless and impatient, depending on what else is in their birth charts. This is said to be a lucky place-ment, but that luck comes from their resilient dispositions.

JUPITER IN THE SECOND HOUSE

This placement makes people idealistic about their values and, unless there are difficult aspects in the chart, it also indi-cates a healthy flow of money over the course of their lives. But wherever there's Jupiter, it's easy come, easy go, and their love of spending is as strong as their love of accumulating. They can be quite for-giving with friends, as they're able to see and validate the efforts that others put forth. As much as they like shopping and social media, they need to make sure that their friendships are based on more.

JUPITER IN THE THIRD HOUSE
People with Jupiter in the third house are likable, have an easy time making and keeping friends, and can spend time with many different people. Boredom is the kiss of death for them because they crave a quick and dynamic tempo. Their minds can hold many details, so they get bored when there's not enough going on that interests them. They should be careful not to talk out of both sides of their mouths or speak before they think. They may tend to exaggerate, and gossip can be one of their favorite ways of connecting with others, but it can also bite them in the buns if they're not careful.

JUPITER IN THE FOURTH HOUSE
These people have an innate sense of belonging, but that doesn't necessarily translate to strong friendships. If there are challenging aspects in their chart, they tend to feel the opposite way—like they're not at all rooted. They are generous and warm and once they make a friend, they'll go to the ends of the Earth for them. They also often convert their friends into family. There's a risk of them being a little needy or selfish for attention, especially when they haven't gotten enough sleep.

JUPITER IN THE FIFTH HOUSE
This placement can make people very creative. It gives them a love of play, flirtation, and risk-taking. If they have

kids, the friendships they make through their children can be especially rewarding. They run the risk of having all their friendships be either placeholders for love relationships or kind of sexualized. They may need to be reminded that friendship isn't just about fun and dynamic play, but also about showing up for the mundane stuff and doing maintenance work with the people they love.

JUPITER IN THE SIXTH HOUSE
People with this placement have a tendency to push things. They stay up too late, eat all the foods that delight them, and have a lot of drinks—and they can be quite bored by things they don't want to do. The greatest spaces in their hearts are held by the people they spend the most time with. If they find themselves in unhealthy relationships with coworkers, however, it's better that they pull it back. They're good at getting along with others, as well as bossing them around. They may need to pay attention to whether or not people can keep up with them, and slow down when necessary.

JUPITER IN THE SEVENTH HOUSE
Very close friendships are important to these people, but they need to be careful not to overcommit themselves. They're generous with their friends and have a tendency to spoil the people they care about. This placement can incline them to be gregarious and pleasant to be around, but they may forget to spend enough time alone, which can lead to irritability and exhaustion. They also run the risk of keeping things on the surface out

of fear that people only like them because they're fun.

JUPITER IN THE EIGHTH HOUSE

These people are inclined either to be tight with their money or to spend it impulsively on a good time. They also have deep and spiritual natures. Their private lives exist on a rich landscape, which, depending on other aspects in the chart, they will either share with their true friends or keep to themselves. They have a healthy relationship to endings and the inevitable ebb in the flow within long-term friendships. Their ability to stay present through other people's difficult times is formidable.

JUPITER IN THE NINTH HOUSE

This is one of the luckiest placements in the zodiac. These folks have a flair for languages and a capacity to be friends with a wide range of different people. They're smart and able to grasp new and complex ideas quickly. They're also fun, gregarious, and good at being the life of the party. They can be quite religious, so friendships made through schools or spiritual institutions are important to them. The risk here is that they will get up on soapboxes and never step down. Their nature inclines them toward having broad-minded, tolerant views, but they may also wear blinders.

JUPITER IN THE TENTH HOUSE

These people are natural-born leaders, and they can be very social, especially when it comes to networking and main-taining appearances. They are self-reliant and, unless there are difficult aspects in the chart, this placement inclines them to live by their word and prize honesty very highly. They can be proud or self-righteous, especially if they forget that other people's validation is not the only indication of a life well-lived. They can also be generous when they feel like life is treating them right.

JUPITER IN THE ELEVENTH HOUSE

Justice is especially important to these people, and they may find that their friendships are oriented around humanitarian, religious, or progressive organizations. This placement inclines them to be fair-minded, but they may also jump to conclusions. They will often skim through the details and just focus on the big picture. Positive aspects will incline them to have long-term friend-ships. With difficult aspects, they're more likely to see friendships as temporary adventures.

JUPITER IN THE TWELFTH HOUSE

These people are empathetic, compas-sionate, and generous of spirit. Art, music, and spirituality are meaningful ways for them to connect to others and themselves. It may feel really essential that at least part of their life is devoted to helping others, but they should also make sure they don't take on martyr roles within their friendships. They need to watch out for codependency and find other parts of their lives to help them fulfill their need to be helpful.

SATURN ♄

Time it takes to traverse the zodiac:
Approximately 29.5 years

Sign it rules: Capricorn

House it governs: Tenth

FRIENDSHIP: SATURN

Saturn is the Daddy of the zodiac, meaning it governs patriarchy, hierarchy, restriction, and obligation. It governs your internal structure as a human being, your drive to succeed and be viewed as successful by others, your need for security, and your relationship to your existential self. For those reasons, Saturn doesn't play a significant role in your casual friendships. Instead, it rules your long-term committed friendships, how you feel about yourself as a friend, and the kinds of friends you attract. It's what spurs your secret fears that you're not good enough, or the difficulties you may have tolerating change and spontaneity. It also governs your feelings of scarcity—that sense there's not quite enough of what you need—and the drive to gather more proof of your validity or safety.

LIFE LESSONS

The lessons Saturn has to teach us are big-picture lessons—the kind we learn over the course of a lifetime, as opposed to the course of a couple of months or years. For this reason, Saturn issues show up in many of our relationships. And the more we can understand and heal those issues, the more likely we are to attract healthy dynamics and relationships.

Unless you're incredibly close, others may not be sharing their Saturnian natures with you. But that doesn't mean it's not impacting your friendships. For example, if you have Saturn in Capricorn, its influence on your chart could make you feel that you should already know everything and have it all figured out. In instances where you feel like your friends all understand something about the world that you don't, Saturn will compel you to fake it 'til you make it, and you'll miss out on the true intimacy and the close-ness that can come with admitting what you don't know. The lesson is that you don't actually have to go it alone—and working with others helps you grow.

WE'RE ALL IN THIS TOGETHER

Saturn has the potential to show us that we're all part of a larger community of humans, but also that we are all alone in an existential way. Your stable, long-term friendships can hold both things. These are the connections you can rely on over the course of time—whether it's with childhood friends who are more like family or friends you've had in your life for many years; in other words, friendships that have stood the test of time. If your intention is to have your friends be your chosen family, it's important to redefine family. That can require giving your platonic loves as much attention and care as you might give a romantic partner.

KEEPING UP WITH SATURN

Saturn itself governs rigidity; it's your bones and teeth. It's also your internal structure and your sense of reality. When your friends are there to validate your reality, it can be a beautiful thing. But what's equally beautiful is having close friends who can challenge that reality in a supportive way.

Saturn governs your ideas about how others should or shouldn't behave, and your sense of right and wrong often comes up in close friendships. For any intimate connection to flourish, you need to be willing and able to confront what isn't working, adapt as your friends change, and be forthcoming to the people who know you best.

HOW TO WORK WITH THIS PLANET

Saturn governs the responsibility we take for our actions, the work we're willing to do to show up for others, and how we ask for help when we truly need it. Take responsibility for the people you choose to let into your life. You need people who are willing to clap when you win and call you out when you falter. How you contribute to the long-term success of your friendships is a matter of both your integrity and your humanity.

SATURN THROUGH THE SIGNS

SATURN IN ARIES

People with Saturn in Aries tend to take themselves very seriously; they can be a little pushy or domineering, but their true friends know that they struggle with identity and don't always have a clear sense of themselves. When they cultivate the ability to listen and ask questions of others—without slipping into what they think it means about them—they can be the fiercest of friends. The ability to distinguish between validation and attention is an important skill for these people to learn.

SATURN IN TAURUS

These folks are very security-oriented. When they learn to structure their lives around the things they value, their capacity to love and be loved expands. They really like to break bread with their friends, and they need activity partners—not just confidants in the digital world. Once they decide how things should go, it's hard for them to change their minds. They should be careful not to over-emphasize appearances—whether it's the appearance of closeness or making friends to make themselves seem cooler or more powerful. At the end of the day, they're loyal, steadfast companions who know how to show up for others and want people to do the same for them.

SATURN IN GEMINI

People with this placement tend to either push themselves hard or absolve themselves of responsibility. They need people they can argue with on occasion, but they should be careful not to spend all their time playing devil's advocate. They are not strangers to loneliness, so their need for friendship is strong. Changing their minds doesn't come naturally, and they can overthink things and get stuck on seemingly random details. Their friendships are most successful when they can contain the most challenging, weighty aspects of life.

SATURN IN CANCER
People with Saturn in Cancer can be uncomfortable showing and receiving love and are acutely sensitive to rejection. They tend to feel connected to the past, and they enjoy looking at old houses, shopping for vintage objects, and listening to music from back in the day. They're loyal and hard-working friends, yet they may be so motivated by security that they opt for safety over authenticity and vulnerability. They can grow very attached to other people and unconsciously re-create their original family dynamics within their chosen families.

SATURN IN LEO
Creative outlets and expressions of joy are important parts of friendship for these people. They may want to surround themselves with fans, but fans won't really get to know them. They have a deep-seated need to feel appreciated, valued, and seen; when that need isn't met, they tend to feel rejected, harmed, or ignored. These people don't always have an easy time keeping it light, but when they can access their lighter sides,

they're awesome to be around. They don't always need to initiate connection within their friendships, and they will benefit from learning to let other people come to them.

SATURN IN VIRGO
These people are contemplative, thoughtful, and discerning—sometimes to the point of being too careful. They're reliable, exacting, and can have a hard time recognizing their own worth. Becoming a part of their routine is a surefire way to become part of their inner circle, and their deepest friendships include long conversations over meals. They tend to show their interest and care through their actions and are willing to do the work that friendship requires. They need to be careful to avoid overinvesting in people who aren't prepared to meet them halfway.

SATURN IN LIBRA
People with Saturn in Libra crave friendship and a sense of belonging, but their desire to be liked can sometimes override their willingness to show up completely as themselves. They would benefit from having friends at different tiers of closeness. They can be accommodating, diplomatic, and loyal—making it hard for them to talk about unpleasant truths. They can also get easily hung up on whether or not things are fair. They may find themselves in friendships where other people make decisions for them, even if they're not always comfortable with that dynamic.

SATURN IN SCORPIO

These people can be insightful confi
dants, and they need really deep platonic
friendships, even if they don't always
prioritize them. They're ambitious and,
in order for a long-term friendship to
succeed, they need their friends to give
them periodic space, without needing
explanations. While they have really
strong intuition, they don't always trust
it. They need the people they can count
on to do what they say and say what they
mean; their friendships may be deep and
intense for long periods of time and then
end abruptly.

SATURN IN SAGITTARIUS

Friends they can travel with are especially
important to these people. Seeking truth
and justice, exploring culture, and learning new things together are also key for
long-term connections. People with this
placement can be dogmatic, opinionated,
and pushier than they realize they are.
Exploring the world is their favorite thing
to do, whether it's through philosophy,
religion, or culture. When a friendship
can hold those things, there's a sense
of security and dependability for these
people.

SATURN IN CAPRICORN

People with this placement are persistent, careful, and ambitious, and have a
profound relationship to responsibility.
They want to feel a sense of family and
belonging, but without all the messiness
of emotional needs. They have a very
transactional relationship to friendship,
which can make them excellent friends,
but oblivious to nuance. They tend to be
loyal—and should make sure they're being
loyal to the right people and situations.
They will benefit from learning that they
don't need to barter for love and attention.

SATURN IN AQUARIUS

These people have a strong need for
friendship, as well as a need for space and
autonomy. This placement can incline
them to be obtuse or fixed about what
works and that can create some rigid
dynamics in their close platonic relationships. They may be more comfortable
asserting their need for respect than their
need for love, and they tend to thrive in
relationships in which people are kept a
little at arm's length, whether that's due
to physical distance or differences in age
or lifestyle. Cultivating comfort with
solitude helps them to be better friends
to themselves and others.

SATURN IN PISCES

These folks have lessons to learn about
boundaries. Feeling seen and heard can
be tricky for them, in part because of
how important those needs are. They are
sensitive but often have strong defenses
around their sensitivities. Their need for
loyalty, friendship, and love is key. It's
important they learn how to verbally
express the hard stuff and also how to
take a physical step back from dynamics and situations they can't engage with
in a healthy way. Friendship needs to be
a sanctuary for them. They have strong
needs for safety and privacy, and while
solitude is healthy for them, hiding away
is not.

SATURN THROUGH THE HOUSES

SATURN IN THE FIRST HOUSE

People with Saturn in the first house are not easy to get to know, in part because they are excellent at controlling the expression of emotion on their face; they're likely to have RBF ("resting bitch face"). They are serious, loyal, and inclined to follow through with their commitments. They command respect and are generally willing to give it in return.

SATURN IN THE SECOND HOUSE

These people *truly* care about the people and things they care about—but they may struggle to consistently prioritize them. This placement makes them a bit tight with money in such a way that they restrict their social activities or indulge in social activities and then feel alone or stuck afterward from overspending. They need to learn how to receive gifts, whether that means material objects or attention and care.

SATURN IN THE THIRD HOUSE

People with this placement have strong ideas about themselves and others, but they can be sensitive to criticism and may struggle to express themselves without defense or justification. One-on-one friendships are preferable to groups, because they don't like competing to have their voices heard. Conversely, with difficult aspects, they can be assertive about having others listen, without doing a great job of listening themselves. They're great to have around in a crisis, and their capacity for doing the work in friendships is strong.

SATURN IN THE FOURTH HOUSE

These people can be homebodies and may be very attached to family and to the past. This placement can give them serious dispositions and incline them to seek consistent validation of their place in relationships. There's a risk of being defensive when they don't feel appreciated. It's important that they have people in their lives with whom they can spend chill time and break bread. While trust is slow to build, once it *is* built, they are steadfast and committed friends.

SATURN IN THE FIFTH HOUSE

This placement is often related to being timid or restrained when others come together to be playful and goofy. It inclines people to be deeply loyal to the people they love, but it can also make them slow to warm up and inclined to play roles with people before they become true friends. Developing an art practice or appreciation is not only good for these people but can be a meaningful way to connect with others.

SATURN IN THE SIXTH HOUSE

This placement yields lessons to learn through health and habits. These people's availability to hang out can be very consistent at times and very inconsistent at others, as they have a very particular way they need to manage their day-to-day lives. They're not terribly assertive. They can be worrywarts and need to avoid running with their fears. They can benefit from learning the value of direct communication. Mutual reliability is important to them when it comes to friendship.

SATURN IN THE SEVENTH HOUSE

As important as friendships are to them, people with this placement tend to have a difficult time with relationships. They may want to make things permanent and safe before they know whether or not there is sustainable compatibility. They also run a risk of prioritizing romantic partnerships over friendships or using friendship as a placeholder for romance. At the end of the day, however, they're responsible and committed friends who will do anything for their besties.

SATURN IN THE EIGHTH HOUSE

These folks can be introverted or private. They have a serious approach to emotional and collaborative matters. They are inclined to prioritize love or sexual relationships over friendships, even if it's not in their best interest. Learning how to be intimate without strings attached is a valuable lesson for them.

SATURN IN THE NINTH HOUSE

These people can have a hard time challenging themselves to see perspectives that are different from their own; they need to be open to asking questions and listening closely to the answers. Traveling through other cultures and lands can be a valuable way to expand what they think is possible and how they are willing to relate to others. The capacity here is for wisdom and deep learning, and the risk is that they can be a bit pedantic if not careful.

SATURN IN THE TENTH HOUSE

Responsibility is a big deal for these people. They're inclined to be so self-reliant that they have a hard time remembering to ask for help. They have a tendency to want to prove themselves even when it's not necessary or appropriate. They often get into overcommitted work dynamics that can interrupt their social lives.

SATURN IN THE ELEVENTH HOUSE

These people feel called to foster their sense of belonging within their communities. They may want to avoid groups or, conversely, to work tirelessly with them. And while they're likely to have real issues within their friend circles from time to time, if they're willing to show up, their capacity for loyalty and long-term friendships is unparalleled.

SATURN IN THE TWELFTH HOUSE

People with this placement have a tendency to seek assurance, safety, or validation from others, as they're not quite sure who or what they are. They're inclined to present a strong front in public but to be plagued by insecurities about their place in the world. Having one-on-one friends with whom they can truly be themselves is key, and they tend to turn their true friends into family.

URANUS ♅

Time it takes to traverse the zodiac: Approximately 84 years

Sign it rules: Aquarius

House it governs: Eleventh

FRIENDSHIP: URANUS

Uranus is the odd planet; it rules eccentricity, uniqueness, and queerness. It's an impermanent force in astrology—its energy shows up to teach us something and then it leaves. Where we have Uranus in our birth charts, we tend to want to do things our own way. It's not really concerned with intimacy—it cares more about learning, growth, and the future.

Uranus rules the part of the chart where we're progressive, open-minded, or downright eccentric, but it's not where we're the most flexible or collaborative. It's not where we want to get bogged down by feelings, but where we are motivated by the idea of connecting to get somewhere or to achieve something. When we're looking at friendship in the context of Uranus, we're really looking at shared interests. Where we find this planet is where we find functional friendships, activity partners, and long-distance relationships—not necessarily BFFs who hang out every day.

UNPREDICTABLE URANUS

When people have a strongly placed Uranus or a number of planets in Uranus in their charts, they can be real friends. Unless they change their minds. Depending on where we find the planet in the chart, we're either interested or utterly disinterested in other people. This planet can also be associated with friend breakups—because where we find Uranus, we're not willing to make compromises. We'd rather cut and bail than stay and suffer.

Friendships governed by Uranus are spent innovating and contemplating plans for what's ahead. This outer planet rules the way we interface rather than interact—in other words, there's a less personal quality to the dynamic. With this planet, the proof is in the pudding. Uranian people don't feel the need to impress anything upon other people; they believe their actions stand on their own, and they don't want to hear the same story twice.

This planet rules the internet, which allows us to be more connected than we've ever been before to a greater number of people and to a much more vast body of knowledge. Uranus has some of the same hermit-like tendencies that Saturn does, but where Saturn says "I'm alone and being alone is work," Uranus's approach is "I'm so interested in what I'm thinking about that I'm not very motivated by other people." It brings a more excited, focused energy.

People who have strong Uranus dynamics in their chart may seem like they're always in a hurry.

They're usually doing something they find interesting—and sometimes that also makes them interesting to other people, but not always. If you can keep up with a Uranian person's pace, you're more likely to be their friend. Their energy can be abrupt; they're there while it works and done when it's over.

YOUR INNER DUDE

An excellent Uranian archetype is The Dude from *The Big Lebowski*—he doesn't fit easily into any one category, and he is always ultimately himself. He's tender and attentive with his friends, but he doesn't owe anyone a damn thing. Uranus rules that type of authentic autonomy. If you're in a room with friends, and you suddenly decide you want to leave because you simply don't want to be there anymore, you're following your inner Dude. Or when you're walking with a group, and you decide you want to travel at a different pace than everyone else, that's also Uranus.

HOW TO WORK WITH THIS PLANET

The key to working with Uranus is to work on staying present. People ruled by this planet want to rush into the future and figure out what comes next. It can be hard work to stay in the present moment, but it's important to because it's the foundation for the next one. Ask yourself: How am I going to have the best impact on my future in this moment?

URANUS THROUGH THE SIGNS

Uranus has an orbit of eighty-four years and spends approximately six years in each sign, meaning that a whole generation of people have these placements in common. For purposes of inclusivity, I've written about the last time Uranus was in each sign, as well as the next time it will be there.

You'll notice that there will be overlap years; that's because planets go retrograde, meaning that for all intents and purposes, they go backward. Astrology, like life, is not always tidy.

URANUS IN ARIES (1927–1934 AND 2010–2019)

When Uranus was in Aries in the early twentieth century, the United States experienced a massive stock market crash and the Great Depression began. The era required that people have more self-will, originality, and assertiveness in coping with survival. The combination of Uranus and Aries can create a lot of originality, willfulness, and daring, but the energy is quite erratic and blunt. These two forces come together to create periods of time of agency and individuation, which can lead to me-first thinking and behavior or the kind of embodiment of self that allows for a greater sense of agency.

What this means about friendship: This generation will redefine maleness and masculinity. There's a strong emphasis on individualism, and much of their identity comes through technology.

URANUS IN TAURUS (1934–1942 AND 2018–2026)

When this placement occurred in the last century, it coincided with the years when the Great Depression set in. Racism and xenophobia also had a new global stage with the arrival of World War II. This was a period that forced individuals to take stands about who they were and what they prioritized. The collective push at this time was a change in the global conversation about values. The same themes are coming up again and will likely play out through this cycle.

What this means about friendship: Personal relationships are increasingly important to this generation. People with this placement are redefining their values and their relationships to women and what it means to be female.

URANUS IN GEMINI (1941–1949 AND 2020–2025)

Uranus was last in Gemini during a period in which we saw advancements in both psychology and metaphysics. This generation grew up to become the students who were the radicals of the 1960s, and they were able to make inventive use of the information they received about

freedom, liberty, and independence. Uranus is revolutionary, and Gemini is the sign of communications.

What this means about friendship: The exchange of ideas and the formation of local communities are important to this generation. Connecting with others is a big part of how they connect with themselves.

URANUS IN CANCER (1949–1956; WILL HAPPEN AGAIN IN 2033–2039)

The age of McCarthyism occurred during this placement. A whole generation of artists and freethinkers were tamped down in the name of protectiveness and patriotism (several elements that are key to Cancer). There was the expansion of media and the arrival of television (and TV dinners, which was the beginning of processed food and provided people with more freedom without more quality, which is in keeping with Uranus). The planet wants freedom quickly, sometimes without consideration of the long-term impact.

What this means about friendship: The tension between the desire to be close and still maintain autonomy is the primary struggle for these people. Learning compromise is necessary for satisfactory friendships. The key here is to find a way to balance self-protection with freedom without choosing one over the other.

URANUS IN LEO (1956–1962; WILL HAPPEN AGAIN IN 2039–2046)

This was a time when entertainment became a much bigger part of Western society and the Vietnam War was in its infancy. Uranus in Leo is a time of forceful engagement. This is a generation of self-confident people who are very creative and also have a strong need for validation by external forces. When this placement happened last, we saw a lot of people exploring their lives' meaning through having children. When it happens next, we may see a cultural shift where people prioritize their autonomy over having children.

What this means about friendship: People in this generation need friends as a means of connecting with their creativity, and they're likely to prioritize that above more practical things.

URANUS IN VIRGO (1962–1969; WILL HAPPEN AGAIN IN 2046–2053)

The last time Uranus was in Virgo, the draft for the war in Vietnam began in the United States, and people rose up in radical resistance; many also dropped out of society. There was an emphasis on personal improvement as a route to social change. This was also when alternative health care began to play a larger role in Western culture. Virgo rules practical process, mundane reality, and day-to-day living. So, when combined with Uranus, it also spurred second-wave feminism, which was very much about writing, speaking, and public analysis. Uranus in Virgo created a generation that experiences a

newfound emphasis on personal agency and new access to lifestyle-improving techniques.

What this means about friendship: This is a highly discerning generation of people who come together to exchange ideas and redefine the values of their time.

URANUS IN LIBRA (1968–1975; WILL HAPPEN AGAIN IN 2053–2059)

This generation is all about changes in social justice, diplomacy, and the arts. This was a time when alternative partnerships and roles in society became more eclectic and diverse, and women had more autonomy in their relationships. This was also when divorce really took a stronger role in society, and romantic partnerships were no longer seen as the only way forward in relationships.

What this means about friendship: This generation tends to approach friendship and community in new and progressive ways. They are making space for chosen family outside of traditional models.

URANUS IN SCORPIO (1975–1981; WILL HAPPEN AGAIN IN 2059–2066)

This combination produced a brave but private generation. This period saw a generation that was reached by more corporations, advertising, and media than ever before. There was an increase in occultism and New Age culture during this time. Androgyny also came to the fore, with the rise of New Wave arts and music, and affirmative action also made legal strides during this time as more alternative voices stepped into the mainstream. Scorpio is a sign concerned with power, privacy, and intense experiences, while Uranus represents our eccentric, outsider, individualistic urges.

What this means about friendship: These people create deep connections but aren't quick to trust. They crave transformative experiences that bring them closer to themselves and others.

URANUS IN SAGITTARIUS (1981–1988; WILL HAPPEN AGAIN IN 2066–2072)

These were the arms race years. This era saw an increase in humanitarian interest as well as in fundamentalism. Kids were encouraged to have global pen pals, and individuals connecting to other individuals to create a global society was an important part of this phase. Sagittarius is a cross-cultural sign, fostering open-mindedness and expansion.

What this means about friendship: This generation has strong intuitive impulses and craves adventure. Friendship plays a very important role in their lives, and they have the expectation of living in a global world.

URANUS IN CAPRICORN (1987–1996; LAST OCCURRED 1904–1912)

These were times when the roles of government and corporations took a stronger hold on society. It was also a time when we could take our individual chaos and problems and come to a more systemic solution. Conversely, there were great upsets to agreed-upon norms and the "right way of doing things." There was a major shift in the AIDS

crisis during this time, as pharmaceutical companies stepped in to "protect us" from the epidemic. The systemic reach of the school-to-prison pipeline grew significantly.

What this means about friendship: This generation has a strong a sense of being alone but also interconnected; for them friendship is key to their identities.

URANUS IN AQUARIUS (1996–2003; LAST OCCURRED 1912–1920)

These were times of great scientific and technological advancement. Google was incorporated in 1998; this and other advances in data and information sharing were the mark of a mass, global shift. Computers made their way into classrooms, so this generation grew up with regular access to other people from around the world. Aquarius is ruled by Uranus—this is its natural sign—so there is both the intensity of humanitarianism and a sense of interconnectedness and reliance on others.

What this means about friendship: This generation is deeply connected by the convenience of the internet, even as their individualism has been reinforced. This was also the case when electricity started to become accessible in the last Uranus in Aquarius generation in the 1920s.

URANUS IN PISCES (2003–2011; LAST OCCURRED 1920–1928)

When this placement happened in the roaring 1920s, there was a shift in morality and a greater emphasis on pleasure and disassociation. More recently, there has been a rise in the role of pharmaceuticals and a growing dependence on them to manage our moods. Uranus relates to distraction, an increase in sensitivity, and the desire to feel pleasant. This generation is more socially conscious than others that came before it and yet has stronger escapist tendencies.

What this means about friendship: When it comes to friendship, this generation can be a bit dissociated—in other words, they drop in and drop out of their social lives. They are highly sensitive and need to learn to effectively communicate their boundaries.

URANUS THROUGH THE HOUSES

URANUS IN THE FIRST HOUSE

These people can be a little unapproachable and are pretty terrible at either hiding their feelings or showing their feelings at the appropriate times. This fact can make them very individualistic and eccentric; other people notice them. They are likely to be outspoken, abrupt, and restless. They want friends who are fascinating, inspiring, and can get involved in challenging relationships—because they love a good challenge!

URANUS IN THE SECOND HOUSE

People with Uranus in the second house have their own very specific set of values, and if you share those values, it will solidify a friendship. They have a tendency to be stubborn about what they think is right, which can lead them to jump to conclusions and assume they know how others feel. They often employ this strategy because they think it's going to promote peace within their friendships—it might occasionally do that, but it's not as effective as listening. Their need for friendships may sneak up on them and take them by surprise because it isn't consistent.

URANUS IN THE THIRD HOUSE

People with this placement have friends for different reasons and different seasons. Nothing makes them happier than having an active lifestyle and friends to share it with, but they may be inconsistent in how they approach their friends—that may be because they have so many or simply because their interests are a bit capricious. They tend to be smart, but they're not always focused. They can find themselves feeling irritable or restless, and there's a need here to cultivate a greater ability to listen and to remember to ask questions.

URANUS IN THE FOURTH HOUSE

These people are driven by a foundational restlessness that makes them both exciting and inconsistent. They don't like to be alone, but they also *need* to be alone a fair amount of the time. Having friendships that involve going out into the world and doing stuff together is important, but it's equally important to have friends with whom they can stay at home and have quiet time together. This placement can incline people to start friendships in the middle and convert people into family quickly—for better or for worse.

URANUS IN THE FIFTH HOUSE

Having creative friendships—whether that involves going out to dance, making art, or just straight-up playing—is the best use of this placement. These people need to make sure not to use friendship as a placeholder for romantic love. Flirtation may be a meaningful part of their friendships because they love getting and giving attention. The potential here is to find the self through the act of play and to connect with others through celebration.

URANUS IN THE SIXTH HOUSE

These people have a preferred way to do things day-to-day, so their successful friendships need to work in and around

that routine. They're not very flexible around some things and wildly flexible around others—which can make it hard for people to read their needs. Uranus is not known for diplomacy, so depending on the rest of the chart, they may need to work on expressing their preferences in a way that others can hear. It's important that they allow their friendships to help expand their sense of the world and include mini adventures—even if those adventures take place in the virtual world.

URANUS IN THE SEVENTH HOUSE

This is a placement of abrupt beginnings and endings. People with Uranus in the seventh house may meet people and feel a sudden and intense connection with them and just as suddenly fall out of resonance with them. Their close relationships may be with inconsistent people, or they may be inconsistent and unavailable themselves. Their style of friendship is to be all in for periods of time and then become super preoccupied. It's important that they make sure their friendships actually work for them. And if they don't, it's just as important that they're willing to change them.

URANUS IN THE EIGHTH HOUSE

People with Uranus in the eighth house are likely to have deep and penetrating minds and a keen sense of observation. They can be secretive and may come across as mysterious or unusual—and that's probably because they are. This placement can have them caught up in edgy friendships where spirituality, sexuality, or other emotionally taut mysteries are the theme. Or, conversely, they may just be straight-up loners who don't need more than two friends. They have a tendency to want what they can't have—in both their love lives and their friendships.

URANUS IN THE NINTH HOUSE

People with this placement have some really eccentric ideas about the world, which is to say they're unlikely to follow a conventional religion or even go very far in college and, as a result, unlikely to have the same social connections that many other people have. They don't like hierarchy. That said, they can be pretty self-assured about what they believe, which appeals to some people and can be off-putting to others. This placement can intensify their drive to exchange ideas, to be part of social reform, and to innovate in the realm of art and culture. Boredom is the kiss of death for them in a friendship.

URANUS IN THE TENTH HOUSE

When they learn to accept the ways they're different, these people can shape their lives based on their true selves, and this makes them self-possessed. There's a danger they'll decide to be leaders and expect others to simply follow. They're likely to have friendships with people who share similar ideas about how to live and who take the world on at a similar pace. Their nature is original and ultimately humanitarian, but they can get lost in technology and forget to come back out if they're not careful.

URANUS IN THE ELEVENTH HOUSE

Having a wide and diverse circle of friends is really important to these people, and this tends to happen pretty organically. In fact, they can probably fit in with several different kinds of people. They may know many people but only have a few tight, intimate relationships. It's important that they have some people in their lives who are wildly eccentric—whether they're creatives or activists—as well as contemplative friends to whom they can bring their serious sides. They may come across as chilly or hard to approach—and they may actually be those things. But more likely they're just so caught up in their own thoughts that they're not considering how it makes others feel.

URANUS IN THE TWELFTH HOUSE

These people's relationships to authenticity and self-discovery are deeply personal. Their friendships either give them relief from that process or help facilitate and support it. Self-control is not something they have a consistent grasp on and this can make them pretty confusing friends at times. It's not that they don't mean to be forthcoming, but they're often confused about *which* truth to focus on. They need a fair amount of time alone, and they're likely to have secrets they feel the need to keep. They're most fulfilled in friendships where they let other people get to know their real selves.

NEPTUNE ♆

**Time it takes to traverse the zodiac:
Approximately 165 years**

Sign it rules: Pisces

House it governs: Twelfth

FRIENDSHIP: NEPTUNE

When it comes to your friendship with yourself, Neptune is key. Where we find this foggy planet, we find our ideals, which shape our sense of what's possible, what we hope for, and how fair we feel things are. It's a planet that inspires creativity and spirituality, as well as selfless behavior and humanitarianism, and it articulates itself through high art and a love of nature and animals. It can also govern anxiety, second guessing, ambiguity, and social awkwardness, as well as our desires to disassociate, to escape, and to give up on ourselves.

Where you find Neptune in the birth chart is where you need to reflect on your sense of belonging—not necessarily to a specific group of people, but to your own body and to the time in which you live. This planet can incline you to feel paranoid or unsure and its influence can inspire a sense of victimhood or martyrdom. Conversely, friendships ruled by Neptune can make us feel seen, heard, deeply supportive, and truly uplifted.

SEEING AND BEING SEEN

This planet governs universal love as opposed to individual love. It shows up in sentiments such as "I love all the cats of the world!" Or "I love the land!" Where we find Neptune in the birth chart can indicate the parts of our personality where we have a hard time accepting the warts and shortcomings of others without taking it personally or feeling demoralized. An important part of getting to know others—and letting them truly know us—is acceptance, which Neptune is both great at and terrible at. Friendships that are creative and revolve around activism, the arts, spirituality, or nature (surfing, yoga, or gardening) can be some of the best ways to engage Neptune.

Getting together with someone to watch TV, play video games, or have a drink as a way to check out or blow off steam is also Neptunian, especially when those activities are accompanied by the sense that you're escaping something. That kind of shared space is vital—we all need a safe place to be in the world. But, when we're not embodied, or when we're interacting virtually, we can project all we want onto others and they can project all they want onto us. The experience is missing the sensory impressions that come from a mindful IRL connection—which is more about the Moon and Mars—and it allows us to project onto others or to put them on pedestals.

THROUGH THE LOOKING GLASS

Neptune wants a life without consequences. It wants things to be beautiful and it wants faith to be enough. Sometimes it is enough, but not always. Just because someone is your BFF doesn't mean they're not going to hurt you, disappoint you, or piss you off. And just because you're hurt, doesn't mean you've been wronged. Life is complicated and where Neptune is in the birth chart, it can be hard to tolerate those complications.

Neptune tends to be devotional. It expresses itself as "I love you, therefore you're perfect. I trust you, therefore I never question you." The problem is that people aren't perfect. In order to have true intimacy, we must use discernment alongside our devotion and accept our very real differences.

HOW TO WORK WITH THIS PLANET

When you are in a depressive or anxious state and feel the need to temporarily disappear on your friends, here's a good Neptune pro-tip: When you don't feel up to using language, use emojis. Text your friends a ghost and a kissy face. Make sure you don't alienate others while you're taking care of yourself.

NEPTUNE THROUGH THE SIGNS

Neptune takes 165 years to complete its cycle through the signs and spends 14 years in each sign. Neptune also reflects the convictions and spiritual ideals of a generation. For this reason, I have focused on the Neptune cycles that will most likely reflect my readers and their parents. I won't be covering Neptune in Aries, Taurus, Gemini, Cancer, or Leo because the cycles won't occur in our lifetimes.

NEPTUNE IN VIRGO (1928–1942)

These were Depression-era babies. Born into a period of scarcity, they needed to make do with less, and their spiritual values had to guide them toward finding meaning when things felt dire. This was a generation that had to put self-care aside to deal with day-to-day survival. People born in this era had to learn to take care of their bodies as a way to take care of their minds, and vice versa. The world became larger with the advent of World War II, yet there was a great deal of fear of what we didn't understand. There was a new boogeyman for this generation culturally.

What this means about friendship: This was a period where psychology and psychiatry became more popular in the Western world. This generation spent time trying to figure out how to find a place of belonging and comradery in a disorienting time.

NEPTUNE IN LIBRA (1942–1956)

This phase coincided with the end of World War II, when ideals around love and a global sense of connection emerged. (The United Nations was established during this time.) Nations came together with a Neptunian ideal of unity and a shared will to protect humanity. Children born at this time grew up to be the "make love, not war" generation. Libra is a relational sign—it's concerned with justice and fairness and expresses itself in a one-on-one context. Combined with Neptune's idealistic, romantic, and highly spiritual ways, Libra shaped a whole generation that wanted to learn to partner with people in genuine ways and strived to have more interpersonal empathy.

What this means about friendship: This peace-loving generation uses the arts as a way to connect and places a great emphasis on platonic love.

NEPTUNE IN SCORPIO (1956–1970)

The generation born during this time faced—and embodied—a great deal of intensity. These people expanded their sense of community, finding new ways to commune and connect beyond school, the military, and church. This is in line with Neptune, which governs universal connectedness. Scorpio, on the other hand, is all about letting go—and it's deeply concerned with death and sex for this reason. It is the sign that holds the underbelly of society. This planetary combination can lend itself to addiction, escapism, and excesses in terms of sex and sexuality—which explains why many of the people born during this time grew up to deal with these issues. Sex became freer, but there were consequences. These children grew up in the AIDS crisis, and they were the first modern generation to suffer such dire health consequences of their sexuality.

What this means about friendship: In order to achieve true universal connectedness, these people feel a strong urge to let go of their attachments and preconceived notions. This can lead both to dogma and to spirituality that transcends religion and a great sense of isolation *or* unity in community.

NEPTUNE IN SAGITTARIUS (1970–1984)

As children, this generation experienced greater connectivity than ever before. The world became much smaller as international travel became more common for the middle class. It was a time of global unity and connectedness. Western culture became less monotheistic, and both alternative religion and spirituality were normalized. Another cultural barrier was broken down during this era after *Loving v. Virginia*, the landmark civil rights case that invalidated laws prohibiting interracial marriage in 1967, making Generation X the first to be born in legal interracial marriage in the US. Gen X is conscious about romance, social justice, and fairness; they value liberty on a social scale.

What this means about friendship: This generation is moving beyond nuclear family to encompass more forms of belonging.

NEPTUNE IN CAPRICORN (1984–1998)

Neptune in Capricorn people are a generation prone to questioning the powers that be. But because of the omnipresence of TV, advertisements, movies, and games, this generation is also easily distracted. Capricorn is associated with capitalism, hierarchies, and structural power. The combination of Neptune and Capricorn creates an idealized notion of authority—and the move to nonbinary relationships with authority. The ideal here is a dissolving of old governments and national boundaries and transforming capitalism. This generation was the first one raised with pharmaceutical use as a part of everyday life. These people were inundated by large corporations that had a huge hand in creating a culture that reinforced their product-driven objectives. This was a time when the environment and societal structure became a greater part of society's daily awareness.

What this means about friendship: This generation is questioning hierarchical authority and striving to find their societal voice. This placement is directly related to a greater self-awareness that can lead to anxiety and questioning belonging as the world becomes more interconnected.

NEPTUNE IN AQUARIUS (1998–2012)

Neptune in Aquarius rules connection to collective consciousness. It's where the intellectualization of ideals comes to fruition. Technology is deeply prominent for this generation. It creates an unprecedented sense of interconnection.

Children born during this time had access to everyone around the world, which engendered a sense that everything was possible. The astrology of this generation was epitomized by the Black Lives Matter movement and the anti-gun violence activism of the era—from Ferguson, Missouri, to Parkland, Florida. They were the first generation raised on social media and they tend to feel a sense of shared ideals.

What this means about friendship: This is the first generation that calls dating "hanging out" and there's a new-found emphasis on social groups and friendships.

NEPTUNE IN PISCES (2012–2026)

This is Neptune's natural placement, which makes it a particularly powerful place for the planet to be (that is, its functions are strengthened in both good and bad ways). Neptune and Pisces combined are marked by significant feelings of uncertainty and confusion. Pisces is the sign of the unconscious, of what is hidden—meaning these children are being raised at a time when things are being hidden from view and also emerging into the light. We may see pharmaceuticals and an overwhelming amount of media facilitate dissociation. (Pisces can be a very dissociative sign; under its influence, people can lose themselves in substance use, video games, and media in general.) This generation is being born in a time of humanitarian and environmental crises. This is also an age of art, as these children are born during a time of greater democracy of the arts; people can self-publish and project their voices without the support of traditional arts and the entertainment industry.

What this means about friendship: This generation will have more self-awareness around mental health than any before it, and they've come into a digital world that it requires them to find a more analog place inside themselves.

NEPTUNE THROUGH THE HOUSES

NEPTUNE IN THE FIRST HOUSE

People with this placement make empathetic and generous friends; they're inclined to be shy and sensitive to what others think and feel about them. It's easy to misinterpret them as harmless, gentle, or weak. Neptune in the first house can incline people to want to hide, which they can easily do in plain sight. There's a strong need to retreat into the self—and spirituality and the arts often offer the safest ways to do that.

NEPTUNE IN THE SECOND HOUSE

These people have a difficult time figuring out exactly what they value. There's a tendency to spend money on the people they care about. They have serious issues with regard to class and prefer to not have to care about money. Friendships with people who inspire them to do more in the material world are important for them. They can be conflict-avoidant and often have a hard time expressing their boundaries before they're totally drained.

NEPTUNE IN THE THIRD HOUSE

People with Neptune in the third house can be idealistic, and they tend to trust the potential they see in their friends over the hard evidence, which can lead to some confusing friendships. They're not fantastic at direct communication, and they have a strong desire to protect the feelings of others, making them conflict-avoidant. As friends, they are good listeners and sensitive to nuance.

NEPTUNE IN THE FOURTH HOUSE

These people tend to see their homes as sanctuaries, and having friends who they can chillax with is a huge part of what constitutes intimacy for them. They may not like to go out because of how drain-ing the world can feel, and they may end up using substances as a way to check out from the anxiety that people can produce in them. Their real friends are the ones with whom they can truly feel at home.

NEPTUNE IN THE FIFTH HOUSE

People with this placement tend to have many romantic friendships, or they may forget to prioritize friendships altogether. They're inclined to be creative and spend a great deal of their energy seeking inspi-ration. They can also be inconsistent in how they express their affections due to a sense of anxiety or emotional ambigu-ity. They may have a hard time saying no, but if they can learn to master it, it will be an important part of learning how to be loved for who they are.

NEPTUNE IN THE SIXTH HOUSE

People with Neptune in the sixth house thrive in friendships with a shared definition of self-care. They're inclined to want to take care of their friends and also have important lessons to learn around boundaries. They are empathetic and sensitive but often have a hard time articulating their issues with friends until things have gone too far. They're not naturally energetic and do best with one-on-one friendships in somewhat controlled environments.

NEPTUNE IN THE SEVENTH HOUSE

These people have an impressive capacity for love and devotion, but they run the risk of putting people on pedestals and idealizing them. They're inclined to see the very best in others and may end up doing too much for the people they care about. They have to be careful not to take on other people's moods, and their empa-thetic nature can lead them to feeling anxious or overwhelmed. It might not be easy to face reality with this placement, but it's a necessary part of having healthy friendships over the long term.

NEPTUNE IN THE EIGHTH HOUSE

Creative, empathetic, and highly intuitive, people with this placement may come across as a little emo and intense, and it certainly gives them depth of character. It's important that they're mindful about the kinds of people they let into their social lives because they're so deeply impacted by others. They need to learn to clearly express healthy boundaries within relationships and not expect others to maintain those boundaries for them. It's important that they make friends with whom they do more than drink or party.

NEPTUNE IN THE NINTH HOUSE

Idealistic, philosophical, and worldly, these people are interested in big-picture themes, as well as different cultures, ideas, and religions. They tend to make friends with people who agree with them and can have a tendency to gloss over differences. They may need to avoid dogmatic thinking. The ninth house is all about belief, and these people are bound to spend a great deal of time exploring their ideas and the perspectives of the people around them.

NEPTUNE IN THE TENTH HOUSE

It's really important to these people that they feel at home wherever they are. They're prone to compromising as a way to get their needs met, whether or not it's effective, and they have a tendency to question the direction of their lives. Their friends can be either a pleasant distraction or a vehicle of self-discovery. They're likely to have work friends, even if these friendships are not always based on meaningful intimacy. Cultivating self-acceptance is an important part of letting other people get to know and love them.

NEPTUNE IN THE ELEVENTH HOUSE

These people have a fluid ability to connect with a range of people, often to the point of being indiscriminate. They can be quite idealistic about friendships. This placement can incline them to be open and nonattached within their friendships *or* to be needy for attention and validation. Having creative connections is incredibly important within their friend circles, and they may also find themselves affiliated with groups that reflect their political, spiritual, or humanitarian ideas.

NEPTUNE IN THE TWELFTH HOUSE

People with this placement need close, intimate friendships more than they need pals and activity partners. They tend to be very sensitive, and the people in their lives often can define their feelings and moods. This placement can also be associated with a fair amount of anxiety and nervousness, so the risk is that they look outside themselves for cues. They need a lot of downtime to recharge because people can exhaust them. It's wise for them to make sure that all their friendships aren't online, because while interacting with people IRL can be messier, it tends to be more valuable in the long run.

PLUTO ♇

Time it takes to traverse the zodiac:
Approximately 248 years

Sign it rules: Scorpio

House it governs: Eighth

FRIENDSHIP: PLUTO

Pluto is the planet of creation and destruction—it's intense, oceanic, and transformative. Where we find this planet in the birth chart, we want to be seen and yet feel compelled to hide ourselves. It's only the people we wish to have truly deep connections with or indulge our self-destructive tendencies with that we show our true Plutonian nature. Pluto governs our survival mechanisms and our fight-or-flight instincts. Depending on where we find Pluto in the chart, we have no chill; it's where our power issues are articulated and where we feel like we don't have a choice.

This is not a mellow planet, because its energies are so passionate. That doesn't mean you can't have Plutonian friendships, but it's just as likely that you and your enemies or frenemies will have strong Pluto connections. Pluto is all the Heathers from the movie *Heathers*.

HEALER AND DESTROYER

When we look at friendship in the context of Pluto, the issues that get triggered are often deep, old, and meaningful. Where you find Pluto in the chart is where you are compelled to deeply share of yourself about what's most real; it's where you can heal through the power of communion. This planet can inspire you to act out of compulsion and often involves in-your-face sexuality; working on deep, taboo topics through art or activism; getting wasted; or looking or acting extreme in one way or another. Your Plutonian friends are the people you have intense feelings about or get to be intense with, where power can be more important than true intimacy.

The twelve-step model has a very Plutonian structure because it involves coming together and sharing the realest, messiest parts of ourselves. Often, when people with addiction issues get sober, they lose their communities and their lifestyle has to change. Twelve-step groups such as Alcoholics Anonymous (AA) provide an automatic circle of friends. It's an important example of how Pluto can facilitate friendships through the act of getting raw and real. This energy concerns the things that are hard to talk about and share openly. Other examples of Plutonian friendships are the kinds where you commune around witchcraft, end-of-life issues, spiritual belief systems, or some form of self-destruction.

If you are a Plutonian person (in other words, you have a strongly placed or heavily aspected Pluto), your nature is going to be intense. You may be driven by profound and negative feelings and consequently end up acting in ways that are perceived as compulsive and dramatic. In the context of friendship, you'll often find yourself in all-or-nothing dynamics. On the one hand, your intensity may cause you to come across as demanding, and you probably have strong feelings about who you choose to show up for and how you express yourself to others. On the other hand, you may shield yourself from other people completely, and go the route of rejecting others before they can reject you. This can be much like being everybody's therapist or parent and never really showing up with your true self.

HOW TO WORK WITH THIS PLANET

If you feel yourself getting dragged into the depths of defensiveness, paranoia, or compulsion, it's important to use the same safety rules that apply when in an undertow in the ocean. Don't struggle against it, don't try to understand. Instead, just go limp. Let go and then return to the topic that you're obsessing over when you don't feel so activated, ideally seventy-two hours later.

PLUTO THROUGH THE SIGNS

Pluto takes 248 years to complete its cycle through the signs and spends 12 to 31 years in each sign. It marks the intense compulsions of a generation. For this reason, I have focused on the Pluto cycles that will most likely reflect my readers and their parents or children. I won't cover Pluto in Aquarius, Pisces, Aries, Taurus, or Gemini because they

won't occur in our lifetimes. You'll also notice that some of the years below overlap. That's because all the outer planets retrograde in and out of a sign. That will often coincide with a planet being in two different signs in one calendar year.

PLUTO IN CANCER (1913–1939)

Pluto is associated with transformation and can be destructive, while Cancer is associated with security, the home, and nation. During this phase, we had World War I, the Great Depression, and the beginning of World War II. This generation had a really rough go of it because they never felt safe, so they are prone to being highly protective or reactive. It was also a bit of a clannish or nationalistic generation (Jim Crow segregation laws were in effect during this period, and the KKK held a great deal of power). It was a real us-versus-them world. The emphasis on family was really strong, as people were struggling through poverty and war.

What this means about friendship: People were looking over their shoulders more. Nationalism divided people around the world. And by the same token, it forced people closer together than they otherwise would have been. Immediate family was really important. These people had it rough and that difficulty put a real strain on their heart connections.

PLUTO IN LEO (1939–1957)

This generation lived through a period of oppressive dictators, including Benito Mussolini in Italy, Adolf Hitler in Germany, Kim Il Sung in North Korea, Ho

Chi Minh in Vietnam, Mao Tse-tung in China, Francisco Franco in Spain, Nikita Khrushchev in the Soviet Union, and many more. So, it only makes sense that the people born during this period were shaken. The era also saw the explosion of the first atomic bombs in Hiroshima and Nagasaki. These folks were dealing with ferocious energy, so themes of control, success, and validation were all strong. There was a great deal of racial segregation and xenophobia. The first Detroit race riots took place during this period—in other words, people spoke out and were shut down violently. This was an era of anger expressed and repressed. Those born with Pluto in Leo were not responsible for these cultural shifts, but they were raised during these shifts—prompted by the generation before them.

What this means about friendship: People of this generation are charismatic and willing to be very assertive about their thoughts and feelings, but it doesn't always go well for them.

PLUTO IN VIRGO (1957–1972)

This generation was raised by Pluto in Leo parents and is much more socially conscious than the immediate generations before them. A lot of substantial changes to laws and shifts in medicine occurred in this period. Pluto in Virgo has the compulsion to shift focus often, seeking the most perfect truth—but since there is no perfect truth, these folks can get caught up in their routines and habits. This generation may have abandonment issues.

What this means about friendship: This generation had a new emphasis on personal development and exploration. Virgo influences the willingness to unpack the pieces and be healed by their reconstruction. This generation has many who tend to be loners, but their need for friendship is really a need to be seen and heard. They also require serious private time to be with their thoughts and parse out their needs. This generation was both made closer and sent further apart because of the social movements. There was the sense of having a mission, a calling—and that often functioned as a reason to connect with friends, or a motivation to not be vulnerable in a real way.

PLUTO IN LIBRA (1971–1984)

After the Vietnam War ended in 1975, there was a return to prosperity and relative peace during this period. This generation didn't need to focus as much on practical survival as the generations immediately before it did, so there was more room for the arts and social justice issues to become a larger part of the culture. Friendships took on a much larger role. Generation X was very conscious about romance, social justice, and fairness. Where there's injustice they took it personally. There was also a spike in the number of latchkey kids. As the world started to get much larger, the concept of stranger danger took on weight, and the cultural conversation became more about only trusting people you knew. The Black Panthers were started in Pluto in Virgo, but the bulk of the movement took place in this phase. The rigidity of gender roles we saw with Pluto in Leo was softened by the time Pluto in Libra came around with the disco era and changes in the film industry.

What this means about friendship: Feminism and LGBTQ issues made major strides during this period. Self-development through the vehicle of relationships became very important. People were hitchhiking; women were in the work world. You could meet people in different ways.

PLUTO IN SCORPIO (1984–1995)

This was the first generation to grow up with computers in their homes. Their sense of connectedness to the larger world can make them feel jaded or cynical. They've been exposed to all of it; nothing is taboo. There is also more androgyny—these kids were exposed to more nuanced and complicated gender identities and sexualities, including pop stars such as David Bowie and Annie Lennox. This generation had sexual images permeating the mainstream culture. They saw gay characters on TV and further expanded notions of gender and sexuality.

What this means about friendship: This generation had more emphasis on friendship—they are able to choose more ways of being interconnected with people that didn't involve partnerships.

PLUTO IN SAGITTARIUS (1995 TO 2008)

This placement also occurred between 1746 and 1762. People born during these periods were brought up with paradoxical understandings of the world. On the one hand, these were times of prosperity; on the other hand, political tensions were reaching breaking points. In the case of this most recent era, the oppressed and poor were becoming more and more impatient with the ruling class. There was an increased awareness of the need for change, and these people were prone to being interested in political reform and revolution. They are excellent at inspiring others with their charisma and energetic personalities. There has been an expansion of gender roles and norms and a burgeoning acceptance of different gender presentations. Social media and self-publishing have become more available, making it possible for a whole range of formerly disenfranchised folks to bypass traditional gatekeepers and have their voices heard.

What this means about friendship: Social connections are just as important as actual friendship for this generation. People under the influence of Sagittarius move through intimacies quickly and can get impatient when things get stuck or feel like they're part of a routine. This can have people rushing toward each other and crashing and burning, or there can be a renaissance of finding meaning based on common interests. Social media also radically changed the landscape of friendship for the first time. It allows barriers to get crossed and for cultures to more easily meld into each other. People have a larger web of friends, and social organizing through technology has become much more accessible.

PLUTO IN CAPRICORN (2008–2024)

The Boston Massacre, the Boston Tea Party, the American Revolution, and the signing of the Declaration of Independence all occurred during the prior Pluto in Capricorn (1762 to 1778). This current generation will undo a lot of the restrictions that were established during Pluto in Sagittarius—particularly as it relates to lack of privacy and corporate control. This generation will be highly committed to change, sometimes rather cynical about the state of the world. They will be serious, be dedicated to their causes, and have rock-solid morals and ambitions. They'll use frameworks of oppression to their advantage, and they'll approach the task of improving the world with grim determination. This generation will also embody power as opposed to preaching or lecturing about it. These people may place practical or external matters in higher esteem than personal ones. They are likely to be capable of great emotional maturity or may be likely to shut down. They will be very capable, but they may be ruthless.

What this means about friendship: These people will place far less value on romantic relationships than previous generations did. Platonic relationships will likely play a stronger role in their lives as they reinforce individuality and focus on equality.

PLUTO THROUGH THE HOUSES

PLUTO IN THE FIRST HOUSE

These people can come across as intense, and they attract other intense people to them. They may avoid or make really focused eye contact. They may also be prone to oversharing, so having healthy boundaries and knowing their own limits is a big part of working with this placement. They're not super comfortable or adept at cultivating platonic intimacy, because they are highly sensitive to rejection. Although their friendships are essential to their identities, they also need a good deal of time alone.

PLUTO IN THE SECOND HOUSE

This placement gives people really intense feelings about money and class, which can manifest in either scarcity issues or superiority issues, feelings of resentment or entitlement. The good news is this placement can give them earning power and, if they are directed in this way, they may have the capacity to heal and transform the values they were raised with into something they truly believe for themselves.

PLUTO IN THE THIRD HOUSE

Communication is a big deal for these people. This placement may make them withhold—to the point that they're not comfortable speaking their truths—or it may make them intense or punishing in how they use language or tone. Because communication and words are so important to them, they may procrastinate or put off difficult conversations or, conversely, rush in and demand to be heard right away.

PLUTO IN THE FOURTH HOUSE

People with Pluto in the fourth house have a great need for privacy and intimacy. These two drives can result in them only having a few really close friends that they allow in deeply. Or, with difficult aspects, they may even decide not to make friends outside of their family. They have an incisive way of understanding power dynamics in social situations and may prefer to hold back when they're not really sure of their places. Their true friends are people they're comfortable inviting into their homes.

PLUTO IN THE FIFTH HOUSE

This placement makes the arts hugely important to them and having friends with whom they can dance or enjoy creativity in general is a huge part of what gives them life. Sensitive to power dynamics, these people may be inclined to be flirtatious with friendships. They run the risk of being manipulative in their quest for attention and validation. That said, they are very talented and generous friends.

PLUTO IN THE SIXTH HOUSE

These people work so hard at their jobs, whether they like them or not, that they can build up resentment toward others for not doing the same. They believe that they always have to try really hard, but that's not necessarily true. Developing healthy boundaries with their own behaviors is essential to being able to chill with their friends. It's possible that food and exercise are really big deals for them—but rigidity around self-care can become a way to keep other people out instead of inviting them in. The best version of placement, this allows them to have deep and meaningful friendships with the people they work with, or to have friends they can work on life with.

PLUTO IN THE SEVENTH HOUSE

Relationships are of the utmost importance to these people—so much so that they can be obsessive about how deeply they connect and with whom. That doesn't mean that it's always easy for them to open up to others, given how much they want assurances. This can incline people to skip the beginning and jump right to the middle and become besties right after they meet someone. Or they may fear losing control of themselves and never really let others in. Relationships can be powerful forces of transformation for them, and even their more casual friendships will bring up intense feelings.

PLUTO IN THE EIGHTH HOUSE

Sex is intense for people with this placement; it can be something that their friendships are predicated on—talking about sex, thinking about sex, and so on—or it can be something they try to keep private from their platonic relationships. This placement makes people highly emo, and their capacity to experience love, grief, and resentment is deep. This placement can also indicate that people have strong psychic ability and can struggle with addiction. There are very few people these individuals truly let get to know them, but those who do will be rewarded with undying loyalty.

PLUTO IN THE NINTH HOUSE

This placement inclines people to have deep and penetrating minds. They can be afraid of those who are different from them or, alternatively, profoundly interested and invested in people from different cultures or religions. Their experience of spirituality is deep and may or may not get channeled through actual religion, but their connection to the divine can be quite profound. Education is important to them, and this can be achieved through institutions, travel, or the school of hard knocks.

PLUTO IN THE TENTH HOUSE

These folks can be fixated on career— and that could mean they're terrified of it, they're avoiding it at all costs, or they're workaholics. They need their friends to support them in whatever paths they've taken. They have a habit of holding on to resentments, but they also have great power to pick themselves up, dust themselves off, and move on, once they've decided to. Their alliances are important to them, in some ways more than their intimacies are. It is crucial that in their drive for success they make sure that resentment or power drives don't trip them up and stop them from having relationships with people who care about them for who they are, instead of what they do or what they offer. This

placement gives them the capacity for achieving great things.

PLUTO IN THE ELEVENTH HOUSE

Friends are incredibly important to these people because they cherish friendships so deeply, but feeling they belong is a tenuous, shifting sands sort of thing. Power struggles can interfere with friendships; they may feel possessive or isolated within groups, and they might reject others for fear of being rejected first. But they're still drawn to figuring out how to have a community. Being a part of something larger, focused on social reform or doing humanitarian work, is a great use of their energy—because they truly care.

PLUTO IN THE TWELFTH HOUSE

This is a very psychic placement, and these people may have scary dreams or a deep sleep life. They are empathetic and very sensitive to other people's energies, but their reactions to these sensitivities can be to either overextend themselves to others or shut down all together. There's a need to cultivate discretion around who they let in and how much. This placement can incline people to feel easily victimized or to befriend people who feel like victims (I'm not referring to true victimhood here, but to feelings). They may also struggle with addiction issues— whether it's addiction to substances, food, or TV—and they can be rigid in their self-care habits.

TWO

HANGING OUT AND DATING

Dating involves a whole range of possible scenarios, but in this chapter, I'm going to focus on two diverging paths: dating with the intent to form a committed relationship and dating to have fun (otherwise known as hanging out). With the former there's hope it can grow into something more; with the latter there's the understanding that what you see is what you get. The two approaches are not mutually exclusive and they both involve flirting, chemistry, and hooking up. They also both have their own set of perks, challenges, rules, and risks. For most of us, most of the time, both approaches usually start off the same way: awkward and uncertain for the first few months. That kind of pre-commitment, pre-certainty, early-stage dating is what I'm going to look at here.

HELLO, HAWAII

When you're really excited about someone new, it's like visiting Hawaii. It's magical, beautiful, and there are rainbows and waterfalls everywhere. But moving to Hawaii is a different story. It can be hard to find a job, the weather never really varies, and it's easy to get island fever. In a nutshell, that's the difference between dating and establishing a relationship.

When we develop feelings for someone, we naturally reflect on the past and project into the future—this is the Moon in action. And when our attraction is primarily visceral or sexual, that's the

influence of Mars. But all of our planets work together, and it's easy to convert sexual desire into intimate feelings without even meaning to—for better or worse. On the other hand, if we're having fun with someone and it's working for us, allowing ourselves to enjoy that union without projecting meaning onto it is a really healthy skill.

Your birth chart can tell you a lot about how you approach sex and love (in ways you may or may not be completely aware of). While some people feel that the two are inherently connected—that revealing yourself physically to another person is an expression of connection, intimacy, and trust—many others see sex as a physical act that is separate from emotional intimacy. The exciting thing about human experience is that there's room for it all. Some people will have phases of their lives when they experience many different kinds of sexual connections. Others may keep sex separate from intimacy. And some may choose to have sex only with people they have closeness and intimacy with. There's no right or wrong way to be when it comes to your sexual preferences and the choices you make with your heart.

It can be hard to talk about sex—not only with our therapist or our besties, but also with the people we're doing it with. And yet, talking about sex is an important part of finding out what really works for you. Identifying your preferences and validating your right to like certain things and not others—or to change your mind about what does and doesn't work for you—is an important part of embodying your sexuality, and therefore birth chart, in a healthy way.

Mercury governs verbal communication, the Moon governs emotional presence, Venus governs how we flirt and socialize, and Mars governs the way we assert our preferences and needs. These planets don't exist in isolation, but whether or not they work collaboratively is another question. Your sense of ease with fluidly moving among these areas is individual to your birth chart—and understanding all parts of the equation can enable you to embody the wholeness of what you are.

FANTASY, DESIRE, AND AGENCY

I'm a big supporter of taking ownership of your own fantasy landscape, regardless of your birth chart, and not allowing your sexuality to be exclusively responsive to one person—unless that person is you.

There's often a gender imbalance when it comes to comfort with and ownership of sexuality. That's because people who are raised male are encouraged to have a wide-open, no-holds-barred fantasy landscape—whatever turns them on is okay. By contrast, people raised female are encouraged to have a more responsive, protected sexuality. Many of us were never encouraged to explore what we liked or wanted; we were told instead to focus on what our partners wanted or what was "appropriate." Women and nonbinary folks are often taught, directly or indirectly, to be ashamed about their

own sexual desires and experiences, while those who are raised male are often reared to believe they can boost their self-esteem and strength with their sexual experiences and sex drive.

Our fantasy landscapes exist in the realm of the imagination, which is governed by Neptune. But what we're really talking about is investigating personal preference, which is the jurisdiction of all the planets. Therefore, it's too simple to say that Mars is the sole driver of our sex lives even though that's the prevailing message of astrology. Human sexuality is complicated, layered, and deeply interwoven with power and safety. The truth is that being willing and able to explore our feelings, ideas, and even our fears is essential to navigating a fantasy landscape. Having a sense of entitlement to want whatever you want is really healthy, even if acting on it is not. In this way, every planet in the birth chart reflects and describes components of your sexuality, which is a beautiful thing to own.

WHY CAN'T I SKIP TO THE LONG-TERM RELATIONSHIP PART?

When you first start dating someone and emotions run high, you can feel like you really know the other person. This can incline you to make commitments and assumptions before you're truly ready. On the following page are my rules to remember when you are totally crushed out.

LANYADOO'S YOU-DON'T-KNOW-A-BINCH RULES

YOU DON'T KNOW A BINCH
until you've fought, and
it was your fault.

YOU DON'T KNOW A BINCH
until you've fought, and
it was their fault.

YOU DON'T KNOW A BINCH
until you've been sick.

YOU DON'T KNOW A BINCH
until they've been sick.

YOU DON'T KNOW A BINCH
until you've been together
during the Christmas season
(even if you don't celebrate).

CONSENT

An important part of sexual health is respecting yourself enough to cut out any binches if they don't respect your sexual boundaries. The people who do that are not your friends, and it's not your fault if they don't stop when you say stop. That said, the onus is on you to make sure you're expressing those boundaries clearly. Consent is simple, but it can feel complicated. It's important to verbally express, even with only one word, when you want someone to slow down, pause, or stop. This requires you to believe you have the right to do so—and you absolutely do. We all do.

But we don't always feel as if we have the skills or the right to clearly express our boundaries. If you are doing something that doesn't feel like a clear, enthusiastic yes, it's healthy and fair to say, "I don't know if I like this. Give me a minute." You don't have to know everything about what you like, because a fun sexual relationship can sometimes involve exposing yourself to something new or pushing some boundaries. Sex is complicated.

We've all been fed the terrible Disney princess story that the perfect partner will always respond to our needs in the perfect way, and we never have to say a word or tell them what we like or how we like it. But that's not usually how life is. Satisfying and healthy sexual relationships require that both parties have a sense of agency and that both parties' sexual desires and preferences get equal attention.

Astrologers have typically associated Mars with sex because it governs the way people express their needs and desires viscerally and at times forcefully. But this is where astrology needs a feminist re-visioning. Every person of every gender has Mars in their chart. The idea that men express sex and women have it done to them is old and tired. It's not an astrological truth. But because of many centuries of patriarchy, women and gender-nonconforming people have more societal and ancestral roadblocks to accessing and fully being in their bodies and expressing their Mars.

SO MANY WAYS TO BE SEXUAL (OR NOT)

Just for clarity, heterosexuality and monogamy are not superior or healthier than any of the myriad options that exist. There are lots of other types of connections and unions that work for people, and they don't necessarily involve anything that resembles conventional sex or romance. This includes asexual folks and people in the kink community who opt for alternative, play-based relationships.

Whether your thing is deep eye-contact with the lights off, missionary sex, or LARPing, there are many ways to connect and build intimacy in a given moment with a given person. What's important is that you honor the truth of what you can do—and really want to do—in a healthy way that is authentic to you.

SUN ☉

Time it takes to traverse the zodiac:
Approximately 1 year

Sign it rules: Leo

House it governs: Fifth

HANGING OUT AND DATING: THE SUN

In astrology, the Sun rules your identity; it is your will and your sense of self. Where it lies in your birth chart determines what people call your "sign." Where the Sun appears in the birth chart, our energies are meant to be expressed. And when they're repressed, our Sun sign also shapes the way we act out.

OUR ESSENTIAL, VITAL SELVES

Who we are, what we like, and how we express all that is governed by our Sun sign. When it comes to dating and hanging out, the Sun is a really big deal, because it's about being seen as who we really are. It can also tell us how we most want to be validated. And it's hot to feel desired for exactly who we perceive ourselves to be.

As the brightest luminary in the sky, the Sun represents your vitality and virility—and I use *virility* to mean "strength," "force," and "the ability to make things happen" (qualities without gender). The Sun governs your essential self, and if you're having a casual hookup or you

don't want it to go much further than sex, the Sun may or may not play a significant role. It might not seem important that the other person gets to know you at all, and you may just be needing to have more experiences that are playful or romantic (it may be less about who you truly are and more about who you are with another person in this moment). Or, conversely, you may just want someone who makes you feel good about yourself and who sees you, even if you don't want to nurture the connection to create a deeper, longer-lasting relationship.

On the other hand, when you're starting what you hope might be a longer romantic relationship, it may be easy to feel that the person you're dating knows you better than they actually do, just because there's chemistry and intimacy between you. But people can only see what we show them—and they see it from their own perspectives. It's human nature to hold back some parts of who we are at first—to pick and choose and curate our identities in ways we think will make people like us or help us get what we want. But the fact is, getting to know a person takes time, effort, and shared experience.

A PERSON IS MORE THAN THEIR SUN SIGN

Because Sun sign astrology is so popular, what you've heard about a person's sign can bias you about them in the first few weeks or months. (She's a Cancer, so she must be super emotional! He's a Scorpio, so he must be super sexual!) But that kind of simplification won't get you very far. Not only are we much more than our Sun signs, but the Sun only gets fully expressed when there's enough safety, trust, time, and experience between people.

As you show up and get to know others, the security and stability of your will (the Sun) and your ego (Mars) have everything to do with how authentic you're able to be. When you start dating someone and you're really not sure where it's going or how you feel about one another, it's not realistic to expect to be your complete self, or to be fully seen. That early stage is when most people are likely to feel scared, shy, and hopeful—which are not disingenuous feelings, but they're not the same as being totally relaxed in yourself. So, whether you're a hunter (Mars) or a gatherer (Venus) in the world of dating, caught up in a cycle of three-month relationships, or dating around and getting to know many people, your Sun is an essential part of what you're leading with. Just keep in mind that a person's Sun probably isn't going to shine at its full capacity at the very beginning.

So, take it slow and let things develop. Make room for your Sun so that you can be as authentic as possible in the early days (unless you just want to hit it and quit it; in which case, you can leave your Sun wherever you want to put it).

WHAT DOES IT MEAN TO BE "ON THE CUSP"?

Astrology is math! Every zodiac sign is one twelfth of a 360-degree wheel, or 30 degrees, and based on that math, you're either one sign or another. My experience has shown that most people who feel "cuspy" do so because they tend to have planets in two adjacent signs.

HOW TO WORK WITH THIS PLANET

Think about the people you're hooking up with or dating, and ask yourself: How much do I trust them? The answer to that question should be directly related to how much of your true self you share with them. It's okay to reveal only the parts that are appropriate for a specific union at a specific time; just make sure you're honest about how you do it.

THE SUN THROUGH THE SIGNS

SUN IN ARIES

These people like to jump into things and have a tendency to rush to conclusions. They can be such leaders that they don't always listen to what others tell them about themselves. They may be well-suited to casual hookups, because they like to get in there, get theirs, and get out. They need to feel like there can be spontaneity in all dating situations. Aries also governs irritability, so a lot depends on whether an Aries likes you right now. This is a fiery, independent, take-no-prisoners placement.

SUN IN TAURUS

Sensual experience is very important to these people. They tend to have good social skills and the process of connecting with others and flirting is appealing to them. But they're not usually casual about sex and dating. People with the Sun in Taurus love repetition and routine; if they're having a grand time with you, they're going to want to do it again and again. They also often struggle with saying what they mean and meaning what they say—especially if they risk hurting the feelings of others.

SUN IN GEMINI

These people are great at asking questions and making conversation, and they always have their eyes out for the next shiny, glittery things. They can also get caught up in their heads. Their ruling planet is Mercury, which means they like to text you quickly, meet up, and explore. They're not particularly concerned with attachments to the future; they want to have fun now.

SUN IN CANCER

These folks ultimately seek love and intimacy, so they can have a hard time in casual dating arrangements. It's tempting for them to want to quickly convert people they've only recently started dating into intimate connections. They can be a little self-protective and hard to get to know, but once they feel good in your presence, they're usually warm, kind, and supportive.

SUN IN LEO

Leos may confuse lust and love; they like flirting, chasing, being chased, and, of course, being adored. In this way, they are well suited to casual dating. But it can also be hard for them to let go of a lover or situation if they're having fun or feel that they're the star of the show. They can be quick to decide whether someone is right for them and need to learn not to jump to conclusions (or into commitments).

SUN IN VIRGO

Virgos can be very cerebral and live largely in their heads. If you can appeal to their interests, they're fantastic conversationalists with great senses of humor. They can be skilled at keeping casual relationships very clear and consensual, because they can decide ahead of time that the relationships won't ever be serious. But they have to be honest with themselves about their willingness to let go at the ends of encounters and not get attached. Virgos can be quite accommodating at the beginning of relationships but make no mistake: They know what they want.

SUN IN LIBRA

Libras are the lovers of the zodiac, making them not well suited to casual sex and dating. They can be accommodating—sometimes at the expense of being authentic. These folks may also be possessive toward the people with whom they have a good time and feel intimate. Because they have a tendency to be partnership-minded, they're also prone to rush relationships and can move them forward before they fully know what they're getting into.

SUN IN SCORPIO

It's not always easy to know where you stand when you start dating a Scorpio because they can be a bit hard to read, and they kind of like it that way. Trust that if they're truly interested in you, they will make it known. The stereotype is that Scorpios are super sexual, and while that's not true for everyone, they do tend to have strong sex drives. When these people start to feel really close to their lovers, they become the most attached of the zodiac and they have a really hard time letting go. For that reason, they need to be somewhat cautious about who they let in.

SUN IN SAGITTARIUS

These people can be really easy to go on a first date with because they're so excitable and adventurous. They want to have love without rules or obligations. The problem with casual hookups with people whose Sun is in Sagittarius is that they usually want more, and they don't like to hear "no." If others try to limit the connections, they're going to feel restless and bothered. This sign is also plagued by foot-in-mouth syndrome, so don't take it personally if they say something abrupt.

SUN IN CAPRICORN

People with their Sun in Capricorn can be very serious and have a tendency to find themselves in fairly traditional relationships. At the same time, their repression can lead them to be pretty kinky people, and casual dating tends to be super casual for them without attachments or a lot of emotional intimacy. The trick is to make sure that they're not trying to evade their own needs by keeping things on the surface. They can be hard to achieve closeness with, but if Capricorns like you, they are very earnest in their approaches to dating and tend to alternate between being cocky and shy.

SUN IN AQUARIUS

The most important thing to an Aquarius is what's interesting to them, so if a lover sparks excitement in them, they're going to want to invest time in the relationship. Of course, they're also great at casual dating, especially if the most interesting thing about their lovers is the sex. These people are fun, eccentric, and open to getting to know others, but deeper affections can kind of creep up on them.

SUN IN PISCES

Pisceans are very sensitive, and if they forge deep physical connections with others, they have a tendency to fall in love. Then again, they also tend to want to feel really free, and sometimes that freedom can come from disassociating with a new person. Because they're so shy, these people can be accommodating in new dating situations—as they adjust. Not the most assertive of the Sun signs, and a bit prone to anxiety, Pisceans often want to know where they stand, even if they're not quick to ask.

THE SUN THROUGH THE HOUSES

SUN IN THE FIRST HOUSE

These people, especially those who have the Sun within 7 degrees of the ascendant in either direction, tend to capture others' attention when they enter a room, and they can be very good at flirting. This placement makes a person want to be seen. They may jump headfirst into experiences that seem fun or validating, but if they feel that they're not getting the kind of attention they crave, it's simply not going to work. They can be great athletic lovers, and when they're bored they can lose interest pretty quickly.

SUN IN THE SECOND HOUSE

Being adored is very important to these people. They want to feel desired, and they need their lovers to express their desires through tangible things, such as food, texts, and gifts. The sensual part of sex is really important to them; they're not great with quickies if they don't include a lot of touching, flirting, or physical connection leading up to it (preheat the oven).

SUN IN THE THIRD HOUSE

A great way to flirt with these people is to appeal to their senses of humor and have clever things to say. They are easily bored or distracted, and if you are the most exciting distraction around you'll go far. They're playful and dynamic, love to be entertained, and are likely to experience many kinds of lovers over the course of their lifetimes. They're down for casual dating or getting to know people, but it's important that they learn to prioritize forthright communication, so they don't mislead others.

SUN IN THE FOURTH HOUSE

While they may enjoy casual dating, these folks are not always super transparent about it. They are more likely than others to either keep something seriously on the down low or to convert crushes into partners too quickly. Because this Sun placement is so emotional, they may have to really pace how much time they spend with new people and avoid rushing to conclusions about their intentions.

SUN IN THE FIFTH HOUSE

Fun is the name of the game for these people, who really like connecting in the moment and have dynamic love affairs and liaisons. All of this continues as long as they feel adored, worshipped, and valued. Compliments will get you everywhere with these people, but because they have such good BS detectors, you better mean it. And a cautionary reminder: Not everything that feels good is good for them.

SUN IN THE SIXTH HOUSE

These people can be a bit shy or reserved and are not given to casual dating. Once they allow someone to become part of their habits, they're inclined to develop feelings for them. In other words, if they're trying to keep it casual, they should avoid having routine morning coffee with their love interest or snuggling together at night (just stick to the facts, ma'am). They may decide to keep their dating lives very contained. It's important for them to learn to give others a chance by being really clear about what their limits and needs are around dating.

SUN IN THE SEVENTH HOUSE

Partnership is a big draw for these people. They run the risk of consenting to casual dynamics in the hope they will convert them into longer-term, more committed relationships. If they're not transparent about their motives, it can get them into serious trouble. An important lesson for them is that even good sex doesn't always equal love or even intimacy. These people will benefit from remembering that intimate love + sex = loving and intimate sex.

SUN IN THE EIGHTH HOUSE

These people can be drawn to secret love affairs. They're inclined toward enjoying sex for its own sake or, paradoxically, can want to merge with those they are passionate about. They need to prioritize being honest about what they like, about who they're hooking up with, and whether they're actually having fun; intense experiences, while exciting, aren't actually all that fulfilling for them.

SUN IN THE NINTH HOUSE

Adventure is very important to these people. They are just as capable of having whirlwind romances that start and stop abruptly as they are of having pretty puritanical values around sex and love. This placement can incline folks to be excited about exploring new people and new experiences, but their fantasy lives can cause them to weave stories out of feelings that may not be true.

SUN IN THE TENTH HOUSE

This placement can come with silent thunder. These people value casual dating, but they have a low tolerance for small talk. This is a goal-oriented placement, so these folks can be quite focused and outcome-oriented, even with dating and sexual encounters. If they decide they're not in serious or beneficial situations, they will likely jump ship.

SUN IN THE ELEVENTH HOUSE

These people are capable of having really lovely experiences with people they hardly know. They cherish their independence and their autonomy, so they may have periods of their lives when they prefer keeping things casual, having friends with benefits, or dating people who live out of town. They're capable of being forthright about how they're available and what they want, even though they don't always take the time to communicate that way.

SUN THE TWELFTH HOUSE

Although they're generally not well suited for it, these folks will often find themselves in casual dating situations because they're sensitive and not always great at asserting boundaries or limits. They're good at catching feelings and running with potential. They may have a hard time truly accepting purely casual relationships. It's important that they practice safe sex as an act of self-care.

MOON ☾

Time it takes to traverse the zodiac: Approximately 29.5 days

Sign it rules: Cancer

House it governs: Fourth

HANGING OUT AND DATING: THE MOON

The Moon rules our feelings and emotional needs and pulls heavily on our past experiences. Understanding its placement in the birth chart can tell us a lot about the kinds of relationships that are best for us. It can also reveal what it takes to move through either casual or more serious dating situations without abandoning ourselves. When it comes to hooking up, it's important to remember that while some people see sex as a physical act—like scratching an itch—many others don't experience it that way (even if they really want to). For many of us, sex prompts all kinds of feelings about ourselves and the people we're with. The tricky part is that we can have sex with people with whom we haven't cultivated trust and intimacy first. And good sex can mimic closeness that is otherwise only earned through time and mutual care. So, it's especially important to figure out whether you're the type of person who can have sex without developing an emotional attachment; understanding your Moon and its placement in the chart can help with that.

ESTABLISHING HEALTHY EMOTIONAL BOUNDARIES

What happens before and after sex is also important. For some, the act of hooking up is less intimate than snuggling, making out, or having coffee in the morning. For others, sex is more intimate than talking about childhood. The point is that we're all different—and your emotional nature is yours to understand and care for. Maintaining healthy boundaries with people you're only hooking up with is not a matter of right and wrong; it's a matter of what's healthy and appropriate for you.

There's this notion that we're not supposed to care about the people we're dating casually—or hanging out with. Now, much like in the 1970s, sexual liberation and sexual autonomy seem to be paired with a pressure to be "cool with whatever." That's really awesome for people who *are* cool with whatever, but, as with many trends, blindly following this one can result in someone's feelings getting hurt—and that sucks. If you're someone who is tender-hearted or relationship-oriented, or if you're seeking security and stability, the chances are high that it's not healthy for you to stay in a casual relationship for very long. And it's important to take your self-care habits especially seriously in the inevitable stage of uncertainty that happens before an expressed commitment.

THE SLOW LUNAR PACE

If you find that you're moving toward a committed relationship, connecting sexually is an important part of the process, but so is emotional intimacy—building trust, safety, and establishing compatibility. If you have strong feelings for someone who shows care in a way that doesn't make you feel cared for, you have a lunar problem. The mind (Mercury) can make connections and figure things out quite quickly. The heart (the Moon), on the other hand, is a lot slower. It needs space, time, and experiences to identify its needs and figure out what makes it feel safe.

In the early stages of a relationship, many of us focus on being liked and determining whether we like someone (which is all ruled by Venus). This is normal, and yet it's only one part of a much larger equation. If the overall goal is love, intimacy, and real closeness, then it's essential that we're honest with ourselves about how we feel and what we really need (in other words, the Moon) from a partner. This is how we can determine whether we have emotional compatibility.

As I mentioned on page 94, you don't truly know the person you're dating (or their Moon) until: You've fought, and it was your fault; you've fought, and it wasn't your fault; you've been sick; your dating partner has been sick; and you spend a Christmas together (regardless of your religious background). In order to truly get to know someone emotionally and have an intimacy you can rely on, you have to share certain experiences with the other person. You have to know how they handle adversity.

Being liked is not equal to liking how you feel about yourself. Be willing to pause and reflect on how you actually feel around a new person. If it seems the other person doesn't like you—or in fact doesn't—don't interpret that to mean you're not likable. The danger with this scenario is that you're giving a relative stranger authority over your self-esteem and your value. When you do that you risk losing track of yourself. When you stay connected to your Moon (that is, your own feelings), you will be more likely to notice whether you're giving away your power or devaluing yourself. If you are devaluing yourself, bringing awareness to that fact can lead you to take better care of yourself in situations where that might happen—and hopefully you'll start doing less of it.

HOW TO WORK WITH THIS PLANET

The Moon is wildly important when you're getting to know someone. It's easy to get caught up in either the excitement of liking someone or the fear that they don't like you. What's most important is not whether you're compatible with the person you're dating or whether you feel cared for—it's that you remain a loving, caring friend to yourself. Choosing self-loving actions in the face of great desire or heartache isn't easy, but your heart is worth protecting.

THE MOON THROUGH THE SIGNS

MOON IN ARIES

These people are strong-willed, independent, and emotionally daring. They're usually at their best when they can lead because they tend to have strong preferences and reactions. They like adventure, play, and the process of getting to know other people. This is not the most sensitive placement for the Moon, and it can give people a bit of a love 'em and leave 'em nature.

MOON IN TAURUS

The way to these people's hearts is through their stomachs; feed them something good and they're more likely to stick around. These people have a sensual relationship to feelings, so physical displays of adoration and care go a long way for them. They're loyal and steadfast once they decide they like a person, yet they can also be a bit superficial in what they're looking for. Whether or not they're good at it, they're impatient with small talk.

MOON IN GEMINI

These people are quite changeable. They're all the way there or not there at all; when with others, they have many feelings for them, but when they're elsewhere those feelings can dissipate. This placement gives folks a strong ability to process emotions through words, so refining effective communication will go a long way. They have a bit of a restless nature and like engaging in multiple kinds of intimacy for different purposes.

MOON IN CANCER

This placement gives people a highly sensitive, emotional nature that is not at all casual. They're inclined to look for family and belonging with the people they're intimate with, and their sense of rejection can be strong. They're not the most direct about their feelings and needs, and their memories and instincts are important to them.

MOON IN LEO

People with their Moon in Leo love attention, validation, and play. While the adoration of multiple partners or casual encounters may be appealing, they ultimately want to be the most important thing to whomever they're with. They're charming and gregarious, but their ability to intuit what others want from them—and deliver it—can make them less authentic than they might otherwise be.

MOON IN VIRGO

These people want to know where they stand in dating situations. They want a clear sense of what the agreements are, the limits of the commitments, and especially when they can expect to hear from you. They're smart, highly discerning, and sensitive to their own needs and the needs of others. This is an introverted placement for the Moon, and while these people may want to rush things to a place of certainty, they'll do better if they can remember to move slowly.

MOON IN LIBRA

Partnerships are very important to these people. They have a deep need to be liked even before they know whether they like the other person back. This can incline them to be in a rush for their relationships to be "going somewhere." Likable and affectionate, these folks have great social skills and can be quite flirtatious. They're not fantastic at keeping things casual, because the differences between liking, loving, and simply craving attention are difficult for them to parse.

MOON IN SCORPIO

People with this placement are incredibly sensitive; their emotions run deep, and their sense of abandonment can be highly tuned. Sex is deeply important to them, and they can be a bit secretive, not wanting to share the rawness of their feelings until they're completely ready. They can be a little paranoid because they're constantly running scenarios, including all the ways things can go wrong. These folks are loyal and, while they can be jealous or possessive, they reward the people they care about with passion and dedication.

MOON IN SAGITTARIUS

Optimistic and hopeful, these people like to inspire and be inspired. Their curiosity and desire to learn and grow can make them either deeply spiritual or thrill-seeking and restless. This Moon placement can bestow a person with FOMO (fear of missing out), and limitations are really uncomfortable for them. They're often intuitive and have flashes of insight that prove to be quite prophetic.

MOON IN CAPRICORN

People with this placement have a tendency to want to control their feelings and like to know what their roles are with other people. They may have a desire to barter for attention or value, which makes them very quick to do things for others. It can be hard for them to know what they actually feel about the folks they're dating because they're so busy trying to protect themselves from unseen personal failures. It's very important that they know what their emotional boundaries are with casual partners.

MOON IN AQUARIUS

People with this Moon sign are rational about their feelings. They have the capacity to reason with themselves, which ironically can make them quite unreasonable and stubborn in matters of the heart. While they're capable of happily keeping it casual, they may have a hard time admitting that they have needs or feel vulnerable until they feel they have no other choice. They can connect with lots of different kinds of people, and they tend to either want to jump in headfirst or be very cautious in new relationships.

MOON IN PISCES

These individuals are acutely aware of their feelings, and they're deeply impacted by people and situations. They're affectionate and have a tendency to place others on pedestals. Learning not to put the needs of others—or their perceptions of those needs—above their own is essential, especially in the early stages of dating. They can be quite idealistic and devotional, which gives them the ability to love many people in many ways. They may fall in love too quickly if they're not careful.

THE MOON THROUGH THE HOUSES

MOON IN THE FIRST HOUSE
This is a heart-on-the-sleeve placement; it's impossible for these people to hide their feelings because these feelings tend to show up on their faces. They can be moody, and their emotions come on quick and strong, which can incline them to jump to conclusions or make assumptions based on how they feel rather than on what's actually happening. People with this placement tend to love attention and are highly identified with their emotions.

MOON IN THE SECOND HOUSE
In order for intimacy or closeness to be achieved, these folks need to feel a sense of shared values. They are deeply sensual with a tendency to keep things pleasant and have an aversion to conflict or drama. While they can keep things on the surface, people with the Moon in the second house are deeply emotional by nature. They tend to form attachments to those they care about, which can incline them to rush to a place of certainty about potential partners before that status has been earned.

MOON IN THE THIRD HOUSE
These people are curious, open, and capable of connecting with lots of people in different ways. They're inherently very interested in others, and joking, talking, and spending spontaneous time together can help them cultivate the kinds of feelings that lead to real closeness. If you can appeal to their silliness, it will go a long way. This placement can also indicate a fickleness and a distractibility, which may come across as unpredictability in some people's eyes.

MOON IN THE FOURTH HOUSE
This is not a super casual placement with matters of the heart because these people are likely to be relationship-minded and get attached once they feel good about someone. Generally accommodating and nurturing people, they're not well-suited to long-term hanging out, however; things need to progress toward a committed relationship or they'll lose interest. These people really need space and time at home to recover from the world around them.

MOON IN THE FIFTH HOUSE
These people want to feel that they're important to the people they date, regardless of how casual the dynamic is. They're likely to be assertive and inclined to lead, even if from the bottom. They're fun and enjoy play, whether that's through sex, the arts, or good old-fashioned flirting. Sex is emotional for them, so it's important they check that there's water in the pool before diving in.

MOON IN THE SIXTH HOUSE
These folks have a way they like things to get done, they take their time quite seriously, and they have a tendency to

scrutinize the attention they get and the day-to-day progress of their relationships. If those with the Moon in the sixth house are controlling, they can find it hard to date because of how unpredictable it can be to get to know others. But if they can allow things to flow, they're excellent at expressing their needs and limits.

MOON IN THE SEVENTH HOUSE

This is a very relationship-oriented place-ment. These people yearn for connection and don't tend to be terribly casual. They need to train themselves to under-stand the difference between dating and relationships, which is largely a difference in pacing and expectations. They need to sometimes be willing to lead, even though it doesn't come naturally to them.

MOON IN THE EIGHTH HOUSE

It's really important to these people that they feel valued and desired by those they're dating or hanging out with. This is a passionate placement for the Moon, but it's also pretty private and tends toward suspicion. These people value connection intensely, and they often have a really strong desire to merge with others. This placement may also give people an obses-sive emotional nature at times.

MOON IN THE NINTH HOUSE

These people are given to want experi-ences that make them feel like they're growing and moving toward something. It's not the most patient placement; they can rush to get to their destination without packing a lunch. They're very open-minded, but once they get fixated

on an idea, it's hard to change their minds. Unless there are strong aspects that indicate otherwise, this placement suggests that they're not usually posses-sive of the people they date.

MOON IN THE TENTH HOUSE

People with this placement are very focused on their reputations and, for that reason, they tend to want to keep their casual relationships private. They can also be status-conscious, so dating anyone who may embarrass them in public is something they are loath to do. They may find themselves dating people for power instead of true compatibility. They're also very focused on footwear, so be sure to pay attention to the shoes you wear if you're trying to impress them.

MOON IN THE ELEVENTH HOUSE

While these people can be great at flirt-ing, they're not always great at noticing when they're being flirted with. They run the risk of putting themselves in the friend zone, and they do prefer to be friends first before getting serious. They're open-minded and not likely to have a consistent type. This placement inclines them to be able to keep things casual or remain unattached, unless their dates get integrated into their social lives.

MOON IN THE TWELFTH HOUSE

People with the Moon in the twelfth house are deeply sensitive; they often find themselves in romantic situations that are private or kept on the down low. This placement inclines them either to be detached and checked out emotionally or super emotionally present with people. They can be self-sacrificing and often choose people who take more than they give. They need a great deal of personal space in order to manage their emotional wellness in romantic or sexual relationships.

MERCURY ☿

Time it takes to traverse the zodiac: Approximately 1 year

Signs it rules: Gemini, Virgo

Houses it governs: Third, sixth

HANGING OUT AND DATING: MERCURY

Mercury isn't the sexiest planet; it governs the platonic aspects of any relationship: talking, connecting, hanging out, and sharing ideas. It's impossible to have more than a quick one-night stand without engaging Mercury because it's in charge of what we think, what we say, how we say it, how we listen, and what we hear. In other words, it rules the cognitive process that inclines us to swipe left or right. The texts we send to our potential love interests, the stories we share about ourselves, how we negotiate plans, how responsive we are—those things are all ruled by this planet.

THE THREE-DAY RULE

A common convention in dating is the "three-day rule," the idea that you should wait three days before getting back to someone to express interest or risk looking overeager and too available. Whether that strategy is wise or not, it is Mercurial. The role of Mercury in dating is communicating interest and ideas, and

sharing your life with someone, even if it's only for a brief period of time.

As the world becomes more Mercurial, and we are more connected and more in communication than ever before, our minds are advancing at a faster speed than what our hearts can truly handle. How we brand ourselves in the world, the stories we choose to tell, and the tone with which we choose to tell them have become more and more valued. Because of this, Mercury is becoming more related to the ego; instead of listening to others or being willing to interact IRL, we have begun to spend more time projecting the images of ourselves that we want others to see. For example, you may engage in a five-month-long relationship over DMs that makes you feel like you're getting to know someone. But, in fact, you're mainly getting to know what they choose to tell you.

The challenge is that Mercury wants union; it wants connection. Depending on your motives while dating, that facet of this planet may play a role or it may not. For this reason, I'm going to separately address two situations: keeping it casual and moving toward something longer term.

KEEPING IT CASUAL

One of the joys of being in a casual relationship is not having to process all of your feelings with the other person. (If you are and you're casually dating someone, it's probably not that casual.

Or you're doing it wrong!) Some people are simply not well-suited to casual dating, and in that case the early stages of dating may really annoy them. For people who are bad at small talk, for instance, first dates can be especially difficult. That said, it's a really essential part of getting to know others—chatting with them, seeing how conversation flows, learning about them. When you try to skip over that phase, you end up missing out on essential components of getting to know someone.

Mercury is the planet of communication; but what we do or don't say isn't exclusively ruled by this planet, it's related to other intimacy issues driven by other planets. From a Mercurial standpoint, if you know you want to keep it casual, you would just say that. If you would want to know where the other person is at, you would just ask them. But life—and the influence of the other planets—makes it more complicated than that.

EARLY STAGE OF DATING (WITH POTENTIAL FOR SOMETHING LONGER TERM)

Mercury fosters union through the open exchange of ideas—so this planet can be incredibly important for the early stages of dating. Listening to the other person and finding ways to accurately communicate who you are can help you understand whether you're compatible. Part of getting to know someone is collecting data and then using that data to come up with an honest evaluation of what is right and true for you. For example, if you're a busy person and you're dating someone who hates making plans—but you need plans in order to fit them into your schedule—you have a compatibility problem, which may or may not be surmountable.

At the start of a relationship, it's important to flex your Mercury; practice disagreeing with your date to see how it goes. Being willing to engage Mercury and talk about difficult things—politics, controversial ideas, and so forth—is considered a no-no in the beginning of a relationship, yet it's one of the best ways to explore how each of you think—and think together—which is essential if you want to turn the getting-to-know-you phase into the I'm-so-glad-I-know-you-let's-stay-together phase. Learning to ask questions and really listening to the answers is important, because doing so can keep you from rushing into a relationship. So many of the problems I see in long-term relationships actually come from a shaky foundation around communication, and that foundation is built in the first several months. Because love and chemistry can make us feel like we "know" someone, it's a good idea to slow down and pay extra-close attention to what your communications are revealing about your compatibility.

HOW TO WORK WITH THIS PLANET

When you're just hanging out or trying to build something new, the way to work with Mercury is to really listen to what people are telling you about themselves and to share the truth of what you think, what you prefer, and what does or doesn't work for you. The exchange of ideas can be sexy and flirty, trust-building, and energizing—or it can just be banter. Make sure that phone calls, texts, and emails don't replace the kind of intimacy that can only happen IRL. Mercury (our minds) shouldn't stand in for feelings (the Moon), romance (Venus), or sexual chemistry (Mars).

MERCURY THROUGH THE SIGNS

MERCURY IN ARIES
Impulsive, direct, and dynamic, these people may be prone to sudden bursts of energy and changes of opinion. They like to take the reins, and they tend to be quite impatient and assertive. They're not great at compromising, and while they can be quick to take offense, they're just as quick to get over it. These folks get bored by small talk, but they're great at flirting when they're in the right mood.

MERCURY IN TAURUS
People with Mercury in Taurus like to give compliments and make others feel good about how they look or the way they're presenting themselves. They're quite impatient to get what they want, but hate being rushed. These individuals may not always be forthcoming about what they really think—because they're also diplomatic—but don't confuse that with them being agreeable across the board. They're sensual and romantic and have good taste—or believe they do.

MERCURY IN GEMINI
Great verbal skills allow those with this placement to carry on conversations with almost anyone. They're smart and quick-witted and love to laugh, but they can also be quite fickle. Planning is not their favorite thing to do, so if they're making plans with you, it's a good sign. Boredom is the kiss of death for these folks; they're especially excited by people who are different from them.

MERCURY IN CANCER
These people can be a bit guarded, reserved, and even contrived until they feel safe. But when they're comfortable, these folks are funny, great at drawing others out, and good at making their dates feel really wanted. While they're not always the most direct, they are great at maintaining warm connections.

MERCURY IN LEO

This placement gives people a flair for the dramatic. They are excellent at flirting or, at the very least, communicating enthusiasm. They may have to allow others to lead at times, though, to make sure that their exuberance doesn't get mistaken for bragging. Those with Mercury in Leo are loyal and steadfast when they choose to be, although they can also be quite inconsistent in their love interests. They will do best when they can remember to ask other people about themselves.

MERCURY IN VIRGO

These people give great DM. When it comes to communicating in emotionally sensitive situations, they are much better at writing than talking. They are thoughtful and detail-oriented and can vacillate between being very risk-averse and jumping headfirst into liaisons with other people. While it's hard for them to let their guards down, they're funny and attentive when they do.

MERCURY IN LIBRA

Friendly, charming, and really easy to talk to, these people have great social skills and are laid back around a wide range of people. On the other hand, they can be quite passive when it comes to expressing their needs. This placement can incline them to be more diplomatic than honest, because the idea of hurting people with the truth usually seems worse to them than telling small lies.

MERCURY IN SCORPIO

These folks are mysterious, deep, sometimes evasive, and tend to be really intense communicators one way or another. Their wit and ability to see into situations is deep, but this is not the most flexible or open-minded placement for Mercury. They have great tenacity and are willing to play the long game with lovers. They are either fantastic at flirting or extraordinarily bad at it.

MERCURY IN SAGITTARIUS

These people have a warm, gregarious way about them that makes others feel invited. They are fantastic and natural flirts, even though they don't always know it. They are honest and straightforward, although not averse to exaggerating. They often speak before they think, which can lead to them becoming more deeply involved romantically than they are fully prepared to be. These folks are especially in the moment, so people who are out of sight can fall quickly out of mind, which can lead them to feel neglected.

MERCURY IN CAPRICORN

This is a very literal placement; if you act too goofy around them or don't say what you mean, you can lose their interest really quickly. They are direct and have a bit of a managerial way about communicating and processing information. Sarcastic and witty, they can be quick to judge and not terribly forgiving if you cross the line of what they believe to be appropriate.

MERCURY IN AQUARIUS

These people are quick and observant and tend to see the symbolism in many things. They're independent and have a unique style of flirting. They want to get to know their crushes as independent people with their own thoughts and interests and get sexy from there. If you can capture their interests, they may get super talkative and stay in touch all day long—but trust that they're probably talking with other people, too. They like spontaneous connection and are often down for spur-of-the-moment plans.

MERCURY IN PISCES

This placement gives people natural sensitivities. They are empathetic, intuitive, and very tuned in to other people. Their feelings can be easily hurt if those they're dating or hanging out with are careless or don't offer them enough attention. They have a devotional and romantic way of connecting, and they're great at making others feel good about themselves.

MERCURY THROUGH THE HOUSES

MERCURY IN THE FIRST HOUSE

These people are fantastic at flirting because they're great at initiating conversations, connecting with people, and making plans. They are dynamic and sincere, although they may sometimes speak before they think. Their thoughts tend to run across their faces, so if you want to know where you stand with them, make sure to hang out IRL.

MERCURY IN THE SECOND HOUSE

Those with Mercury in the second house are really good at making others feel valued. They are naturally sensual, graceful, and good at expressing care. They can also be quite diplomatic and not always forthcoming about their preferences, so figuring out how to please them can sometimes be challenging. For these stubborn folks, crushes come and go, but enemies are forever.

MERCURY IN THE THIRD HOUSE

Smart, quick, and genuinely interested in others, these people really love connecting. Their interest is earnest when it's felt, but they can also change their minds pretty spontaneously. They're versatile, dynamic, and not put off by a challenge when it comes to dating. They might find that their dating history reflects a wide variety of people.

MERCURY IN THE FOURTH HOUSE

Mercury in the fourth house is very family-oriented. Sex, flirting, or casual relationships tend to make these people a little uncomfortable, since this placement is more focused on emotional safety than the adventure of getting to know others. They shouldn't invite their dates to sleep over if they don't want to develop serious feelings.

MERCURY IN THE FIFTH HOUSE

These people are motivated by sex, play, and creativity, and they love to have fun. They can be stubborn and opinionated, but they also really enjoy hearing other people's perspectives. Having lovers is a great way for them to get to know themselves. These folks are a touch dramatic, and they can get into conflicts with people easier than most. They're not always great with other people's boundaries—so they may agree to see you on the weekend and then text you by Wednesday to hang out.

MERCURY IN THE SIXTH HOUSE

This placement makes people very detail-oriented in their daily life. Their need for clear communication and consistency in dating situations is very strong. They tend to not like surprises, although this trait depends on other aspects of their chart. Their turn-ons include witty repartee, a well-versed interest in the world, and consistent communication. Their turn-offs include dishonesty, last-minute plan breaking, and erratic behavior.

MERCURY IN THE SEVENTH HOUSE

Partnership is very important to these people, so unless they already have a close BFF or three, they'll more likely want to fill that space with serious commitments than casual connections.

This placement inclines them to be very diplomatic and motivated to facilitate the flow of communication in their relationships. They're so good at saying what others want to hear that they may mislead people without knowing it.

MERCURY IN THE EIGHTH HOUSE

These people are very intuitive and able to pick up on the subtlest nuance in any situation. They can also be quite private and prefer to keep their flirtations on the DL. They are masters of the sext, and their flirting skills really shine in writing. They tend to hold grudges, and they hate being lied to—although they themselves may withhold the truth at times.

MERCURY IN THE NINTH HOUSE

Bored by details, these people really like to feel they are moving in the direction of their desires. They can be a bit dogmatic in their views, while also being the first to tell you how open-minded they are. These folks have excellent intuition but need to learn how not to jump to conclusions. They love expanding their horizons and being inspired by the people they date. Although they have busy lives, they tend to like being in frequent contact.

MERCURY IN THE TENTH HOUSE

These people are concerned with where things are going and with how to move relationships, plans, and interactions forward. They are quite goal-oriented and can have so much going on in their lives generally that they can end up being very easily distractible within their relationships. They enjoy having lots of different kinds of relationships, and they respond well to the humor of others, although they don't always lead with it themselves.

MERCURY IN THE ELEVENTH HOUSE

Friendships and socializing are really important to these people but, without a sense of shared interests, you won't get very far with them. Smart, sharp, and insightful, they have an unconventional approach to getting close to people, and they're interested in others and the world around them. They're so good at keeping conversations light and fluid, that they can unintentionally put themselves in the friend zone with people they like.

MERCURY IN THE TWELFTH HOUSE

People with Mercury in the twelfth house can be a little daft when others are flirting with them, and they may have a tendency to keep things digital at first, because of how shy and sensitive they are. Determining the truth isn't always easy for those with this placement, so they need to move slowly enough to be able to track what others think and gauge how much feels safe to share. These folks will often chase the potential they perceive in others even if it doesn't match up with the reality of who they are.

VENUS ♀

Time it takes to traverse the zodiac: Approximately 1 year

Signs it rules: Taurus, Libra

Houses it governs: Second, seventh

HANGING OUT AND DATING: VENUS

In the realm of dating, Venus is the gatherer, while Mars is the hunter. Venus governs our need for connection and closeness, and our urge to get along. It also rules our desire for stability, security, and ease. This planet is essential to look at when talking about the way we like people and flirt with them, as well as when discussing the sensual side of hooking up.

Many people see Venus as the planet in charge of sex, dating, and relationships. That makes sense because it's associated with love, beauty, and connection. The truth is, however, that many of us hook up and choose partners from an entirely different set of desires and compulsions. Both Venus and Mars are inclined to "date with their dicks" (spiritually speaking, of course). In the case of Mars, there's a strong drive to hook up; whereas Venus drives us to date people who represent the way we want to be perceived. This planet governs aesthetics, class, social status, and our sense of belonging in the world. This planet has the power to help us either show up with our whole

selves or skim the most superficial of surfaces.

VENUS THE DIPLOMAT

This planet's big intimacy issue is that it can cause us to be accommodating at the expense of authenticity. Under the influence of Venus, we try to turn ourselves into what we think others want. For instance, we may choose to be nice over being kind, which is to say we can be disingenuous in an effort to preserve the appearance of happiness, desire, and closeness. Venus rules diplomacy, and diplomacy is a valuable skill that we all need from time to time. The trouble comes when we overuse it and deny our true feelings and responses. Say someone suggests you meet for pizza on the first date, and you don't like pizza. You may choose to compromise because it's not a big deal, and you want them to like you—after all, we are all told we're more likable when we're agreeable. Small compromises like this are wise to make, but when we make too many of them, our crushes don't get to know what we truly like and dislike. True closeness can be gritty, because true kindness and intimacy require that we are willing to be authentic at the expense of what someone else wants or prefers. Of course, it also requires actual compromise and a little finessing at times.

As we get to know people, we may find certain behaviors obnoxious: the way they kiss us, the way they undertip at restaurants, or the fact that they take twelve hours to text us back. Yet, the influence of Venus can cause us to tamp down on the negative sides of our feelings and the sharp edges of our preferences. This is neither good nor bad, but it can signify a larger problem if you're not allowing others to get to know your actual feelings, preferences, and thoughts. In other words, things can start to fall apart after three months when you do begin to share more of what you think and want—and the other person realizes that you're different from what you seemed to be. When that happens, you're not being rejected for who you are; you're being rejected because you didn't show up as your true self from the beginning.

HOW TO WORK WITH THIS PLANET

Ultimately, Venus governs the part of us that wants to be desirable, and that's a huge part of what dating is—the potential for being seen as charming, hot, and valuable. The problem comes when we place too much emphasis on those values or can't get beyond them. Many of us have a hard time expressing dissent, disagreement, or even contrast unless we feel sure it will be well received. So, here's the best way to handle Venus and an invaluable tool for dating in general: Align with what you value and commit to being authentic.

VENUS THROUGH THE SIGNS

VENUS IN ARIES

People with Venus in Aries are dynamic and great at initiating new connections as well as moving things along. This placement inclines them to be outgoing, positive, and good at the hustle of getting to know people and making dates go well. There's a tendency to have hot, fast feelings for others, but that flame can burn out just as quickly, so it's wise for these folks not to make proclamations based on their first round of feelings.

VENUS IN TAURUS

People with this placement are passionate and know how to make others feel desired. They can be quite indulgent and love sensual connection, flirting, and teasing. On the other hand, they don't like not knowing where they stand with others, and they are not huge fans of surprises. They tend to be possessive, even when they themselves are feeling ambivalent about what they want.

VENUS IN GEMINI

These people often find themselves attracted to those who use words and language well—they get turned on by creative and charming conversations. If you capture the interest of someone with Venus in Gemini, you'll have more than that person's attention—you'll have their heart. Such people may enjoy having multiple love interests at once, and thrive on the process of getting to know people. They're also curious and easily distracted and may be plagued by FOMO.

VENUS IN CANCER

This is known as the "smother-love" placement. These people like to give and get a lot of attention and reinforcement, which is not always appropriate when you've just started dating someone. They can be quite self-protective because of a yearning for real emotional connection. While these folks really don't like it when others play games, they may find themselves doing so out of shyness or insecurity rather than a real desire to be manipulative.

VENUS IN LEO

These people are great at flirting, value pleasure very highly, and thoroughly enjoy sexual and romantic attention. Due to their prideful nature, they can inordinately prioritize how their dates handle themselves in public and around others. Appearances are really important to them, and having romantic adventures is something they find rewarding.

VENUS IN VIRGO

This is a notoriously feminist placement for Venus and these people need to see equality play out in their relationships. Though shy or introverted, they are funny and weird and have particular ways of dating that do and don't work for them. Even though they're not quick to get emotionally attached, these folks can get pretty obsessive; they have to make sure not to treat crushes or lovers like projects.

VENUS IN LIBRA

Diplomacy is especially important to these people, as they are naturally charming and sensitive to the needs of others. They should avoid prioritizing being liked over determining compatibility in the early stages of dating. As soon as they have feelings for someone, they want to behave like they're in a relationship, even if trust has not yet been earned.

VENUS IN SCORPIO

These people are passionate, sensual, and very sensitive to rejection. They have deep emotions and deep attachments, and they tend to vacillate between being quite shy and being incredibly forward. Sex and sexual connection are important parts of how folks with this placement relate to others, whether they are sexually held back or enjoy being very slutty.

VENUS IN SAGITTARIUS

These people love to jump headfirst into liking and loving other people. They're fun, funny, and adventurous, and they get really excited by people they're into. Easily bored or distracted, they may have to be careful that they don't weave false narratives to support their ideas or feelings about their crushes. They're great at flirting, but if they're not careful they may use humor as a way to deflect romantic attention.

VENUS IN CAPRICORN

These people are not playing hard to get, they *are* hard to get. They can be really sarcastic and mean in a sexy, flirty way. Alternatively, they can be quite reserved.

The rigidity of Capricorn can express itself as kinkiness or an excellent game, or it can incline people to be passive for fear of doing things "the wrong way." They're most comfortable when they know the rules of conduct.

VENUS IN AQUARIUS

These folks are playful, funny, and open to experimentation. They can be aloof and reserved, less out of shyness and more out of pure introversion. This placement can give people somewhat open or non-monogamous natures. Their romantic feelings can abruptly change, and they are attracted to many different types of people. Because they're so easily bored by routine, they really like being surprised.

VENUS IN PISCES

This placement makes people especially sensitive and romantic, but they're not necessarily great at managing boundaries. They love giving and getting affection and care, but they can fall in love with that process, as opposed to the actual person they're dating. Learning how to pace themselves and vet relationships before committing is a very useful skill for these folks to cultivate. Otherwise, they can be self-sacrificing and have a tendency to fall into codependent dynamics with people who are not super available.

VENUS THROUGH THE HOUSES

VENUS IN THE FIRST HOUSE

These people come across as really pleasant and easy to get along with. They often have lovely complexions, and other people tend to find them attractive. They have natural social skills and are generally great at flirting. They dislike conflict, especially when they're at the center of it; they'd rather negotiate a peaceful détente than engage in conflict directly. Learning not to date for appearances and finding ways to be more authentic at the onset are skills they'll benefit from developing.

VENUS IN THE SECOND HOUSE

This placement can incline people to be very conflict avoidant and stubborn, but often they're so fun and charming that they get away with it. They want to feel worshipped; they may also be quite status conscious and materialistic, which can get in the way of being open to people who may be good for them but who don't have as much to offer in a material sense. That said, if you're trying to woo this type, a thoughtful gift will go a long way.

VENUS IN THE THIRD HOUSE

People with Venus in the third house are great communicators, especially when it comes to making small talk and getting to know people. While they're adept at asking questions and drawing people out, they may not share their real selves with people they're dating, since it's easiest for them to hide behind other people's preferences and interests. They can be diplomatic and charming, but the downside is that they can also be superficial and indulgent at times.

VENUS IN THE FOURTH HOUSE

Once these people feel comfortable in a dating situation, they are charming, engaging, and invested in the people they're getting close to. They don't love beating around the bush or the process involved in getting to know people, so they're inclined to want to meet friends of friends instead of finding someone through a dating app. This placement isn't fantastic for casual sex either, as it associates sexual satisfaction with intimacy.

VENUS IN THE FIFTH HOUSE

This placement bestows people with a genuine ability to flirt, play, and enjoy the objects of their crushes. Others tend to be attracted to them, and they find having love affairs genuinely enjoyable. It's important that these folks have some clarity about what they want while dating so that their pleasure-seeking is connected to a sense of purpose and doesn't convert to disappointment.

VENUS IN THE SIXTH HOUSE

Although a little introverted, people with this placement tend to be generous, kind, and totally willing to show up. If they really like someone, they'll either be really slow to let them in or feel driven to make them part of their day-to-day lives; they often want to land square in the middle stage of dating, skipping over the essential getting-to-know-you part.

VENUS IN THE SEVENTH HOUSE

These people really *love* love. This is a very partnership-oriented placement, and so these folks have to be careful not to seek shortcuts when getting to know the people they date in an effort to get to something more serious. Others are attracted to them because they're quite easy to get along with. As is often the case with those who have planets in this house, they should be careful not to place diplomacy over directness.

VENUS IN THE EIGHTH HOUSE

Sex is a really fun way to get to know a person, and people with this placement are down to do the necessary investigations. They're willing to go deep when connecting with others, but they can ultimately be quite shy. These people also have a tendency to attract lovers who want to take care of them or offer them some other kind of material support. This placement can make them very hedonistic, which is great when it's kept in check. But when it's not, that tendency may lead to risky sexual behavior.

VENUS IN THE NINTH HOUSE

This placement empowers people with great social skills. They are fun and inspiring to be around and know how to encourage others. They're also fantastic at flirting because they genuinely like connecting with people and making others feel good. They may not have much of an obvious type when it comes to dating, as they tend to respond more to vibe than they do to aesthetics.

VENUS IN THE TENTH HOUSE

These people are naturals when it comes to shaking hands, kissing babies, and making others feel good about themselves. But it can be challenging for them to take the risk of being authentic for fear that they won't be liked. People who they define as their type are not necessarily the ones who are best for them; they benefit from allowing their preferences to mature. They may also need to work to balance their desire to nurture others and their own self-care.

VENUS IN THE ELEVENTH HOUSE

These people rarely meet a stranger they can't connect with, but they don't always choose to exercise those skills. Bored by small talk, they also usually want to feel like they're connecting with another person for a reason. Depending on other placements, hooking up may simply be an act they enjoy rather than a way to get close to others.

VENUS IN THE TWELFTH HOUSE

These folks are super sensitive and have a tendency to romanticize their feelings and connections. They may develop crushes strictly on unavailable or unattainable people, and they're really bad at hiding their attraction to other people. They may have a tendency to create fantasies about others without realizing it. They can send mixed messages to the people they're dating because they tend to be quite ambivalent themselves.

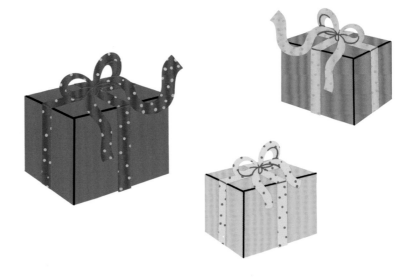

MARS ♂

Time it takes to traverse the zodiac: Approximately 2 years

Sign it rules: Aries

House it governs: First

HANGING OUT AND DATING: MARS

When it comes to sex and dating, Mars is the hunter. It governs our physical body, what we do with it, and the energy behind that action. It presides over dancing, running, and all manner of getting sweaty, whether solo, with a partner, or in a group. Mars determines the sexual type that our bodies crave, the chemistry we share with others, and our confidence as we go about putting ourselves out there and getting our sexual needs met. Personal accountability, or accountability to the body, is an important part of sex. Your body is a source of pleasure and a vehicle for engaging with others and meeting other people's needs. It's also a resource, and it's your job to protect, maintain, and respect it.

This planet is, by its very nature, self-centered; it is highly concerned with its self. Therefore, it's related to the ego, ambition, anger, and entitlement. While that's not inherently good or bad, it can be either. Mars governs "dating with your dick," which is to say our most instinctive reactions and impulses.

THE HUNTER

Mars is a fighter and the planet that gets things done. Its energies want to be expressed viscerally. Whether you're a top or a bottom, proactive or more passive in your style, where there is sex, there is Mars. Depending on where this planet shows up in your birth chart, it may seem closer to or further from the surface of your awareness.

The way we act to show the person we're dating that we really like them is ruled by Mars. And when we can go on dates, make out, or fornicate from a place of complete embodiment, we're activating our Mars in a healthy way. Part of the equation with this planet is the assertion; Mars is all about going after what you want. The other part is being able to respond to the needs of others in an active process, versus letting things happen *to* you.

The body wants what it wants—and once Mars has its sights set on someone, it can be really hard to convince it otherwise. We don't always make decisions based on the heart (or the Moon) when Mars is in control. Living according to your boundaries is an act of will that requires self-awareness, clarity of intent, and actions that reflect those two things. Whether you're emotionally unavailable to the person you're hooking up with, or you're trying to build toward something more meaningful, your forthright presence is required. There has to be some form of collaboration between your body and your heart in order for sex to be truly healthy. And doing something physically gratifying at the expense of your emotional wellness can have consequences in the long term.

A note on Mars and inclusion: All people with physical and developmental disabilities have Mars in their charts and their sexuality is just as important as everyone else's. There can be an infantilizing of people who are differently abled, but from an astrological viewpoint, the expression of Mars is an inalienable part of the human experience.

HOW TO WORK WITH THIS PLANET

Strive to stay in your body in relation to sex. Be present for the needs of your ego, rather than just for your physical needs, so that you can navigate the space between the two with integrity. When you approach your goals, needs, desires, and even your frustrations from an embodied place—where you're truly present—you not only get more of what you want, but you offend fewer people along the way.

MARS THROUGH THE SIGNS

MARS IN ARIES
This is Mars' natural placement, making it a very strong one. These people are assertive, dominant, and energetic. They can be quite irritable and pretty bad at hiding it. They have a natural magnetism and a strong sex drive. They have strong athletic ability in and out of bed. They're also enthusiastic and hot tempered, quick

to feel desire, and equally quick to get over it.

MARS IN TAURUS
This placement can make people stubborn; it may be hard for them to change their minds once they've developed an attitude toward something or someone. They enjoy all the steps that lead toward sexual connection—and they're likely to have impressive stamina as well. Once they've decided they like someone, they can be quite driven to make it official.

MARS IN GEMINI
These people are really fun to be around and generally game to do whatever. They're willing to compromise at first, as compromising helps them understand what they really want or need. This can have the unintended consequence of making them seem fickle when they change their minds. They may enjoy casual sexual relationships for periods of their lives and then they may change their minds and begin only wanting something more serious that allows them to focus; in other words, they need to feel like they can be many ways over the course of their lives.

MARS IN CANCER
This placement makes people deeply caring, sensual, and motivated to treat others well. They can also be quite moody and self-protective. If there's a sense of mutual care and emotional connection, they can really enjoy sex. But they're not always direct about their needs and preferences, so it can take

longer to get to know them than it might first appear. They may try to take care of themselves by taking care of others.

MARS IN LEO

These people are gregarious, fun, self-confident, self-willed, and generally good at expressing sexual interest. They can be quite generous, possessive, and really want to be wanted. They can be deeply hurt (and demanding) if they don't feel like they're getting the kind of attention they deserve. They're impatient, sexy, desirable, and playful.

MARS IN VIRGO

When people with Mars in Virgo develop feelings for those they're dating, the feelings tend to be passionate and intense. These people are likely to have singular focus and can catch themselves over-thinking new relationships at all stages. Because they're so attuned to detail, they may be overly picky when meeting new people, especially because they themselves can be quite shy and awkward in the early stages of dating.

MARS IN LIBRA

These people are compromising, indecisive, and quite sociable. They can have a difficult time being alone and so may strive to advance their relationships more out of the desire to avoid loneliness than because the relationships are ready. They prefer things to be fair, and they're not always comfortable letting their partners know their sexual preferences because they want to be seen as easygoing.

MARS IN SCORPIO

Deeply self-reliant, these people are not the most trusting. They prefer to do things their own way, at their own pace, rather than risk becoming too reliant on others. They're quite sexual and able to lose themselves in passionate moments. This placement has no chill, however. They can make hard and fast decisions about people or dynamics and have a hard time being flexible.

MARS IN SAGITTARIUS

These people love romantic trysts; they can be quite dynamic when they're excited. They have a pretty fixed sense of right and wrong, so they are likely to have strong feelings around fidelity, monogamy, and open relationships (they have a nature that allows them to keep things open). These folks can be sexually exploratory, but while they're very enthusiastic, they may lose interest easily. They also might be pillow queens.

MARS IN CAPRICORN

Once they're clear about what they want, these people are really dogged about making it happen. They really care about how their lovers seem to others, and they don't take kindly to being embarrassed, especially in public. With Mars in Capricorn, people like to know where things are going; when they don't, their insecurities can expand exponentially. They have great sexual stamina and can go all night.

MARS IN AQUARIUS

People with Mars in Aquarius are open-minded and can vacillate between being very experimental and having a solid sexual routine. They are motivated to make relationships happen, but are not the best at compromising. They have a really varied type, and it's easier for them to maintain interest when things take a more surprising route. They don't need relationships to take a traditional trajectory in order to be happy.

MARS IN PISCES

These people have very deep sensitivities, and it's important that they learn how to have healthy boundaries. Romance and a sense of connection are very important to them. This placement inclines them to be either very emotionally embodied or quite disassociated—or they may swing between those extremes. They can be hesitant to put themselves out there and very sensitive to the people around them, which may incline them to be more accommodating than is healthy.

MARS THROUGH THE HOUSES

MARS IN THE FIRST HOUSE

Anything but wallflowers, these people are assertive and have strong physical presences. They're great at flirting, making things happen, and getting the ball rolling with people who interest them. They can also be bullish, combative, and not great at picking up cues from others; they may easily offend others without realizing it. Impatient, these folks like to know whether the time they invest in other people will pay off and they often assess the situation too early.

MARS IN THE SECOND HOUSE

These people can be anxious to move dating situations to a place of certainty as soon as possible. They're deeply sensual but can also get so fixed about what they want that they're not properly listening to what their love interests want. Their drive for security or reassurance may also incline them to pick partners who will ultimately bore them. It's important that these folks make decisions ahead of time about what they're really looking for in a relationship so that they don't get unduly influenced by their new love's desires.

MARS IN THE THIRD HOUSE

Impulsive, restless, and interested in many things, those with Mars in this house seem to change their minds easily. They really like the beginning of relationships and can be easily distracted if their partners aren't dynamic enough. They need to be mentally stimulated in order to maintain arousal. It's important that they allow themselves to have at least one period of their lives when they dip in and out of a wide variety of experiences—sexual and otherwise—with other people.

MARS IN THE FOURTH HOUSE

Overall, this is not a very casual placement. For these people, sex can be either quite compartmentalized or really connected to relationships and intimacy. They may be quick to seek reassurance; developing relationships is incredibly important for them (although they can be restless once they have what they want). Once they've been hurt, they may be highly reticent to put themselves out there again. They have strong emotions and can be especially attentive lovers.

MARS IN THE FIFTH HOUSE

Folks with this placement really enjoy sex and can be quite athletic in bed—unless they have other difficult aspects in their charts. They can be impulsive and indulgent and therefore not always inclined to practice safe sex—but they would be wise to keep it in mind. They love beginnings in relationships and taking risks. They are driven to have creative exchanges that are like mini adventures with others.

MARS IN THE SIXTH HOUSE

These people are great at advancing plans and making things happen. They're not great at knowing when others are flirting with them, however. Because they're likely to keep their lives quite busy, this placement can indicate that either folks are good at moving relationships ahead on a material level or they can have a

really hard time making space for new people in their lives. Their passions can be quite particular, and they're willing to work hard to advance their interests.

MARS IN THE SEVENTH HOUSE

Relationships are really important for those with Mars in the seventh house, and they are either assertive and managerial or drawn to people who are that way. This placement indicates that they prioritize relationships and need to have many people with whom they're close. They may also be attracted to people who are quite dominant and want to have their own way.

MARS IN THE EIGHTH HOUSE

This is a very sexual placement. These folks may find themselves hooking up with the "wrong people" and having secret affairs. They often confuse passion and chemistry with compatibility, and will jump into things if the getting is good. They may also be prone to sudden attractions—and then have a hard time letting go, even when the moment has passed.

MARS IN THE NINTH HOUSE

Friendly, outgoing, and gregarious, these folks aren't always the best at listening or compromising. They can tend toward proselytizing, so there's a need to allow space for others to show them who they are—instead of deciding (or telling) people who they think they are. They're restless and flirtatious, and they'll put up with a lot of things they don't love if there's adventure to be had.

MARS IN THE TENTH HOUSE

People with Mars in the tenth house can be quite concerned with how things appear to others and doing what's right. They can be a little hard to get to know, as the way they present themselves can be curated and polished. They'll often choose to date people who have a functional purpose. These folks would be wise to allow others the space to reveal themselves, but they may also need to make an effort to share more of themselves.

MARS IN THE ELEVENTH HOUSE

Great at meeting new people, these folks tend to put themselves out there and get the party started. While they're great at connecting with others, they can also be quite forceful and a little tone deaf socially. They are most likely to meet potential dates and lovers through their friends. They're not opposed to meeting people online either, because the unpredictable quality appeals to them.

MARS IN THE TWELFTH HOUSE

These people are shy and will often respond to thoughtful assertions from romantic partners. They can be very passionate, but they need to feel safe because they're not always terribly grounded in their bodies. This placement may also give them a tendency to engage in secret relationships or wildly romantic unions that involve having to give something up to get their needs met. They may have very high and low cycles in regards to their sex drive.

JUPITER ♃

**Time it takes to traverse the zodiac:
Approximately 12 years**

Sign it rules: Sagittarius

House it governs: Ninth

HANGING OUT AND DATING: JUPITER

Jupiter is the gambler of the zodiac, the one willing to hop into a stranger's car and drive into the sunset. It has the potential to help us have growth experiences that are fun and expand what's possible. This planet is also distractible; it can make us feel as if where we are is the only place we've ever been. Jupiter is associated with luck and expansion. In the context of dating, it may influence us to act before we think, in pursuit of experiences that feel good. Because of this, where we have Jupiter in the chart is where we are most likely to be impulsive, spontaneous, and ready to take risks.

A FOCUS ON FUN

If this planet is very strong in your chart, you are likely to seek out electric, exciting attractions. You may also get bored easily; mundane things such as planning and being on time may frustrate you. The tendency is to be so impatient to get to the fun part of a relationship that you neglect to make sure that the dynamic is based on anything real, let alone healthy, safe, or sustainable.

Jupiter is associated with drinking—a common way to manage social anxiety when we're getting to know new people. But too much cocktail-fueled escape can make it hard to keep clear tabs on how a date is unfolding—if for no other reason than we might not clearly remember what went down after the fact. And flirting or hooking up under the influence doesn't help facilitate meaningful connections, if that's what you're seeking.

Jupiter's energies are great for short affairs and fun, low-key relationships that don't get too messy. But they're not as good for the steps involved in forging a lasting connection with someone. Regardless of whether alcohol is involved, when you're moving too fast, you're likely to skip over the foundational phase of getting to know a person—and you can end up making assumptions, which may create cracks in the foundation.

Dating unavailable people or telling yourself that they will be available if you're fun enough can be another mistake made under the influence of Jupiter. It's easy to tell a story about what's happening between you and someone else, but you won't know what that story means until it has stood the test of time.

IS WHAT FEELS GOOD ACTUALLY GOOD FOR YOU?

Another trouble with Jupiter is that, because of its resiliency, it can take you pretty far into an unhealthy situation. So, it's important to do reality checks to make sure that what you're choosing actually feels good *and* is the best way for you to feel healthy, happy, and whole—or, at the least, it isn't blocking you from achieving those things. The key here is motive: If you can motivate yourself to compromise, or to slow down by understanding that doing so will help you get more of your actual needs met over the long term, you're totally talking Jupiter's language.

HOW TO WORK WITH THIS PLANET

Jupiter is the champion of short-term compromises that offer long-term gains. Try not to confuse what's fun with what's expansive (both are qualities of this planet). When you're hooking up with someone who you wish liked you more, are you really having fun? Seek the most honest good time you can get, rather than the quickest route to a good time. Some compromise is inevitable. Just make sure you aren't compromising yourself.

JUPITER THROUGH THE SIGNS

JUPITER IN ARIES

Always on the hunt for dynamic experiences, these folks are willing to put themselves out there to have fun. This placement can give them a sense of entitlement that can make them come across as arrogant or cocky and can also incline them to rush into things that seem exciting before they figure out what they really want. They're flirtatious and open to growing through connection and exchange.

JUPITER IN TAURUS

Feeling desired is very important to these people; if this need isn't fulfilled, they can become distracted or a little needy. This placement can mean a good amount of stubbornness, so it's important for these folks to remember that their first impressions aren't gospel. They value stability and security and delight in material and sensual pleasures. Sharing meals, going to beautiful places, and showing physical affection are all very important ways to build intimacy with them.

JUPITER IN GEMINI

Unique and playful, these people love entertaining and being entertained. They tend to have odd, original ways of connecting, making them truly delightful to hang out with. They're easily distracted, restless, and have an idiosyncratic way of sharing and processing information. Other people tend to love their quirks—or not. They can be quick to make snap judgments about people; regardless of how good their judge of character is, these folks need to allow others to reveal themselves when and how they're ready to.

JUPITER IN CANCER

This placement gives people a strong ability to connect with others emotionally. They can be sentimental and are likely to get attached when they're having a good time. They're not great at casual hookups, because people with Jupiter in Cancer want to do everything family style (they don't even like to eat alone). They can also be self-protective, which is a great thing unless it's out of balance, in which case it can incline them not to let others in.

JUPITER IN LEO

These folks love to shine; they're playful, flirtatious and great in social situations, and may have a bit of a wild streak. They also really like validation; they need reminders and proof of other people's attraction to them. Depending on what else is in their birth chart, they may have a tendency to sexualize things as a way to get attention rather than find a way to connect deeply (this isn't inherently bad or good, but it is something to be mindful of).

JUPITER IN VIRGO

In order to fully enjoy themselves, these people need to feel as if they truly understand what's happening. They can be hyper analytical, practical, habitual, and smart. They tend to show kindness through their actions. And while they're not inclined to take a casual approach to

dating situations, if the expectations and roles are clear, they can be happy in all forms of relationships. These folks can also get lost in the details and forget to stop and look at the big picture.

JUPITER IN LIBRA

Those with Jupiter in Libra prioritize being agreeable and honoring what they believe to be right, but they have a tendency to choose being chill over being real. They can jump to conclusions without evaluating all sides. In this placement, people are inclined to want even the most relaxed connections to have a partnership vibe about them. So, if they're trying to keep it casual, it's important that they're forthcoming, because their actions may suggest otherwise.

JUPITER IN SCORPIO

These people are quite intense and willful—they know what they want, how they want it, and they're also willing to do what's necessary to get it. They have a deep capacity for enjoying attention and the mating rituals of pursuit, and their tastes can be quite indulgent. Sex can be a great way for them to grow and connect. They have an innate ability to stick around through deep, heavy, and otherwise taboo stuff.

JUPITER IN SAGITTARIUS

Terrific initiators, these people are capable of seeing opportunity and getting excited about it in a way that's quite infectious. They're inspiring to be around, but their capacity to see potential can be a double-edged sword. They may be either perpetually excited and optimistic or exhausted and demoralized by how far their lives are from their ideals.

JUPITER IN CAPRICORN

This placement makes people methodical and willing to take the steps needed to grow something. They can also be self-serious about dating and flirting, especially with PDA (they're either very drawn to it or very opposed to it). While they're capable of doing the work to build up a romantic connection, they can also be quick to cut others off if they feel they're not getting what they want.

JUPITER IN AQUARIUS

These folks can get really excited about the idea of dating—and run with it, which can incline them to love having flirtations and love affairs with many different kinds of people. They tend to be up for romantic adventures and hate being pinned down. They consider themselves open-minded, but, as a fixed sign, they can actually be quite rigid when it comes to what they're willing to see as possible or true.

JUPITER IN PISCES

These people are generally compassionate and sensitive. This placement inclines them to be idealistic and tenderhearted about the people they're intimate with; once they like a person, they have a devotional way of expressing it. They need to spend a fair amount of time alone or in repose, so learning to pace themselves in new dating situations is really important for their emotional health.

JUPITER THROUGH THE HOUSES

JUPITER IN THE FIRST HOUSE

These people are funny, confident, assertive, and playful. They can take up a lot of space, have big personalities, and often come across as optimistic. They're easily bored and can rush headlong into new relationships. They often prioritize seeking pleasure and play over doing the messy work of getting to know someone.

JUPITER IN THE SECOND HOUSE

This placement gives people host-with-the-mostest qualities; they're accommodating and have great social skills. They're good at positively reinforcing others and doing the little things that make the people they're dating, flirting with, or hanging out with feel attended to. They enjoy being generous and appreciate the best in life (objects, money, fine foods).

JUPITER IN THE THIRD HOUSE

These people give good text; connecting, chatting, and keeping in touch are their strong suits. This placement indicates that they have powerful intuition when it comes to other people. That said, they're also vivid storytellers, which is really exciting in a dating situation but not always reliable because they tend to exaggerate and embellish. They're sexually attracted to people they find smart, witty, and interesting—so come prepared.

JUPITER IN THE FOURTH HOUSE

These people are interested in growing through strong personal connections with others based on real stuff. They're loyal and deeply emotional; however, they're not always attentive to the signs that other people are not those things. Because of how important their relationship to home is, they need to be careful about bringing someone into their personal space too soon.

JUPITER IN THE FIFTH HOUSE

Big love, big connection, and big chemistry are all attractive to these people. They can be creative and have a great sense of joy and adventure—sexually and otherwise. This is a fertile placement, so they should wrap it up if they have the kind of sex that can make babies. This placement might like to get in there, get it done, and keep it moving. Their sexual style is quick and dirty, even with an established partner.

JUPITER IN THE SIXTH HOUSE

These people tend to have such busy lives that it's not always easy for them to make time for dating. Because they have so much going on, it helps if they have overlapping interests with their love interests. Having post-sex coffee, running errands, and doing other simple things together can make them more likely to develop serious feelings for the people they're dating.

JUPITER IN THE SEVENTH HOUSE

People with this placement adore relationships; even if things are casual, they have a tendency to make a partner out of their new love interest. They have great social skills and are good at maintaining the peace, even if they're not always perfectly forthcoming about their preferences. It can be easy for them to confuse fun with compatibility.

JUPITER IN THE EIGHTH HOUSE

This placement inclines folks to take risks. Sex is important to them and can be very healing, but they are not known for their self-control; hedonism can get them in trouble if pursued without limits or pacing. These people may jump too quickly into sexual intimacies, which can lead to promiscuity (neither a good nor a bad thing). They may become easily bored by their lovers.

JUPITER IN THE NINTH HOUSE

This placement gives people confidence, at times causing them to come across as arrogant. Adventure is incredibly important to them, and if they don't feel entertained and engaged, they're unlikely to stick around. These folks are good at putting themselves out there with new people. They're prone to be disappointed when others fail to live up to their perceived potential. They need to learn how to listen to others and pace themselves through the early stages of dating so they don't jump to conclusions.

JUPITER IN THE TENTH HOUSE

These people have a pretty strong set of ideas about how life should go and how people should treat one another. They will often have an agenda that they may or may not remember to share with those closest to them. They are also self-reliant and can be socially active. Because their goals are so important to them, they may find themselves in short and quick relationships that don't distract from their long-term vision.

JUPITER IN THE ELEVENTH HOUSE

This is a very social placement. These folks enjoy connecting with others, getting to know new people, and pursuing a variety of dating scenarios. Casual and early-stage connections are easier for them than intimate, touchy-feely stuff. They have great intuition and are good judges of character, and they have the potential to be really good storytellers.

JUPITER IN THE TWELFTH HOUSE

These people are generous and intuitive. They also have good inner resources, which they may sometimes forget to use. With Jupiter in this house, they can be quite self-reliant but run the risk of associating their inner wellness with the people or situations that bring them pleasure. They need to learn to distinguish between a stimulant of their happiness and the root of their happiness.

SATURN ♄

Time it takes to traverse the zodiac:
Approximately 29.5 years

Sign it rules: Capricorn

House it governs: Tenth

HANGING OUT AND DATING: SATURN

Saturn is the boner-killer of the zodiac. Where we find this planet, we find scarcity, fear, rules, rigidity, paralysis, and other feelings that are neither sexy nor spontaneous. That said, Saturn also is associated with the kinks that come from repression.

REALITY BITES

Saturn governs our experience of reality and how we cope with it. It also rules our bones and teeth—the stuff that holds us up. This planet is related to our internal structure, and it governs all the ways in which we are inclined to be self-reliant. It offers us the tools to learn from our life experiences. For that reason, Saturn plays an important role in who we date and how. Are you scared someone doesn't like you so you do stuff for them to compensate? Do you judge people too quickly because you're afraid of rejection? Have you been seeking someone to create security for you because you're convinced that you don't know how to create it for yourself? These are Saturnian questions,

and you may need to learn more about your own Saturn to answer them.

IN IT FOR THE LONG HAUL

This planet is a big player in long-term relationships. When we rely too heavily on it near the beginning and rush to create stability and security, we may end up requiring more than is appropriate from people and situations. And when we're in that state, we're not likely to be spontaneous or open-minded. On the plus side, where we find Saturn, we are capable of having clear boundaries, because we're likely to know what our needs are. Learning to express those boundaries and needs in a way that others can truly hear is a challenge—but it's one that's worth taking on.

When it comes to intimacy, Saturn's energies can prompt us to pull what I call the "George W. Bush." It has us convinced that there are weapons of mass destruction out there threatening our liberty and safety, and so we find ourselves ready to bomb whoever makes us feel threatened, even when there's zero evidence to support that impulse.

FREEZING UP

Under the influence of Saturn, the response to fear is always some kind of action. And to be clear, that includes inactivity, paralysis, and evasion. When we feel afraid, Saturn may prompt us to freeze up or stop, but it's an active form of stopping—a strategic decision. Whatever we establish in ourselves in reaction to Saturn becomes a tangible part of our internal structure, even if we don't intend that to happen.

Saturn may incline you to feel that if you don't get what you believe you need out of a dating situation, you've failed; but that's not at all the case. Having the chance to learn about yourself, another person, and your relationship patterns is not a failure—it's just not the experience you wanted. The only way to truly fail is not to learn.

Saturnian people aren't usually comfortable with flirting; they only have a few moves: sarcasm, teasing, and sexy meanness. So, if you have a lot of Saturn in your chart, don't hide your Mean Girl light away. Understand and perfect your approach to teasing, and make sure you're not just being mean; the odds are good you'll find people who are receptive.

HOW TO WORK WITH THIS PLANET

The pressures of dating can cause people to freeze up and resist participating fully. It's okay if you don't like dating or small talk, but you have to start somewhere. Practice remaining present in the getting-to-know-you stage and tolerating that early, inevitable uncertainty—as excruciating as it might be sometimes. There's no falling in love without falling.

SATURN THROUGH THE SIGNS

SATURN IN ARIES

Cultivating a sense of self is really important for these people, as they may be quite fixated on what they want instead of what they truly need. They'll benefit from learning how to be better listeners—and seeing listening as an active skill. Compromise is not easy for them, and it's helpful to remember that getting to know people requires collaboration and patience.

SATURN IN TAURUS

The desire for security and stability may incline people with Saturn in Taurus to rush relationships before they're ready. This placement can indicate a tendency to be stubborn or to make compromises without sufficient forethought (and later regret or resent it). Taurus's natural sensuality may be restrained by Saturn's restrictive nature.

SATURN IN GEMINI

These people are easily distractible and tend to change their minds about what they want or need once they've gotten it. There's a risk of nervous tension about dating and relationships with this placement. It's important that these folks are forthcoming about their preferences about how often they prefer to be in touch and other mundane details in the early stage of getting to know others.

SATURN IN CANCER

These people have a real sensitivity to vulnerability, and this makes them hesitant to put their heart out there or quick to look for certainty within intimate dynamics. They crave love and validation, and they can be quite defensive if they feel that neither is forthcoming. People with this placement can be easily hurt and a touch paranoid.

SATURN IN LEO

These people crave reinforcement and validation. They want to feel that they're important to those they're dating. When they don't feel that way, they can become oddly stubborn. Creativity and sexual expression are hugely important to them, but they need to avoid being heavy handed about their preferences and desires.

SATURN IN VIRGO

Offering these people insightful attention is the way to their hearts; when you're texting them, make sure you don't have any spelling errors. They can be contemplative and have a good sense of humor. They're not terribly spontaneous and can benefit from learning the difference between judgment and discernment, so that they can allow for a more fluid relationship to love and play.

SATURN IN LIBRA

Partnering and relationships are incredibly important for these folks, and because of this they may approach dating with a heavy hand. Learning to pace themselves with new people is a skill worth cultivating.

Getting to know others without minimizing their own needs is also important. It's healthy for them to learn to strike a balance between self-care and relating.

SATURN IN SCORPIO

People with this placement are given to lurking or obsessing about others, instead of getting to know them in a more organic, graceful way. They can be given to possessiveness or jealousy and need a fair amount of validation. It's important that they avoid being rigid because they have such very clear drives and desire. Deep, sexy, and intense, they're great at drawing others out.

SATURN IN SAGITTARIUS

People with this placement either like to jump into things or have a tendency to hesitate before starting. They are interested in finding the truth, but they can also be quite fearful of what they'll find. It's important that they moderate their tendencies toward dogma, as this placement's drive toward the truth can lead to overexplaining, patronizing, or jumping to conclusions.

SATURN IN CAPRICORN

These people tend to take themselves very seriously and have a hard time with the ambiguity inherent in the early stages of dating. They go after what—and who—they want in a thorough way. They are also highly sensitized to their own vulnerability, which can make them reticent to opening up. But once trust is established, they're equipped to do the work to bring things to the next level.

SATURN IN AQUARIUS

This placement can incline folks to be quite detached, which is excellent for keeping things casual. They are good at parsing out what all parties are bringing to a dynamic. This empowers them to maintain a clear sense of what is and isn't personal to them. They can vacillate between being reasonable and being quite uncompromising.

SATURN IN PISCES

Identifying and maintaining boundaries doesn't come easily to these people. They may struggle to recognize and maintain a sense of their own worthiness. It's important that they move slowly in dating scenarios so that they don't lose sight of their own feelings and experiences and get caught up in the agendas of others.

SATURN THROUGH THE HOUSES

SATURN IN THE FIRST HOUSE

These people are reserved, shy, and can be hard to read. They're so acutely aware of themselves and their vulnerabilities that they hold back or control their self-expressions. They're not comfortable with casual dating because of how seriously they take themselves. If a love interest can find a way to break down their walls, they will find unique, funny people who are worth getting to know.

SATURN IN THE SECOND HOUSE

Folks with Saturn in the second house really value security and stability, and they can have a difficult time with the uncertainty inherent in getting to know others. They can be reliant on compliments and gifts, often desiring material evidence of others' affections. They're very loyal, but their loyalty may arise before the people they're with have really earned their trust. They need to learn that diplomacy should not come at the cost of honesty.

SATURN IN THE THIRD HOUSE

These people are not always confident about their intelligence, so teasing them about it is a great way to ruin dates. They love humor and are very sensitive to being listened to and feeling heard. This placement can indicate literal thinkers and people who may not feel that they're as resilient as they really are.

SATURN IN THE FOURTH HOUSE

This placement indicates that people are quite shy. They tend to feel attached to home and family—chosen or otherwise. For this reason, they have an impulse to convert lovers into partners quickly, or they can be terribly hesitant to do that at all, ever. They either want to be left alone or they have a hard time tolerating being alone; and a lot of that has to do with their childhoods and families of origin.

SATURN IN THE FIFTH HOUSE

Sex and dating are incredibly important to these people, but they may be quite controlling about how those things go down. Their need to "get it right," can override their desire for fun. Because Saturn governs inhibition, they may be super kinky, as kink often comes from repression. This position also denotes stamina, so if they're down to play, they can play all day.

SATURN IN THE SIXTH HOUSE

These people are not the most flexible, and they may end up overthinking how things unfold in dating situations. They are likely to be hypochondriacs, so prioritizing safe sex in casual situations is important for their own mental and emotional well-being. They're at their best when they choose to pace themselves through romantic liaisons, because when they feel out of control, they either go on autopilot or tap on the brakes.

SATURN IN THE SEVENTH HOUSE

People with Saturn in the seventh house can develop pretty fixed ideas about other people, themselves, and their relationships based on their negative past experiences. Insecurity can make it difficult for them to see the whole picture. Allowing relationships to develop in their own time is an important lesson for these folks. This can be an uncomfortable process, but ultimately valuable, as relating is an important key to self-knowledge.

SATURN IN THE EIGHTH HOUSE

Sometimes they're hot; sometimes they're not. Sex can be important to these people at one moment and then completely irrelevant the next. This placement can incline them to be either super kinky or pretty conservative in their willingness to explore what brings them pleasure. Both Saturn and the eighth house are concerned with power, so these folks tend to clock the power they hold in a romantic dynamic, as well as the power their love interests hold.

SATURN IN THE NINTH HOUSE

These folks can find new ideas and experiences quite intimidating—but those things are also important for them to explore. Love relationships often take an unexpected turn for them. They're funny, and—when they're not dogmatic—they can be quite open-minded and willing to learn from the people they date. It's important that they resist the impulse to edit while in the writing stage—so that their judgments don't keep their relationships from organically unfolding.

SATURN IN THE TENTH HOUSE

Self-reliant and driven, these people are not always focused on love relationships. This can incline them to have either "filler" people (those who fulfill specific needs) in their lives or serious (that is, relatively predictable) partners. The problem is that all serious relationships have to start somewhere, and these folks are impatient in the beginning. Ultimately, they may find that cultivating that specific kind of patience is key to their happiness.

SATURN IN THE ELEVENTH HOUSE

Community is very important to these shy, often socially awkward people. They like to be able to meet romantic partners through their social circles and often end up developing feelings for friends, which can get complicated or messy. These people are loyal and like showing their love and affection through clear, solid actions. They appreciate well-articulated boundaries.

SATURN IN THE TWELFTH HOUSE

These folks tend to look for the strong, silent types (aka "daddies" in a nonbinary way) to help them navigate the world, even though their big lesson in life is to learn to navigate on their own terms. They are quite private, may be shy, and can find themselves in secret affairs or love relationships on the DL. Sex can be very important at times; at other times it doesn't even occur to them.

URANUS ♅

**Time it takes to traverse the zodiac:
Approximately 84 years**

Sign it rules: Aquarius

House it governs: Eleventh

HANGING OUT AND DATING: URANUS

Uranus is the most independent and
autonomous planet in the zodiac; it rules
the part of us that is thoroughly satisfied
to be on its own. It's original, independent, and craves exciting experiences.
Where there's new terrain to be traversed,
Uranus is often lurking nearby. For this
reason, casual encounters, short-term
affairs, long-distance relationships, and
alternative relationship structures are all
very Uranian. This planet's energy is fun,
exciting, and unpredictable. Then again,
because it's unpredictable, it can also be
stressful and upsetting, and it tends to
create abrupt beginnings and endings.

At its best, Uranus inspires us to be
transparent about who we are as individuals, what we have to offer other people,
and what we desire. But relationships, no
matter how casual, are about compromise, and Uranus isn't terribly interested
in compromise. This planet rules the
belief that our way is the best way, and
it can incline us to be obstinate.

HOW QUEER!

Uranus is also associated with queerness—in the old-school sense of the
word, which is to say eccentric, odd, and
unconventional. It also fits in the modern
context. This is not about gayness
or sexual preference, per se, but that
which is outside the gender binary or
the hetero-typical norm.

AUTHENTICITY AND INDEPENDENCE

Where you find this planet in the chart,
you are meant to act in authentic ways.
Uranus governs the central nervous system, as well as brilliance, innovation, and
the ability to make quick connections. On
an interpersonal level, this planet's influence can often lead to distraction, much
as innovators are often distracted by their
own inventions. In the context of dating
and hooking up, distraction can prevent
you from staying present long enough to
make a genuine connection, and that won't
be super endearing to most of your lovers.
But if other factors in the chart are aligned,
a person with strongly placed Uranus in
their chart will be adept at expressing what
they want and communicating clearly
about what they have to offer.

People who are strongly influenced
by Uranus tend to need to learn how
to be independent. That need may be
expressed consciously, but when it's not,
they may express it by projecting it on
others, meaning that they will often find
themselves feeling attracted to people
who are unavailable (because they're

already partnered, live far away, or they're just shut down and are not emotionally available).

HOW TO WORK WITH THIS PLANET

Where you have Uranus in your chart is where you tend to "future trip" or obsess about what comes next. But getting to know someone, whether that means dating or keeping it casual, requires that you stay in the present. Pay attention to when you are fully present and to when your attention slips.

URANUS THROUGH THE SIGNS

You'll notice that some of the following years overlap. That's because all the outer planets retrograde (or appear to move backward) and move in and out of a sign over the course of a year. That will often coincide with a planet being in two different signs in one calendar year.

URANUS IN ARIES (1927–1934 AND 2010–2019)

When Uranus was in Aries early in the twentieth century, the United States experienced a massive stock market crash and the Great Depression began. The era required that people have more self-will, originality, and assertiveness in coping with survival.

The combination of Uranus and Aries can create a lot of originality, willfulness, and daring, but the energy is quite erratic and blunt. These two planets come together to create periods of time of agency and individuation, which can lead to headstrong, me-first thinking and behavior, or the kind of embodiment of self that makes the meeting of individuals possible through a greater sense of agency. It's not a terribly compromising placement, so the downside is that people born during this era might find themselves looking for something perfect and being unwilling to compromise.

What this means for hanging out and dating: These people are highly individualistic and are really looking at "what works for me." They will have less conventional drives toward partnership, which entices them to have more dating experiences or partners, or just simply to experiment with those things.

URANUS IN TAURUS (1934–1942 AND 2018–2026)

This placement in the last century coincided with the years when the Great Depression really set in. Racism and xenophobia also had a new global stage with the advent of World War II. This was a period that forced individuals to take stands about who they were and what they prioritized. The collective push was a change in the global conversation about values. I'd argue that the same themes are coming up again and will likely play out over this cycle.

What this means for hanging out and dating: This placement is focused on security. The drive toward conventional relationships is stronger under its influence. These people want to find themselves through relationships but can err on the side of seeking the material markers of closeness or compatibility.

URANUS IN GEMINI (1941–1949 AND 2020–2025)

Uranus was last in Gemini during a period when we saw advancements in both psychology and metaphysics. This generation grew up to become the students who were the radicals of the 1960s, and these people were able to make inventive use of the information they received about freedom, liberty, and independence.

What this means for hanging out and dating: Uranus is revolutionary, and Gemini is the sign of communication. The people born during this placement are innovative and see the ability to learn new things as a pathway to autonomy. When it comes to dating, they are also prone to explore alternative ways of relating and communicating their desires.

URANUS IN CANCER (1949–1956; WILL HAPPEN AGAIN IN 2033–2039)

The last time we saw this placement was during the age of McCarthyism. A whole generation of artists and freethinkers were tamped down in the name of protectiveness and patriotism (several elements that are key to Cancer). There was the expansion of media and the arrival of television (and TV dinners, which were the beginning of processed food and provided people with more freedom without more quality). The key here is to find a way to balance self-protection with freedom without choosing one over the other.

What this means for hanging out and dating: This placement can incline this generation to be deeply protective of their uniqueness. It can also mark a generation that radically redefines family and the emotional boundaries that happen within intimate relationships.

URANUS IN LEO (1956–1962; WILL HAPPEN AGAIN IN 2039–2046)

This was a time when entertainment became a much bigger part of Western society. The Vietnam War was in its infancy; Uranus in Leo is a time of forceful engagement. This is a generation of self-confident people who were very creative and also had a strong need for validation by external forces.

What this means for hanging out and dating: These are people who can get so caught up in attention that they mistake it for love. This generation has placed a new kind of emphasis on sexuality—which can be reflected by either sexual liberation or oversexualization. These people also have the potential to transform the role of sex and sexuality within their generation.

URANUS IN VIRGO (1962–1969; WILL HAPPEN AGAIN IN 2046–2053)

This period saw the draft for the war in Vietnam begin in the United States, and people rose up in radical resistance. Many also dropped out of society. There was an emphasis on personal improvement as a route to social change. This was also when alternative health care began to play a larger role in Western culture. Virgo is practical process, mundane reality, and day-to-day living. So, when combined with Uranus, it also spurred second-wave feminism, which was very much about writing, speaking, and public analysis.

What this means for hanging out and dating: Uranus in Virgo created a generation that experiences a newfound emphasis on personal agency and new access to lifestyle-improving techniques. This can facilitate more self-appropriate ways of relating to other people, or it can incline a generation to be more introverted or private, thereby de-emphasizing casual dating in favor of self-reflection and betterment.

URANUS IN LIBRA (1968–1975; WILL HAPPEN AGAIN IN 2053–2059)

This generation was all about changes in social justice, diplomacy, and the arts. This was a time when alternative partnerships and roles in society became more eclectic and diverse, and women had more autonomy in their relationships. This was also when divorce became more prevalent, and partnerships were no longer seen as the only way forward in relationships.

What this means for hanging out and dating: The tension between autonomy and partnership can make for really exciting re-envisioning of dating and sexual roles. This combination of planets can also mark a time of innovation within gender roles in society.

URANUS IN SCORPIO (1975–1981; WILL HAPPEN AGAIN IN 2059–2066)

This combination produced a brave but private generation. This period saw a generation that was reached by more

corporations, advertising, and media than ever before. There was an increase in occultism and New Age culture during this time. Androgyny also come to the fore, with the rise of New Wave arts and music. Affirmative action also made legal strides during this time as more alternative voices stepped into the mainstream.

What this means for hanging out and dating: Scorpio is a sign concerned with power, privacy, and intense experiences, while Uranus represents our eccentric, outsider, individualistic urges. People born during this time have a strong desire to be recognized as individuals, and they may have a hard time compromising for partners. This generation is also exploring sexual expression and redefining "perversion."

URANUS IN SAGITTARIUS (1981–1988; WILL HAPPEN AGAIN IN 2066–2072)

The 1980s were the arms race years. This era saw an increase in humanitarian interest as well as in fundamentalism. Kids were encouraged to have global pen pals, and individuals connecting to other individuals to create a global society was an important part of this phase.

What this means for hanging out and dating: Sagittarius is about open-mindedness, expansion, and cross-culturalism. The devil is in the details, and this placement inclines people to be somewhat averse to the little compromises that make up a relationship. This is a generation prone to exploring alternative agreements around monogamy, polyamory, and so on. These people really want to expand their horizons and be free, so they may also balk at the idea of commitment.

URANUS IN CAPRICORN (1987–1996; LAST OCCURRED 1904–1912)

These were times when government and corporations took a stronger hold on society. It was also a time when we could take our individual chaos and problems and come to a systemic solution. Conversely, there were great upsets to agreed-upon norms and the "right way of doing things." There was a major shift in the AIDS crisis, as pharmaceutical companies stepped in to "protect us" from the epidemic. The systemic reach of the school-to-prison pipeline grew significantly.

What this means for hanging out and dating: This can be quite a kinky generation. Because Uranus rules eccentricity and Capricorn rules repression, there's the potential for a kind of eroticization of oppression. These people have the potential to redefine what is considered normal when it comes to courting, dating, and connecting with others.

URANUS IN AQUARIUS (1996–2003; LAST OCCURRED 1912–1920)

This was a time of great scientific and technological advancement. Google was incorporated in 1998, and this and other advances in data and information sharing were the mark of a mass, global shift. Computers made their way into classrooms, so this generation grew up with regular access to other people from around the world. Aquarius is ruled by

Uranus—this is its natural sign—so there is both the intensity of humanitarianism and a sense of interconnectedness and reliance on others.

What this means for hanging out and dating: This generation is marked by the expansion of the role of "queerness" in society—including alternative relationship structures and gay rights. These people are really open-minded but they have a hard time tolerating the emotional vulnerability inherent in human connection. They're also freethinking and willing to do things in new ways.

URANUS IN PISCES (2003–2011; LAST OCCURRED 1920–1928)

The earlier placement happened in the roaring 1920s, when there was a shift in morality and a greater emphasis on pleasure and dissociation. More recent, there has been a rise in the role of pharmaceuticals and a growing dependence on them to manage our moods. Uranus is an easily distracted planet, signaling an increase in both sensitivity and the desire to feel pleasant. This generation is more woke than others that came before it and yet has stronger escapist tendencies.

What this means for hanging out and dating: These people may experience a struggle between self-sacrifice and indulging personal impulses. They may struggle with compromising the self within a union, and they may try to mold themselves into being what the other person wants. For them, substance use, media, and sexuality can be great forms of either escape or self-insight.

URANUS THROUGH THE HOUSES

URANUS IN THE FIRST HOUSE

These people are fantastic flirts with great wit, but they're not always good at picking up on social cues. This placement makes them highly individualistic and slightly odd; there's usually something about the way they look or take up space in a big way that is wholly unique. They're not super touchy-feely or mushy either; instead they prefer boundaries and periods of separation from others.

URANUS IN THE SECOND HOUSE

A unique combination of innovative, eccentric values sets these people apart. They can be very strong-willed and have an impulse to assert their needs and preferences over other people. They see themselves as very open-minded, but when push comes to shove, they're more stubborn than they think. These folks may also have big ideas about what works, without the emotional tools to back them up. If things don't go their way in a new dating situation, they may try to get ahead of the situation and attempt to control the way things unfold.

URANUS IN THE THIRD HOUSE

People with this placement are adept at connecting with lots of different kinds of people. They're good at enjoying what others have to offer them in the moment, meaning that relationships don't have to "go somewhere" to be satisfying—they just have to be interesting, engaging, and fun. These folks to have lots going on and a busy day-to-day life; they're constantly running around. They can have changeable desires because their feelings about their circumstances shift so quickly.

URANUS IN THE FOURTH HOUSE

Restless by nature, these people have a hard time feeling settled or rooted; they'll often find themselves reacting to change or upsets around the home. Depending on the rest of their chart, this can incline them to seek lovers who serve as anchors or who reflect the unpredictability of their lives. These folks tend to have powerful emotions, and once they've let others into their hearts, even in casual relationships, it can be a pretty big deal for them.

URANUS IN THE FIFTH HOUSE

These people have many different types of relationships, and may have a varied "type." This placement can work well for non-monogamous relationships or for those who want to pursue more than one love affair at once. They may be attracted to unavailable people if they don't own their own needs for autonomy and personal space. They tend to have very versatile taste in the bedroom, and they're also likely to pursue sex for its own sake.

URANUS IN THE SIXTH HOUSE

This house indicates that these people may be a bit high-strung and nervous, which can lead them to spend time looking outside themselves for answers—especially in new relationships. But regardless of how much they want attention, these folks also need space. This placement inclines people to be quite introverted or independent, and they may also have particular or stringent rules around dating.

URANUS IN THE SEVENTH HOUSE

The need for autonomy and independence in these people is strong. They get excited or bored by others rather abruptly; shorter-term relationships often meet their needs and work well for them. They may impulsively jump in and out of relationships, so it's a good idea for these folks to be forthcoming about the limits of what they want and what they have to offer. It's also important that they don't make a call too quickly in the early stages of dating. Much like those with this planet in the fifth house, they may find themselves attracted to unavailable people until they own their own needs for autonomy and personal space.

URANUS IN THE EIGHTH HOUSE

This is a fantastic placement for casual hookups. These people can be sexually open, enjoy a good kink, or have unusual sexual interests. Conversely, they may identify as asexual for periods of their lives. They have the ability to get in there, get what they need, and keep on going. They may need to be mindful of other people's feelings; taking the time to communicate their availability will help them do that.

URANUS IN THE NINTH HOUSE

These people are adventurous and down to have fun, unusual experiences with others. While they're motivated to learn about the people they hang out with, they can also be really distractible. Casual, flexible relationships may be the best option for them, because these free them up to explore. These people need to be careful not to spend too much time in their own heads. They can waste a lot of energy weaving stories about what could have been; they would do well to be open to many versions of what's possible.

URANUS IN THE TENTH HOUSE

There's so much that these people feel driven to do with their lives that they may not always have time for a real relationship. For this reason, having purely sexual arrangements with others may make a lot of sense to them. At the same time, they may be more sentimental than they like to admit. They'd be wise to remember that intrigue and relationships enrich their capacity to be happy.

URANUS IN THE ELEVENTH HOUSE

These people value their pals, and when friendships turn romantic or sexual, things can get messy. While they can get excited about the idea of having lovers, the reality doesn't always match up to their vision, and they may get bored or disinterested rather abruptly. These folks are well equipped to "hit it and quit it," if other parts of the chart are in agreement, because they have the tendency to compartmentalize their relationships.

URANUS IN THE TWELFTH HOUSE

Freedom and space are important to these people, but they may have a hard time accepting or owning their need for autonomy. In the context of dating, space allows them to figure out what's working—or not. They may be good at having casual relationships because these allow them the freedom to do what they need to take care of themselves by maintaining a rich inner life, or they may find that they are quite needy and want to use relationships as distractions.

NEPTUNE Ψ

Time it takes to traverse the zodiac: Approximately 165 years

Sign it rules: Pisces

House it governs: Twelfth

HANGING OUT AND DATING: NEPTUNE

Neptune is the source of our most romantic, dreamy tendencies. Because it's an outer or "generational" planet (see page 6), it has often been overlooked by contemporary astrology in relation to something as personal as sex and dating, but this is a mistake as it plays a very important role.

The influence of this planet is deeply spiritual and devotional. It can express itself through very romantic sexual encounters, asexuality, or hooking up just to be liked or loved. It inclines us toward love without boundaries and limits. So, wherever we have Neptune in our birth chart is where we're most inclined to love freely and where we need to cultivate healthy, sustainable boundaries.

REALITY OR FANTASY?

Neptune governs illusion and disillusionment and the sense that you know someone based solely on your feelings about them. When it comes to the early stages of dating, this planet can incline you to run either away from personal risk or toward what you're convinced is love's ultimate potential. Neptune inspires us to see what's possible, which is usually what we perceive to be the very best or very worst of what could be. In this way, it governs high romance, fantasy, and anxiety. It makes us very sentimental—about things that happened in our past, are happening right now, and haven't happened yet. This planet rules our tendency to run with a feeling and associate it with reality. The problem is that Neptune also has a hard time accepting unpleasant reality when it contradicts our sense of what's possible. So, listening to what other people are actually telling us—with their actions and words—is an important skill to develop.

SACRIFICIAL TENDENCIES

Learning that sex and dating is not meant to be a sacrifice—and that consent is imperative at all times—is an important lesson for people with strong Neptune in their charts. Sacrifice is an important and healthy part of long-term intimate relationships, but if there's no intention of taking it to the "next level," or if others have said that they're not available, sacrifice can become martyrdom instead of a healthy choice. Where we have this planet in our charts, we can avoid clearly expressing our boundaries and limits until they've been trampled on. Its influence can incline us to struggle with sexual boundaries—in the context of safer sex (that is, using latex), as well as handling our emotions and our psyches.

People exploring polyamory tend to have strong Neptune in their charts. This is a planet that rules love without limits and our ability to share without possession; it's associated with relationships that go beyond conventional boundaries. In an ideal state, this planet would allow for love and closeness to happen without limitations or rules. The trouble here is that in order to be successfully polyamorous, people need to be able to negotiate their needs and responsibilities with honesty, even when those negotiations are rough. And Neptune can urge you to disassociate from the truth or deceive one another instead.

HOW TO WORK WITH THIS PLANET

It's not possible to be intimate while putting someone on a pedestal, and so accepting how other people are showing up is essential for making healthy choices. Honor your feelings, but don't confuse them for facts. While you're at it, don't forget to breathe.

NEPTUNE THROUGH THE SIGNS

You'll notice that some of the following years overlap. That's because all the outer planets retrograde (appear to move backward) in and out of each sign. That will often coincide with a planet being in two different signs in one calendar year.

Neptune takes 165 years to complete its cycle through the signs, and it spends 14 years in each sign. It marks the convictions and spiritual ideals of a generation. For this reason, I have focused on the signs that will most likely reflect my readers (and their parents) and won't cover Neptune in Aries, Taurus, Gemini, Cancer, or Leo.

NEPTUNE IN VIRGO (1928–1942)

These were Depression-era babies. Born into a period of scarcity, they needed to make do with less, and their spiritual values had to guide them toward finding meaning when things felt dire. This was a generation that had to put self-care aside to deal with day-to-day survival. People born in this era had to learn to take care of their bodies as a way to take care of their minds, and vice versa. The world had become larger with the advent of World War II, yet there was a great deal of fear of what wasn't understood. There was a new boogeyman for this generation culturally.

What this means for hanging out and dating: In a time of scarcity and spiritual tension, people turn to sex as a means of escape. However, casual dating was not a cultural norm at this time, and there tended to be an idealization of the beginning of dating in an effort to rush into things. Women dated with the hopes of converting their connections into marriage, whereas men could present their interests as they saw fit.

NEPTUNE IN LIBRA (1942–1956)

This phase coincides with the end of World War II, when ideals around love and a global sense of connection emerged. (The United Nations was established during this time.) Nations came together with a Neptunian ideal of unity and a shared will to protect humanity. Children born at this time grew up to be the "make love, not war" generation. Libra is a relational sign—it's concerned with justice and fairness and expresses itself in a one-on-one context. Combined with Neptune's idealistic, romantic, and highly spiritual ways, Libra shaped a whole generation that wanted to learn to partner with people in genuine ways and strived to have more interpersonal empathy.

What this means for hanging out and dating: People born during this period were raised in a society that could finally release its breath after the war and begin to think about how to have fun again. These folks eventually became the first modern generation to prioritize sex for spiritual connection and pleasure, and not just for procreation.

NEPTUNE IN SCORPIO (1956–1970)

The generation born during this time faced—and embodied—a great deal of intensity. These people expanded their sense of community, finding new ways to commune and connect beyond school, the military, and church. This is in line with Neptune, which governs universal connectedness. Scorpio, on the other hand, is all about letting go—and it's deeply

concerned with death and sex for this reason. It is the sign that holds the underbelly of society. This planetary combination can lend itself to addiction, escapism, and excesses in terms of sex and sexuality—which explains why many of the people born during this time grew up to deal with these issues. Sex became freer, but there were consequences. These children grew up in the AIDS crisis, and they were the first modern generation to suffer such dire health consequences of their sexuality.

What this means for hanging out and dating: This generation was raised with very rigid gender and sexual roles, yet they also came of age when these things underwent a revolution. Sex became both freer and more complicated as boundaries were loosened.

NEPTUNE IN SAGITTARIUS (1970–1984)

As children, this generation experienced greater connectivity than ever before. The world became much smaller as international travel became more common for the middle class. It was a time of global unity and connectedness. Western culture became less monotheistic, and both alternative religion and spirituality were normalized in this time. Another cultural barrier was broken down during this era after *Loving v. Virginia*, the landmark civil rights case that invalidated laws prohibiting interracial marriage in 1967, making Generation X the first to be born in legal interracial marriage in the United States. Gen X is conscious about romance, social justice, and fairness; they value liberty on a social scale.

What this means for hanging out and dating: When it comes to sex and dating, this generation is primarily concerned with freedom. They want to know that they have options and are inclined to snack at the buffet instead of gorge at the table.

NEPTUNE IN CAPRICORN (1984–1998)

Neptune in Capricorn people are a generation prone to questioning the powers that be. But because of the omnipresence of TV, advertisements, movies, and games, this generation is also easily distracted. Capricorn is associated with capitalism, hierarchies, and structural power. The combination of Capricorn and Neptune refers to the idealized notion of authority—and the move into a nonbinary relationship to authority. The ideal here is dissolving old governments and national boundaries and transforming capitalism. This generation was the first one raised with pharmaceutical use as a part of everyday life. These people were inundated by large corporations that had a huge hand in creating a culture that reinforced their product-driven objectives. This was a time when the environment and societal structure became a greater part of daily awareness.

What this means for hanging out and dating: This generation is all about boundaries because Capricorn has hard rules and Neptune blurs them. These people are concerned with conversations about sexual consent and relationship structures.

NEPTUNE IN AQUARIUS (1998–2012)

Neptune in Aquarius rules connection to collective consciousness. It's where the intellectualization of ideals comes to fruition. Technology has created an unprecedented sense of interconnection for this generation. Children born during this time had access to everyone around the world, which engendered a sense that everything was possible. The astrology of this generation was epitomized by the Black Lives Matter and anti-gun violence activism of the era—from Ferguson, Missouri, to Parkland, Florida. It was the first generation raised on social media, and they tend to feel a sense of shared ideals.

What this means about hanging out and dating: This generation has fewer expectations of marriage and babies in their 20s. They're re-envisioning relationships, but there's a tension between their capacity to meet many people through the internet and their ability to choose partners who uniquely work for them.

NEPTUNE IN PISCES (2012–2026)

This is Neptune's natural placement, which makes it a particularly powerful place for the planet to be (its functions are strengthened in both good and bad ways). Neptune and Pisces combined are marked by significant feelings of uncertainty and confusion. Pisces is the sign of the unconscious, of what is hidden— meaning these children are being raised at a time when things are being hidden from view and also emerging into the light. Again, we see pharmaceuticals and an overwhelming amount of media facilitate dissociation. (Pisces can be a very dissociative sign; people in this generation can lose themselves in substance use, video games, and media in general.) This generation is being born in a time of humanitarian and environmental crises, but also in an age of art and a time of greater democracy of the arts; people can self-publish and project their voices without the support of traditional arts and the entertainment industry.

What this means about hanging out and dating: This generation has had an online presence before individuals have had a sense of self. They're learning to curate their public identity, which can create hurdles to getting to know others without preconception or projection.

NEPTUNE THROUGH THE HOUSES

NEPTUNE IN THE FIRST HOUSE

This placement makes people quite shy, and others have a tendency to project what they want to see onto them. They can be awkward when it comes to flirting, and daft about being flirted with. They are often on the lookout for love, but they may have a tendency to confuse potential with reality. Casual sex isn't their strong suit because they're very permeable; once they let in the energies of others, there's nothing casual about it.

NEPTUNE IN THE SECOND HOUSE

These people love falling in love, and therefore are not fantastic at keeping it casual. They value romance and closeness but loathe having things feel messy or ambiguous. They prefer not to allow themselves to get thrown off course by people they have feelings for, even though that's exactly what they tend to do. Having a sense of shared values or ideals is an important part of connecting and getting to know folks; they have to be careful not to make too many assumptions about others or to compromise what they believe.

NEPTUNE IN THE THIRD HOUSE

This is the house of platonic relationships, so it may be the least relevant in the context of sex and early dating. That doesn't mean that those who have Neptune in the third house don't do those things—this placement just isn't a strong indicator of how it works. These people can be quite vague, which frustrates those they're getting to know. They tend to tell themselves stories and weave theories about what things mean. They are suckers for sweet talk, and they may develop feelings for friends—which can get messy quick.

NEPTUNE IN THE FOURTH HOUSE

If these people are going to bother getting to know someone, they want it to "go somewhere." There's a strong yearning for sanctuary and closeness, so it's wise for them to pace themselves in how quickly they get close to potential loves. Their tendency to make assumptions or jump the gun is high, because they have a great ability to see the potential for union. Intimacy is what they're really looking for, so these folks would be wise to take steps to enforce the kinds of boundaries that protect their hearts.

NEPTUNE IN THE FIFTH HOUSE

These people prize being fun over having fun. Because of that, they don't consistently prioritize their own satisfaction when hooking up or engage in safer sex. A big lesson of Neptune in the fifth house is about having sexual boundaries and a meaningful part of that is choosing to use latex, not just because of the health risks, but because certain forms of closeness must be earned. A good rule of thumb with this placement is if they can't do it sober, they shouldn't do it at all. It's also important for these folks to remember that they're free to change their minds.

NEPTUNE IN THE SIXTH HOUSE

Dating new people can be un-grounding for these people in a way that can make them feel destructive or uncertain. That said, they are quite romantic and can be very devoted. This placement indicates an introverted nature; they need space to process what they're feeling because of how impacted they are by the emotions that come up in the people around them. They can also be hypochondriacs, so it's important that they practice safer sex as a way to prioritize self-care.

NEPTUNE IN THE SEVENTH HOUSE

Highly idealistic and romantic, these people need to make sure they're honest with themselves about what works for them when it comes to loving, liking, and dating. Because this is the house of partnership, and Neptune is the idealist of the zodiac, this placement doesn't lend itself to random hookups. These folks are usually looking for a partner with whom they can have a romantic connection. They also have a tendency to try to take care of people they like before trust is earned, which can cause martyred dynamics. The boundaries between love, romance, and friendship can also be a little blurred for them.

NEPTUNE IN THE EIGHTH HOUSE

People with Neptune in the eighth house can have periods when sex is not at all important to them. They have a deep way of connecting, and they are quite private when it comes to their intimate lives. They're not well-suited to casual sex because they tend to fall in love with those they enjoy snuggling with and sleeping beside. They can be hard to get to know and need to prioritize letting relationships develop in stages.

NEPTUNE IN THE NINTH HOUSE

These folks like to dive in before checking to see if there's water in the pool. This placement denotes a spiritual nature, which can translate very literally to a person feeling connected to something larger or to somebody who just likes to have fun and keep things on the surface. These people love falling in love, but need to pace themselves. They're attracted to people who are culturally different or those who share their spiritual and philosophical values.

NEPTUNE IN THE TENTH HOUSE

Folks with Neptune in the tenth house can get so fixated on what they think they are supposed to want that they're not always present; this can get in the way of getting to know new people, especially romantically. They can be shy and don't like their love interests to make big shows of how they feel about them in public, unless it's agreed on in advance. Once they know themselves, they tend to have a lot more fun and confidence while getting to know others.

NEPTUNE IN THE ELEVENTH HOUSE

These people can have a tender way of connecting with folks to whom they're not close, which can make them seem more flirtatious than they realize. They're quite capable of having casual encounters or getting to know new people, but within that they tend to have a deep well of feeling; their sense of caring or empathy can lead them down paths that they would otherwise not take. If they don't make a mental connection, it's not very likely that a sexual connection will follow.

NEPTUNE IN THE TWELFTH HOUSE

This is not a casual placement. These people are highly empathetic and sensitive; developing healthy boundaries—both emotionally and behaviorally—is essential to happy, healthy, and hot relationships. They can get distracted by the potential they see in a dynamic and confuse it for what's actually happening. They have to be careful not to rush in or take care of others as a way to make something happen with them.

PLUTO ♇

**Time it takes to traverse the zodiac:
Approximately 248 years**

Sign it rules: Scorpio

House it governs: Eighth

HANGING OUT AND DATING: PLUTO

Pluto is a big deal in astrology because it governs our fight-or-flight mechanisms, destruction and healing, compulsive feelings, manic impulses, and the actions that come from them. Its energies in the birth chart can represent where we have trauma and the most powerful resources for transforming it. Pluto represents a place of pain, intensity, and compulsiveness—all inevitable aspects of being human. Where we have this planet in our birth charts, we have a tendency or desire to blame others, or to aggressively blame ourselves. But in order to heal, we must throw away the blame and focus instead on what needs to come next.

In the early stages of dating or hooking up, when it's not clear what it is or where it's going, Pluto is an active player because sex, attraction, and love all tap into our survival mechanisms and our sense of self-worth—and that's this planet's home territory. Pluto's intensity can also bring about some big either/ors: either you never date anyone or you compulsively date people, for example. This is because Pluto is so extreme in its expression that its effects can often feel very all or nothing.

Where we have Pluto in our charts, we will either have deep and compulsive feelings or be highly guarded. It's where our abandonment issues—and many of the other kinds of baggage we carry into relationships—reside. It rules our sense of safety, what we believe to be inevitable, and our darker sides; it drives our behavior but in a way that we can't always see.

Pluto is associated with taboos such as kinky sex and promiscuity. It can tell us a lot about our emotional survival mechanisms, our passions, and our drive to feel wanted. It can be found where there was sexual trauma, and it also articulates our inner resources for sexual healing. In simpler terms, it can tell us how we are or are not able to let others in when sex and romance is on the table.

There's nothing casual about Pluto. It's where our feelings are so intense and compulsive that we have a hard time gauging what is destructive and what is safe. We feel compelled and driven to have an experience with someone, to track an ex or a crush, or to have sexual experiences that validate our worth (for better or worse).

OWNING YOUR DESIRES

Where you find Pluto in your chart is where it's important to get comfortable with your sexual preferences—and not just about what gender you like to get down with; it's broader and deeper than that. How do you enjoy sex? When are you able to own your fantasies and drives? How are you impacted emotionally when the act is over? Can you be comfortable in your own skin in your relationship to your own desire?

This is where our most driving impulses are not always our most reliable ones. Sometimes, the people we are attracted to and the acts we most fantasize about don't actually meet our needs IRL; they don't make us feel valued, loved, or secure. Some of that is inevitable. But this is also an area where we have a great opportunity for self-understanding, self-love, and re-orienting our actions to be healthier and more sustainable.

HOW TO WORK WITH THIS PLANET

Where you have Pluto in your birth chart is where you're most intense. As this planet governs your compulsions, this is where your most powerful feelings are not necessarily your wisest ones. Make sure that you are aligning with your hopes and intentions as much as with your fears and responding with intention instead of just reacting.

PLUTO THROUGH THE SIGNS

Pluto takes 248 years to complete its cycle through the signs, and it spends 12 to 31 years in each sign. It marks the compulsions, convictions, and spiritual ideals of a generation. For this reason, I have focused on the signs will most likely reflect my readers (and their parents).

You'll notice that some of the years below overlap. That's because all the outer planets retrograde in and out of a sign. That will often coincide with a planet being in two different signs in one calendar year.

PLUTO IN CANCER (1913–1939)

Pluto is associated with transformation and can be quite destructive, while Cancer is associated with security, the home, and nation. During this phase, we had World War I, the Great Depression, and the beginning of World War II. This generation had a really rough go of it because they never felt safe, so they are prone to being highly protective or reactive. It was also a bit of a clannish or nationalistic generation (Jim Crow segregation laws were in effect during this period, and the KKK held a great deal of power). It was a real us-versus-them world. The emphasis on family was really strong, as people were struggling through poverty and war.

What this means for hanging out and dating: There was an intensifying of gender roles during this period and a tension between sexual liberty and sexual convention.

PLUTO IN LEO (1939–1957)

This generation lived through a period of oppressive dictators, including Benito Mussolini in Italy, Adolf Hitler in Germany, Kim Il Sung in North Korea, Ho Chi Minh in Vietnam, Mao Tse-tung in China, Francisco Franco in Spain, Nikita Khrushchev in the Soviet Union, and many more. So, it only makes sense that the people born during this period were shaken. The era also saw the explosion of the first atomic bombs in Hiroshima and Nagasaki. These folks were dealing with ferocious energy, so themes of control, success, and validation were all strong. There was a great deal of racial segregation and xenophobia. The first Detroit race riots took place during this period—in other words, people spoke out and were shut down violently. This was an era of anger expressed and repressed. Those born with Pluto in Leo were not responsible for these cultural shifts, but they were raised during these shifts—prompted by the generation before them. Due to technical advances in the home and greater access to education, women gained more power and autonomy during this period.

What this means for hanging out and dating: These people crave a great deal of attention and validation. This generation felt great pressure to have children, which meant that casual dating was still geared to the end goal of marriage. The damsel in distress and the femme fatale were the only two romantic ideals in the Western world.

PLUTO IN VIRGO (1957–1972)

This generation was raised by Pluto in Leo parents and were much more socially conscious than the immediate generations before them. A lot of substantial changes to laws and shifts in medicine occurred in this period. Pluto in Virgo has the compulsion to shift focus often, seeking the most perfect truth—but

because there is no perfect truth, these folks can get caught up in their routines and habits. This generation may have abandonment issues.

What this means for hanging out and dating: The social movements of the time and newfound sexual freedoms brought people closer together and drove them further apart. They saw new levels of sexual liberation, more access to drugs, and expanding male and female gender roles. There was a letting down of formality in courting at this time.

PLUTO IN LIBRA (1971–1984)

After the Vietnam War ended in 1975, there was a return to prosperity and relative peace during this period. This generation didn't need to focus as much on practical survival as the generations immediately before it did, so there was more room for the arts and social justice issues to become a larger part of the culture. Friendships took on a much larger role. Generation X was very conscious about romance, social justice, and fairness. When there was injustice, they took it personally. There was also a spike in the number of latchkey kids. As the world started to get much larger, the concept of stranger danger took on weight, and the cultural conversation became more about only trusting people you knew. The bulk of the Black Panther movement took place in this phase even though it started in Pluto in Virgo. The rigidity of gender roles we saw with Pluto in Leo had softened by the time Pluto in Libra came around with the disco era and shifts in the film industry.

What this means for hanging out and dating: This generation started to embrace androgyny, and there was further expansion of gender roles. This was the beginning of the trend toward delaying marriage and having kids. These people have pursued experimental and creative ways of connecting in relationships.

PLUTO IN SCORPIO (1984–1995)

This was the first generation to grow up with computers in their homes. Their sense of connectedness to the larger world can make them feel jaded or cynical. They've been exposed to all of it; nothing is taboo. There is also more androgyny—these kids were exposed to more nuanced and complicated gender identities and sexualities, including pop stars such as David Bowie and Annie Lennox. This generation had sexual images permeating the mainstream culture. They saw gay characters on TV and further expanded notions of gender and sexuality.

What this means for hanging out and dating: The people in this generation want intense and transformative experiences, but struggle with how much personal risk they want to take. The urge to merge is strong, but that doesn't mean it's always the healthiest impulse to follow.

PLUTO IN SAGITTARIUS (1995–2008)

This placement also occurred between 1746 and 1762. People born during these periods were brought up with paradoxical understandings of the world. On the one hand, these were times of prosperity;

on the other hand, political tensions were reaching breaking points. In the case of this most recent era, the oppressed and poor were becoming more and more impatient with the ruling class. There was an increased awareness of the need for change, and these people were prone to being interested in political reform and revolution. They were excellent at inspiring others with their charisma and energetic personalities. There was an expansion of gender roles and norms and a burgeoning acceptance of different gender presentations. Social media and self-publishing became more available, making it possible for a whole range of formerly disenfranchised folks to bypass traditional gatekeepers and have their voices heard.

What this means for hanging out and dating: Self-expression is essential for these people, as is having autonomy and authority over their lives. They like to jump into intimate experiences and are open to many ways of intimately connecting.

PLUTO IN CAPRICORN (2008–2024)

The Boston Massacre, the Boston Tea Party, the American Revolution, and the signing of the Declaration of Independence all occurred during the prior Pluto in Capricorn (1762 to 1778). This current generation will undo a lot of the restrictions that were established during Pluto in Sagittarius—particularly as it relates to lack of privacy and corporate control. They will be highly committed to change, sometimes being rather cynical about the state of the world. They will approach the task of improving the world with grim determination, dedicated to their causes, with rock-solid morals and ambitions; but they will also use the framework of oppression to their advantage. They'll embody power as opposed to preaching or lecturing about it. These people may place practical or external matters in higher esteem than personal ones and be capable of great emotional maturity or may be likely to shut down. They will be very capable, but they may be ruthless.

What this means about hanging out and dating: Because Capricorn is associated with repression, the combination of Pluto and Capricorn may create a generation open to exploring taboos or evading them totally. We will see either a meaningful doubling down on mores and roles or a radical redefinition of them.

PLUTO THROUGH THE HOUSES

PLUTO IN THE FIRST HOUSE
People with Pluto in the first house either wear their sexuality on their sleeves or are intensely private about it. Their sexuality may be something they received a lot of attention for—positive or negative—in their early years. They can become pre-occupied with being liked and pay less attention to whether they like the person in return, or they may be really quick to write people off for minor infractions. If they feel abandoned or rejected, their response is swift and intense. Chill interactions are not their forte.

PLUTO IN THE SECOND HOUSE
Money, and the power that comes from having it, plays a significant role in terms of who these people want to date. They have pretty fixed ideas around what's right for them, whether or not those ideas are correct, so cultivating more flexibility and a willingness to investigate is a smart move. This placement denotes a strong need for attention, and these folks may attract people who don't give them the kinds of attention they need until they learn how to advocate for themselves.

PLUTO IN THE THIRD HOUSE
These people have intense communication issues, which is to say they have a talent for flirting and quick, witty repartee and deep cognitive abilities, but they don't always choose to communicate directly. And while they really prefer knowing where they stand with the people they're dating, they don't want to

initiate those conversations. Learning to keep it simple but honest is an invaluable tool, especially when they're first getting to know others.

PLUTO IN THE FOURTH HOUSE

These people are easily attached and have a strong drive toward safety—both emotional and physical. Once they start dating someone and having good sex with that person, it's very hard for them to let go, even if it's clear that the situation isn't working. They need to work on understanding the differences between attachment, compatibility, and happiness.

PLUTO IN THE FIFTH HOUSE

Sex and love affairs have especially deep meaning for folks with Pluto in this house. They are driven by a desire for attention and validation, and they may struggle with their urge to have a creative life versus their desire to immerse themselves in romantic entanglements. They are capable of both deeply enjoying sex and using it as a tool for winning intimacies and keeping people around.

PLUTO IN THE SIXTH HOUSE

People with this placement are often workaholics, and their commitment to work can distract them from dating and personal intimacies. They may give more to the people they're hooking up with than they can really afford to and then feel resentful. If a relationship doesn't seem connected to something real, sustainable, or long term, they find it hard to let others in or be vulnerable. They often want to start in the middle, instead of

going through the early work of getting to know someone.

PLUTO IN THE SEVENTH HOUSE

Love, partnership, and connection are of obsessive importance for these people. Themes of control, safety, and power-lessness can be exaggerated for them. Relationships can be either a means to transformation or a self-fulfilling proph-esy, for better or worse. The intensity of their feelings for others makes the beginning phase of dating really compli-cated and hard for them, as they have a hard time pacing themselves and keeping perspective.

PLUTO IN THE EIGHTH HOUSE

This is the natural placement for Pluto, and sexuality is a really big deal for these people. They can lose themselves in the transformational experience of sex and their capacity for emotion and healing is profound. This can mean that they are fixated on the pursuit of hooking up, or terrified of sex. Either way, the power it holds can be overwhelming and lead to shameful feelings. Their urge to merge is really strong, so they tend to be codepen-dent. They may compartmentalize sexual impulses from emotional ones—or with-hold attention and freeze up with people who are truly there for them.

PLUTO IN THE NINTH HOUSE

These people love to jump in the middle of things and have a difficult time with pacing, tending to favor an all-in/all-out approach over a metered one. The potential here is for them to have deep experiences with people who teach them something about themselves. The risk is that they make snap judgments about relationships, or that they get so fixated on the story they're telling themselves about a dating scenario that they stop seeing what's actually happening.

PLUTO IN THE TENTH HOUSE

Ambition is so important to these people that they spend a great deal of energy pursuing their goals or evading them all together and then beating themselves up about it. In regard to dating, this can incline them to jump around from person to person, seeking answers that are meant to be found within. Or they may seek partners who fit into the image of themselves that they're trying to create. Learning to listen to others is a skill these folks would do well to cultivate. They have an easier time in conventional relationships because security is so important to them. They can be either highly attuned to when other people are flirting with them or totally obtuse about it.

PLUTO IN THE ELEVENTH HOUSE

It's likely that these folks will meet potential romantic partners within their friendship circles or have unrequited feelings for friends. This placement can inspire them to be super focused on spending time with friends or to be really antisocial. In either case, there's a tendency to go into a social mode that inhibits others from truly getting to know them; while they do it to feel safe, it's hard to build any kind of closeness from that place. Sexual tension brings

up mixed feelings in them—sometimes it can make them feel out of control or overwhelmed.

PLUTO IN THE TWELFTH HOUSE

While these people may engage in casual hookups, ultimately what they want is to be known deeply and have really profound intimacy. They need a great deal of time to recover from the world because they're so sensitive. They have the ability to go deep with their intimate connections, and will often attract lovers who appear for some kind of transformative reason yet don't necessarily last. These people may also be attracted to scenarios with power struggles that come from victimhood, such as anger problems or addiction.

THREE

LONG-TERM RELATIONSHIPS

Every planet has a role to play when choosing one or more partners and building a life with them—putting ourselves in situations where our finances, home life, life choices, and career all impact one another—but some stand out more than others.

HAPPILY EVER AFTER?

Pop culture would have us believe that the person we have the most romantic feelings for is the same person we'll end up partnering with and staying with over the long term. But history—and astrology—tell a different story. In reality, people often marry or build long-term partnerships for safety, stability, and family. And because gender roles were so entrenched for so long, men and women often came together for security, the realm of Saturn. Those choices were made at the expense of Venus (romance), Uranus (autonomy), the Sun (a sense of personal, individual identity), and Mars (freedom of motion).

For the vast bulk of human history, becoming an adult happened in conjunction with getting married and having kids. It's easy for people born in the 1980s or later to lose track of how recent women's sovereignty is and the impact it has had on our relationships. But until the middle of the twentieth century, many women didn't leave their parents' home until it was time to get married, and only in the late 1990s did we begin experiencing any real progress toward equality for LGBTQ people.

ON ROMANCE

The idea of marrying or partnering for romance is quite modern, yet it's also an unquestioned assumption in today's world—at least on the surface. That assumption only rarely lines up with reality. Long-term relationships are about loving, liking, and deeply seeing and supporting the people we choose, and they're also about compromising, weighing options, collaborating, and co-creating.

While our birth charts can tell us about the types of relationships we may seek out or gravitate toward, and what works best for us once we're in them, we all have free will about what we prioritize within our long-term relationships. One person may choose to partner with someone based on romance and passion, even if communication is lacking or they don't share the same values. Another person may forgo a fantastic sex life in exchange for intellectual intimacy or a secure home life.

JUST THE BEGINNING

Regardless of how relationships are portrayed in Hallmark movies, finding your partner is not the destination; it's not the end of the story. It's actually the beginning, and every story ebbs and flows, dips and dives. If you're with someone for long enough, there will be years when you don't get along and you want to murder your partner's face off. There will also be months and years when you feel extremely grateful to have merged your lives together.

Some people stay in relationships until the end, but many of us end up seeking out multiple long-term partnerships throughout the course of our lives. As much as people like to complain about divorce and separation—and it's certainly no fun—the truth is that people grow and change. We have the freedom to leave when a relationship is no longer working—and that agency is a beautiful thing.

The point is not to have permanent relationships; it's to have healthy relationships. The specific issues that emerge in a long-term partnership require you to be your healthiest self. Because if you stop taking responsibility for your own happiness, growth, and welfare, you inevitably, if unconsciously, invite the same inaction into the relationship.

parts of us that may be inclined toward non-monogamous relationships; Neptune rules polyamory; and Pluto rules the parts of us that feel deeply possessive (it's our survival instincts).

While we all have all these planets in our charts, they are stronger for some of us than for others. There may be parts of your chart where you may be quite possessive or insecure, while another part may allow you to feel open-minded and interested in exploration. Also, just because you're open to alternative agreements doesn't mean your partner is or vice versa. Relationships are collaborations, after all. And there are many other factors—cultural and religious among them—that impact how a person experiences different parts of their nature.

MONOGAMY ISN'T THE ONLY GAME IN TOWN

There are many ways to be in a long-term relationship. The default in hetero-normative relationships, and relationships in general, is monogamy, but that's not the only way that humans thrive in partnerships. Regardless of structure, a long-term committed relationship between consenting adults is ours to co-create with one partner or with multiple people. Throughout this section we'll look to certain planets that tend to have an impact on our interest in and approach to seeking out alternatives to monogamy. Saturn makes us inclined to be monogamous; Uranus rules the

THE PLANETS AT A GLANCE

Here's a rundown of what all ten planets have to offer us if and when we choose to embark on a long-term relationship:

THE SUN governs how we support each other in shining, how we feel seen, and how we cheer each other on as whole individuals.

THE MOON governs how we care for others, the closeness we feel with each other, and the intimacy we share.

MERCURY governs how we communicate and listen, and how our days stream together.

VENUS governs our sense of closeness, and how we enjoy each other socially, romantically, and sensually.

MARS governs how we fight and fornicate, and it's literally how we move through the world.

JUPITER governs our sense of adventure, our ability to grow together, and our potential to share morality and a world view.

SATURN governs longevity; it's how our relationship ages and how we age together.

URANUS governs our autonomy and our sense of curiosity about ourselves and our relationships.

NEPTUNE governs romance and spiritual connection.

PLUTO governs our ability to dive deeply and let things go.

SUN ☉

Time it takes to traverse the zodiac: Approximately 1 year

Sign it rules: Leo

House it governs: Fifth

LONG-TERM RELATIONSHIPS: THE SUN

The Sun governs our sense of self and our will. It's chiefly concerned with what we show people on purpose. We all need to feel seen for who we truly are—and it's natural to want our long-term partners to be a major source of validation.

Our will, and how we use it, is an important part of all of our close relationships. But the Sun is not just about us as individuals, it's about us in the context of our circumstances, our past, and the people around us. The Sun also represents the style in which we show up for others. As humans, we tend to take care of our partners and the other people we love in a way that's consistent with how we want to be cared for.

BRIGHT LIGHT

The Sun shines a big, bright light and, as long as one person doesn't fall in another's shadow, all partners can grow in complementary ways. When one person's Sun is over- or underexpressed in a relationship (when one person is taking up more space, shining at the expense of the other), it can be hard for us to maintain satisfaction and happiness. In long-term relationships, one person will often make major life sacrifices for another—for example, when one person packs up their life to move for their partner. As long as such gestures are eventually reciprocated, the sacrifices don't happen at the expense of their own Solar expression. Everyone deserves the kind of validation that encourages them to grow, change, and pursue their dreams, even if it often happens in a lop-sided way or takes place over the course of a relationship.

The Sun is all about finding yourself and prioritizing yourself—and within long-term partnerships, everyone hasn't always been able to do that. Historically, marriage was predicated on imbalance—women were expected to stay home and care for family, while men were encouraged to prioritize being ambitious and taking up space. In recent decades, we've seen that shift, as people other than cis men get to explore their identities and grow in society and within partnerships. But it isn't always easy to build relationships wherein all people have equal opportunity to shine. For couples who choose to have children, there's a never-before-seen negotiation over roles, power, and autonomy within partnerships.

Some astrology texts will tell you that the Sun is related to maleness, and in particular the male parent, because it rules assertion, strength, and vitality.

Meanwhile, femaleness has been associated with passivity and the Moon, or our emotions. But those ideas aren't in line with modern life. As people of all genders have increasing freedom to express all sides of themselves—including the pursuit of power—it's clear that these principles can no longer be tied to gender.

WHAT DOES IT MEAN TO BE "ON THE CUSP"?

Astrology is math! Every zodiac sign is one twelfth of a 360-degree wheel, or 30 degrees, and, based on that math, you're either one sign or another. My experience has shown that most people who feel "cuspy" do so because they tend to have planets in two adjacent signs.

HOW TO WORK WITH THIS PLANET

Over the course of time, you will grow and change; part of being successful in relationships is feeling like you and your partner get one another and truly see each other for who you are—in other words, valuing and validating one another's Sun. Practice being forthcoming about who you are and who you're becoming and afford your partner space to do the same.

THE SUN THROUGH THE SIGNS

SUN IN ARIES

These people are not known for their innate ability to listen and collaborate, but these are traits they need to cultivate in order to be in successful long-term relationships. It's their job to make sure that their lives are active and dynamic outside of their relationships, which will help them to be present for their partners without feeling compromised. To have satisfying intimate sex over time, people with their Sun in Aries need to have active fantasy landscapes that don't always involve their partners. They thrive in spontaneous connections.

SUN IN TAURUS

People with this placement may at times misinterpret requests for something new or different in their relationships as criticism. They can evade being direct as a way to be nice, but it's not nice if they're being dishonest. Although they risk getting into a rut or routine around what works and what their partner wants sexually, they're willing to do the work. Prone to holding grudges and digging in their heels, these people need to cultivate flexibility and trust that forgiveness is not giving in.

SUN IN GEMINI

Boredom outside the bedroom can lead to bed death for Geminis, but passion can be reignited if they cultivate interest in their partnerships by initiating conversations, asking questions, and pursuing activities out in the world together.

These people shouldn't be surprised if what they like about their partners and what they like to do with them shifts over time. The key is for them to be open to things evolving and to share the burden of initiating change. Reciprocity is especially valuable to Geminis, and they'll do best if it's alive in the dynamic over time.

SUN IN CANCER

Cancers are dedicated and loving partners and feeling valued and cared for is important to them. They can get caught in ruts and routines over the course of time, because they're creatures of habit—especially in matters of the heart. Treating lovers like family members can be a wet blanket on the sex life. The key is for them to continue "dating" their committed partners. If Cancers are open to changing things up and continuing to discover new things about their sweethearts, it becomes a lot easier to really enjoy themselves romantically and sexually over the long term.

SUN IN LEO

A big factor for long-term happiness with Leos is how they feel about themselves, and being adored is really important to them. If they don't like themselves in the dynamic, their sexuality (and affection) will become harder to access. These people have a reputation for dancing on tables and partying until all hours—but a lot of Leos can be more private. They need a broad fantasy landscape and multiple sources of creative engagement in order to keep the home fires burning.

SUN IN VIRGO

People with the Sun in Virgo may find that their drive to connect physically runs in cycles; sometimes they crave touch and sometimes they want space. Virgos in long-term relationships need to communicate to their partners when a lack of energy, and not a lack of interest in them, is the result of their natural cycle. When it comes to long-term relationships, it's essential to be honest in general, but Virgos will benefit from taking a less-critical approach. Communication is essential, but sharing every detail is not.

SUN IN LIBRA

Libra is the most partnership-centric sign of the zodiac, and these people's desire to form long-term relationships can be driving and intense. They believe deeply in compromise, and they're willing to do the work to maintain a functioning relationship. However, when they prioritize accommodating their partners over authenticity and honesty, the result may be passive aggression or resentment over the long term. It's important that they remember that their partners can't meet their needs if they don't know what those needs are.

SUN IN SCORPIO

Scorpios tend to brood and hold on to resentments. If those resentments become repressed or overexpressed, it can be at the expense of intimacy, sexual desire, collaboration, and the ability to show up emotionally. A dynamic sex life is especially important to them; Scorpios need date nights and time set aside for connection. Their intensity is a result of how deeply they feel things, so having outlets for processing emotions before they bring them to their partners is a great tool for avoiding unnecessary drama.

SUN IN SAGITTARIUS

Sagittarians are enthusiastic and optimistic, but when they're down in the dumps, they can go fast and hard into a dark place. They want their relationships to be spaces where they can be authentic and grow. These people may get fixated on things being a certain way, and that can keep them from listening when their partners give them reality checks. If sex dries up in a long-term relationship, it can be a symptom of other things drying up, such as their sense of freedom or excitement about the future.

SUN IN CAPRICORN

Capricorns take themselves very seriously and don't love feeling vulnerable. Letting people in deeply is not something they do lightly, but once they do, they tend to be very loyal. When trust gets bent or bruised in a long-term relationship, romantic and sexual intimacy is also likely to take a hit. Capricorns will want the same thing over and over again in bed—until one day they want something completely different, over and over again. The key to good sex with a Capricorn long term is building trust and being willing to be surprised.

SUN IN AQUARIUS

Aquarians have a reputation for being eccentric and aloof, and that can be true, but they can thrive in partnerships where they feel seen. As highly independent people, they need space to come to their truths on their own terms. When it comes to sex, they may want it to be fast and functional—to get in there, get it done, and move on with the rest of their day. If there's not enough change or growth within their partnerships, Aquarians will get bored.

SUN IN PISCES

People with the Sun in Pisces are highly sensitive and need to feel like their relationship is a sanctuary. They need to connect to their own bodies in a way that's fun and autonomous, in order to be able to truly share themselves with their partners. Because their sensory impressions are so strong, they may find that they need space to figure out what they're actually going through—and it's important that their partners are supportive and respectful of their process.

THE SUN THROUGH THE HOUSES

SUN IN THE FIRST HOUSE

These people are assertive and command attention when they enter a room, whether or not they mean to. They are encouraging and dynamic to be around, but they need to remember to take a step back and let others reveal themselves in their own ways, so that they can collaborate throughout the course of their relationships.

SUN IN THE SECOND HOUSE

Physical and material forms of love, attention, and reassurance are all very important to these people. They like to give and receive validation, whether that's through hugs, gifts, or compliments. Not always forthcoming with their partners, they can be passive-aggressive in the face of conflict. These people tend to be fixed in their perspectives but, given time, they can also be quite reasonable.

SUN IN THE THIRD HOUSE

People with the Sun in the third house are very active and value communication, in part because they're great at it. They can get distracted by the little things and need a partner who doesn't take that personally. They may be of so many minds that it's hard for them to stay wedded to one idea, making them hard to pin down. They can be quite versatile in terms of their sexual appetites, and depending on other aspects, they're generally game to explore their partners' needs.

SUN IN THE FOURTH HOUSE

Family-oriented, these people can get quite attached to the past, whether to their own childhood experiences or to the way things once were in their relationships. They are loyal, committed, and love building a sense of home within their relationships. These folks are willing to do the work necessary to go the distance with others, but their family of origin may be demanding or extra important to them—which can be challenging at times for their partners.

SUN IN THE FIFTH HOUSE

For these people, feeling seen is critical for feeling desired and cared for. It's important that they learn the difference between attention and love, so that they don't run the risk of either committing to being with people who don't really get them or seeking attention from others in periods of boredom. Having creative outlets—whether through children, the arts, or exercise—is an important source of self-maintenance that will support their ultimate happiness.

SUN IN THE SIXTH HOUSE

People with this placement can be quite particular about how they take care of themselves and their environments on a day-to-day basis. Their work lives tend to be important to them and typically either energize them or demand a fair amount of their energy, depending on the circumstance. They need to remember to get off their phones, unplug, and be present with their loved ones. Cultivating a work-life balance will only strengthen their relationships.

SUN IN THE SEVENTH HOUSE

Partnership is extremely important to these people, who tend to thrive when they're in committed relationships. They need to be careful that they don't become codependent or too idealistic about their partners and overinflate the value of their partnerships. It's important that these folks compromise in conscientious ways, so that they bend enough but not too much.

SUN IN THE EIGHTH HOUSE

These people attract partners who either give them life or take a lot of their energy. Sex is an important part of how they relate and achieve intimacy, but if resentment about minor compromises builds up, it can get in the way of a healthy sex life. Merging finances with their partners requires transparency and a willingness to work through their own personal money issues—but it's in their best interest to do that work.

SUN IN THE NINTH HOUSE

Folks with the Sun in the ninth house have ideas about the world that are incredibly important to their nature and, when others disagree, they tend to take it personally. They're generous, tolerant, and ever so supportive. If they feel that their relationships aren't fair, or their partners aren't tolerant or supportive, they can get quite despondent. Vacations and travel are important parts of their long-term relationships.

SUN IN THE TENTH HOUSE

People with this placement are driven to direct the flow of their own lives. Because of this, they can forget to compromise while making plans that directly or indirectly affect their partners. They are ambitious, hard-working, and status conscious, and they really don't want their partners to embarrass them in public. They're also commitment-minded and willing to do the work to make a relationship last.

SUN IN THE ELEVENTH HOUSE

These folks are very sociable. They are driven by a sense of purpose that is larger than their relationships, and they need their partners to support those purposes, either by participating directly or giving them space. This is not to say that they don't also prioritize partnerships, but when they commit to someone, they don't stop having other personal priorities. As a result, these people don't do well in possessive relationships or when there's not enough flexibility around how they use their time and energy.

SUN IN THE TWELFTH HOUSE

Those with the Sun in this house need a good deal of time to reflect and be by themselves. They aren't always clear about who they are and what they need, and this can land them in relationships with domineering partners. Cultivating a sense of self is ultimately an investment in the longevity of a relationship. Learning how to be forthcoming about their needs and desires and to give themselves the space to figure out what they want is essential when it comes to building long-term relationships.

MOON ☽

Time it takes to traverse the zodiac:
Approximately 29.5 days

Sign it rules: Cancer

House it governs: Fourth

LONG-TERM RELATIONSHIPS: THE MOON

When it comes to intimate relationships, the Moon is an essential planet to consider. It rules our feelings, needs, and sense of safety, as well as our home and family. It governs the way we express affection, love, and care—and it affects what we want and need from our partners in return. The Moon also governs our reactions and our pasts, as well as our own personal styles of connecting intimately. The emotional landscapes that began to take shape when we were children and that we're still wading through as adults? That's all the Moon's territory.

SO MANY FEELS

Your capacity to trust, to be vulnerable, to share on an emotional level, and to be close is all found with the Moon. In this way, it's arguably the most important planet to consider when looking at long-term relationships. It's also possibly some of the most essential territory to zero in on when it comes to becoming more mature and self-aware.

The Moon controls the tides; its influence is one of ebb and flow. Our feelings ebb and flow as well, and when we can allow for that fluidity without getting attached, we may paradoxically feel more secure in our relationships. The Moon moves through each degree of every sign in an approximately 29-day cycle. This means that our feelings, our needs, and our sense of intimate connection are also cyclical: They wax and wane just like the Moon. And when it comes to relationships, the changeability of the Moon might explain why your partner can feel like your best friend at noon and the very reason you can't get ahead in life by 6 p.m.

TRIGGER VERSUS TRAUMA

The Moon's location in your chart can signal the part of your life where it can be hard to know the difference between a real-time trauma and a trigger of something from the past. Emotional triggers (something that is similar to or reminds you of a pain in your past) don't always need to be acted on; they don't all need to be fixed or even directly addressed. But when something in your relationship is actually traumatic (it brings harm or is destructive), it deserves direct attention and intervention. Doing the solo work of self-care can help you to determine what you need to confront within a relationship, versus what you simply need to share about what you're feeling.

SELF-CARE AND YOUR RELATIONSHIPS

When we rely on our partners to provide for our emotional wellness, instead of taking responsibility for our own feelings, our relationships may become unequal or static. A common mistake that people make is to treat the Moon like they do Mercury. In other words, we often over-think, convert feelings into ideas, and use analysis as the primary tool for coping with feelings. Being present for your part-ner's Moon, or emotions, isn't always easy either. But if you and your partner are on the same team, the work is to listen, be receptive, and show kindness toward their emotional experiences. None of that nec-essarily means that you're agreeing with them. But it is never kind to offer counter-points just for the sake of disagreeing, nor is it a good idea to placate or police their behaviors. The Moon requires that we be lovingly present with our partners, even in turbulent times.

When another person's feelings stop the conversation, it can be an intended or unintended manipulation, which doesn't build closeness. For intimacy to occur, strive to share your feelings—not as a way to control, but as a way to be close and honest. Practice allowing space for others to do the same in their own way, in their own style. Feelings are not weaknesses, and they're not tools for gaining the upper hand, either.

HOW TO WORK WITH THIS PLANET

Working with the Moon is simple but not easy. There's no replacement for emotional accountability or kindness; you just have to do it. Try to be receptive to your own feelings and experiences in the moment. It's always okay to let your partners know you need space before you can respond to them emotionally. And if you're taking good care of yourself, you might also find that working through the Moon's intensity is less complicated than you think.

THE MOON THROUGH THE SIGNS

MOON IN ARIES
This placement gives people sharp and passionate feelings. Their emotions run hot, and they can be impulsive and reac-tive, but they have emotional resiliency and inner strength they can call on when needed. These folks need to be careful not to rush or run roughshod over their partners, especially if they've partnered with people of more retiring emotional natures. They can be quite assertive and decisive, so it serves them to remember that their primary partners need to be part of their decision-making process.

MOON IN TAURUS
These people can be loyal, sometimes to a fault, and they need to learn that disagreement doesn't necessarily compro-mise loyalty. Those with this placement run the risk of being disingenuous when things get complicated in an effort to

maintain peace. They're great at being in partnerships because of how deeply they value having mutually beneficial intimate relationships. But they may need to watch out for possessiveness and remember to do the work of building and refining trust with their partners, in part by being reliable themselves.

MOON IN GEMINI

Because they can be absorbed in their thoughts and have an especially cerebral way of processing emotions, these people can come across as inattentive. They prefer to relate to their partners in a fun, chill, and humorous way, and they crave a great deal of variety in their day-to-day lives. If they don't maintain dynamic and interesting lifestyles, they're likely to get quite frustrated with their partners, so it's important that they take responsibility for making their own lives interesting and cultivating skills as an active listener (by giving verbal or physical feedback).

MOON IN CANCER

These people can be very supportive, loyal, and willing to do the emotional work of maintaining closeness over the course of time. They're deeply family-oriented and value turning their partnerships into family, whether that includes children, cats, or goats. This placement can incline a person to be quite sensitive and self-protective, so they can be a little guarded if they feel hurt or rejected in any way. The crab doesn't only move sideways, it moves on its pinchers, so these folks need to be careful about being too passive-aggressive.

MOON IN LEO

People with the Moon in Leo like to be the HBIC. They love giving and receiving attention and love, and can be fiercely protective of whom and what they love, and are drawn to creating something that's a reflection of their love, whether a child or a home. It's important that they ask their partners for what they need and show up in ways that keep the passion and adventure alive while maintaining everyone's basic needs. Even though they can be prideful, with a healthy dose of humility, these people will go to the ends of the Earth for the people they love.

MOON IN VIRGO

These people value emotional stability and consistency. They make for steadfast, caring partners, but they can be rigid about what they want and need. Because they're inclined to place their habits above relationships or people, being flexible with their self-care routine will bring them more intimacy and happiness. Access to their bodies isn't always organic, so they're likely to go through both sexual phases and asexual ones. The trick is for them not to get so caught up in their heads that they lose track of their hearts. It's important that they remember to prioritize happiness and only seek perfection in efforts to meet that goal.

MOON IN LIBRA

These people are relationship-oriented and care deeply about fairness. They're willing to make compromises for their partners and their relationships, although they may run the risk of being accommodating to a fault. They really want activity partners they can grow alongside. These folks usually want long-term relationships to convert to marriage, because they crave security and promise. Their desire for guarantees can at times keep them stuck, but they'll have an easier time if they can remember to create stability behind their happiness, instead of the other way around.

MOON IN SCORPIO

Emotionally intense and deep, these folks are slow to trust, but once they let you in they may have pretty high expectations. They can be moody, possessive, and deeply sexual, and they're willing to do the work to grow with their partners over the course of time, especially if they feel respected and valued. People with this placement do best when they have enough time alone to experience and process their feelings. They tend either to be bluntly honest or to compromise the truth as a way to avoid discord and would do well to learn to express what they need from their partners in clear and effective ways.

MOON IN SAGITTARIUS

These people are big-hearted and want partnerships focused on growth—not just in their own lives but also for their partners. They prize fairness and compassion but can also get wrapped up in dogma or self-righteousness if they're not careful. They're spontaneous and can get so absorbed by other things they're

passionate about that they may need to remember to prioritize their partners and home life. Luckily, they tend to be responsive to those reminders.

MOON IN CAPRICORN

These people tend to be uncomfortable with vulnerability, which can make them private, emotionally hard to reach, and difficult to read. Once they get close enough to forge intimate connections, they're likely to hold their partners to the standards they hold themselves to—which can be exacting and demanding. While these folks are loyal, commitment-minded, and considerate in practical terms, they can hold on to grudges for a long time. That said, with patience and clarity of intent, they can bring emotional accountability to their relationships.

MOON IN AQUARIUS

Because they're so astute, these folks run the risk of not fully sitting with their feelings. They tend to be detached and quick at emotional processing because they take an analytical approach to feelings. While they may rush to understand or fix their feelings, this can lead to long-term challenges with anxiety or emotional presence. As these people get caught up in their heads, they can come across as cold, so it's important that they develop relationships wherein their partners are comfortable with their style of emotional expression.

MOON IN PISCES

These people are so sensitive to their environments and their feelings that it can make it hard for them to parse through what they need at times; they benefit from downtime—with or without their partners—to recover from the world. They can be romantic and sentimental and have a devotional form of loyalty. If they're not careful, they can use their partners' needs or desires to avoid tending to themselves. While they can be a little inconsistent or flighty, they're empathetic, emotionally generous, and willing to compromise.

THE MOON THROUGH THE HOUSES

MOON IN THE FIRST HOUSE

These people are courageous, warm-hearted, and want their feelings to be validated. They want to build a relationship wherein they can share a rich emotional connection over the course of time. As they wear their emotions on their sleeves, these folks can seem quite reactive. Learning to take responsibility for how their emotions impact others is key to avoiding unnecessary drama and prioritizing what matters. They can be quite sentimental, and they take great pains to show up for their partners.

MOON IN THE SECOND HOUSE

These folks do best when emotional connections are nested in a sense of shared values. They crave proof of their place in the hearts and lives of others. Physical touch is also an important part of how they give and receive love. These people can sometimes prioritize a sense of security over real happiness, so they need to be careful not to cut off their noses to spite their faces when it comes to getting their needs met.

MOON IN THE THIRD HOUSE

These people process emotion intellectually; they tend to want to talk a lot about their feelings. They need to be able to verbalize lots of ideas and feelings that may not actually be their truth. The trick for them is to talk to friends or write things out in a journal before processing with their partner, because they need to cycle through their feelings first.

MOON IN THE FOURTH HOUSE

This Moon placement indicates a love of home and a strong desire to build a solid foundation with another person. People with the Moon in the fourth house are supportive, loving, and expressive. That said, their emotions run so high and they can get so caught up in their feelings that they stop collaborating with their partners or truly listening to them. Whether or not they have children, having a multigenerational life is important to them.

MOON IN THE FIFTH HOUSE

These people need to have passion and play in their lives. Sex is an important expression of love, and it's important that these folks nurture desire in their dynamic with their partners as well as in their own bodies. Feelings tend to come on strong, so these people need to practice tolerating their emotions long enough to wade through their reactions in order to express their authentic needs.

MOON IN THE SIXTH HOUSE

Day-to-day habits can be a meaningful source of self-maintenance for these people, and they do best when they can establish (and maintain) rituals for staying emotionally present and connected to their partners. When they don't take responsibility to create and maintain such rituals, those with the Moon in the sixth house may end up feeling isolated or being hard to reach.

MOON IN THE SEVENTH HOUSE

These people feel a strong desire to be linked with others they care about. They're at their best when they're in long-term relationships and have besties they can confide in. They require a lot from their partners emotionally, but they're also willing to give a great deal. Codependency is something they need to watch out for; they should find ways of being emotionally present that are not exclusively responsive to others.

MOON IN THE EIGHTH HOUSE

These people tend to have deep emotional wells; in turn, they can be quite self-protective or secretive. When resentment or hurt builds up, they run the risk of isolating themselves from their partners; they'd do well to prioritize dealing with things head-on so that problems don't fester over the course of time. They can be deeply sexual and sometimes find it easier to connect intimately without words.

MOON IN THE NINTH HOUSE

This placement tends to have a devotional approach to love. Their emotional nature runs in leaps and bounds, which is to say their hearts can gallop toward or away from people. Taking trips or sharing spiritual philosophies with their partners may help them maintain excitement and intimacy. Forthright communication can usurp their tendencies to create stories based on their feelings before making sure they're objectively true.

MOON IN THE TENTH HOUSE

Career is really important to these people, and they need partners who support their visions, even as they change over the course of time. They are socially sensitive, and they can be uncomfortable when they believe their partners reflect poorly on them. They're not terribly comfortable with vulnerability and can be kind of bossy as a result, but their capacity to be loyal and to do the work is very strong.

MOON IN THE ELEVENTH HOUSE

These people consider themselves very open, and they can be, but they may also be dogmatic about what they feel is right. Because of this, they may have to remember that being right isn't more important than being close. They thrive when they can be close to more than one person and so have multiple outlets for their feelings, needs, and endless curiosity. Obsessing about the future and trying to second-guess their partners' feelings and actions are two things they should try to avoid.

MOON IN THE TWELFTH HOUSE

A good deal of space is necessary for these people to reflect on what they're feeling and needing. They should be wary of sacrificing too much or martyring themselves for the people they love. They're very devoted to their partners, and it's important for them to have healthy boundaries, which begins with them identifying their needs and feelings and validating their right to have and express them.

MERCURY ☿

**Time it takes to traverse the zodiac:
Approximately 1 year**

Signs it rules: Gemini, Virgo

Houses it governs: Third, sixth

LONG-TERM RELATIONSHIPS: MERCURY

Mercury governs communication, making it a key player when seeking to understand long-term relationships. This planet rules our attitudes, our thoughts, what we say, and how we say it—our words and our tone. In a relationship, when we feel like we're on the same team, it gives us a sense of unity even through disagreements or misunderstandings. When we or our partners are defensive or even distracted, it can be easy to forget that we're teammates; we may stop truly listening and sharing, which creates an oppositional dynamic. In the context of Mercury, the tool we have to repair this kind of rupture is the exchange of ideas and information, and that requires both trust and practice.

LISTENING IS LOVE

Regardless of how long you've been with your sweetheart, it's ultimately your responsibility to ask questions and really listen to the answers before formulating a response; in other words, engage your Mercury with intention. It's also your responsibility to show up and share what's happening with you on the inside. Mercury also plays a significant role in how we disagree with and learn from our partners. When we insist that our attitudes, beliefs, or ideas are right, we tend to stop listening and only respond when we have an opportunity to make a point.

Mars technically governs the ego, but Mercury rules what we believe about ourselves. In an increasingly Mercurial world, our ideas of ourselves can supersede our actual experience in the moment. Instead of listening to another person's perspective, we can hold firm to our version of events and defend points rather than being truly collaborative. Such is the downside of Mercury in relationships. When we get impatient, we're less able to face the kinds of challenges that are inevitable in any relationship. It's important not to generate narratives that match our theories. When applied to relationships, our stories might show us only what we want to see about our partners and not what they're actually revealing. In this way, Mercury is quite egotistical, because our ideas can replace or overlay our actual experiences and the potential inherent in a relationship.

PACE AND PARTNERSHIP

When it comes to compatibility, it's important to keep in mind that everyone has a different pace at which they process, understand, and verbalize ideas. Getting to know—and accept—both your own mental pace and your partner's is really important, especially when it comes time to talk about difficult things or make important life decisions together. Understanding where Mercury falls in the birth chart can help with this.

Mercury rules the foundational friendship that develops when you know someone over the course of several years, which can be one of the best parts of a long-term relationship. Most friendships have their phases of more or less compatibility, and all friendships require work from both parties. We don't need to agree with our partners about everything (that would be boring), but we do need to be able to share ideas in a way that fosters reciprocity and connection.

HOW TO WORK WITH THIS PLANET

Listen—truly listen—to your partner and ask questions that reflect authentic interest. This is not realistic every day of the week. There will be stretches of time when you're just less interested in them, but when that goes on for too long, it sows the seeds of discontent. If you're struggling, it's okay to draw on tools such as multiple-choice questions (word games are also very Mercurial) to get at what's really going on for your partner.

MERCURY THROUGH THE SIGNS

MERCURY IN ARIES

These people are enthusiastic and direct, but prone to interrupting. They may have me-centric thinking, and they're not the most compromising, which is not super endearing to their partners. That said, they are brave, protective of those they love, and willing to do the work of moving things along in their relationships.

MERCURY IN TAURUS

Stubborn, diplomatic, and resourceful, these people tend to have methodical ways of processing, which they do through their senses. If they don't have enough time to do that, they can get a bit rushed and defensive. This means that they need extra time to truly take in information, especially when things get heated or unpleasant with their partners. They may experience periods of inertia wherein they need to find ways to recharge.

MERCURY IN GEMINI

This placement gives people a quick, logical nature. They're able to grasp ideas and communicate them efficiently, but they may get easily distracted or keep things on the surface. They tend toward duplicity if they're not careful; not because they're intentionally lying but because they are speaking to different truths at different moments. It's important in relationships that these folks honor their word and not rely heavily on their ability to convince or talk circles around their partners.

MERCURY IN CANCER

People who have Mercury in Cancer will express themselves indirectly, but their tone of voice will often betray their emotions—especially when they're talking about things that are difficult for them. This can give them a reputation for being passive-aggressive. That said, they are loyal and tend to be supportive and responsive to their partners' needs. Because Cancer is such an emotional sign, they may change their points of view often.

MERCURY IN LEO

This placement inclines people to be enthusiastic and fun and to have a flair for the dramatic in how they tell stories, communicate, and relate to the people they're close to. They may also be a little self-indulgent. They have an authoritative way of speaking and can have a bit of a "do as I say not as I do" tendency. Their stubbornness can become a challenge in relationships, especially if these folks lose sight of their intentions to be creatively connected to their partners.

MERCURY IN VIRGO

These people can be highly critical or thoughtfully discerning. They can get fixated on what they believe to be the truth, and they won't rest until it's verified or validated. There's a tendency to get lost in the details and distracted by the little things. On the plus side, people with this placement can have an endless well of loving curiosity about their partners, especially when they can remain curious in their own lives.

MERCURY IN LIBRA

This placement leads to indecisiveness, which can become uncertainty and insecurity over time if these folks aren't careful. The drive and willingness to compromise is useful in a partnership, but when it gets to a point where people aren't making their own decisions and taking responsibility for what they bring to the table, that indecisiveness can be a real problem. While admirable, their desire to be nice can sometimes lead them to be less than honest in their communications.

MERCURY IN SCORPIO

This is not the most forthcoming placement, as Scorpio tends to be a private, sometimes secretive sign. This is not due to a lack of integrity in these people but instead to the depth of emotion that comes along with their ideas. These folks are quite intense and have very strong attitudes and opinions about people and situations. They're excellent at picking up on subtlety and must learn to resist the urge to clock their partners' every move or bring up the past when discussing charged issues.

MERCURY IN SAGITTARIUS

These people have to be careful not to write checks with their words that they can't cash with their actions. They are quite capable and honest but can also justify almost anything. They love sharing stories, and, as much as they value honesty, they tend to color outside the lines to make things more interesting. Their relationships will work best when they make sure to listen to their partners and when they don't feel as if they're just being swept along for the ride.

MERCURY IN CAPRICORN

Literalists until the end, these people can be hard to predict, and their attitudes vacillate between uptight and wild. They may have rigid mindsets about how things should be and fixed ideas about the past. They also have pretty serious mental dispositions, which empowers them to do the work that relationships require, but it doesn't always make them the most romantic or sentimental communicators along the way.

MERCURY IN AQUARIUS

These people are very detail-oriented and tend to pick up on everything at once. They're given to having eccentric ideas and inventive speech patterns. Attuned to symbolism, they can be active listeners or may project onto others. These folks have to be careful not to interrupt, because even though they think they can anticipate their partners' words, everyone deserves the space to express themselves in their own ways.

MERCURY IN PISCES

This is a very sensitive placement for Mercury. These people are supportive, sentimental, and have genuine empathy for others, but they can be a bit passive when things get difficult in their relationships. They loathe the idea of hurting feelings or being wrong. Since their sensitivities can make them quite moody, it's important they take the space that they need to truly show up within their partnerships.

MERCURY THROUGH THE HOUSES

MERCURY IN THE FIRST HOUSE

People with this placement are quick, but their thoughts tend to play across their faces, making them no good in games of poker. They're highly identified with their opinions, which doesn't make them flexible, but they are forthcoming. Skilled conversationalists, they're genuinely interested in others, but their talkativeness can also get them in trouble if they're not careful.

MERCURY IN THE SECOND HOUSE

Because they don't want to muddy themselves in the details, these folks may rush to find the solution to a problem before fully understanding its complexity. They value communication but have a tendency to keep things on the surface or have a hard time letting things go. They want to feel secure within their relationships, and they're willing to do the work to get there, even if it's begrudgingly at times.

MERCURY IN THE THIRD HOUSE

These folks are excellent at staying connected and sharing information, and as long as their interests are maintained, they're great listeners. They're quick, smart, and funny, but their biggest challenge is that they're distractible and have so much going on at any given moment that they don't always give their relationships the attention they deserve.

MERCURY IN THE FOURTH HOUSE

People with this placement can be quite self-protective and are not always forthcoming until they've worked out how they feel about what they're thinking. They can become quite attached to their beliefs or their version of events, which can become a roadblock to conflict resolution. These people tend to feel a strong sense of "us against them," which can incline them to be either quite loyal or defensive, depending on the circumstances.

MERCURY IN THE FIFTH HOUSE

This is a creative aspect, and children—and other creative ventures—can be quite important to these people. People with this placement are fond of attention, love flirting, and like their partners to stay in touch as a way to feel close. They are dynamic and lively and need to feel as if their ideas have sway over their partners. As they are a bit slap-dash with facts or details, they tend to follow their strongest feelings even though they prioritize loyalty.

MERCURY IN THE SIXTH HOUSE

This placement gives people a practical and thorough form of intelligence. They are quite versatile in how they like to live and what they like to do day to day; in terms of partnerships, they have the capacity to foster healthy collaborative conversations if they can learn to let the little things go. Resisting the impulse to be controlling or to nitpick will allow space for their partners to approach things differently and, therefore, their relationships to thrive.

MERCURY IN THE SEVENTH HOUSE

These people are chatty, and they need partners they can talk to. They may put greater emphasis on talking than on listening or prioritize speaking over action. This is a diplomatic placement, and they are uncomfortable with fighting and raised voices. They may find themselves in May–December romances (dating younger or older people). Partnership is incredibly important to them, and they feel completed by committed relationships.

MERCURY IN THE EIGHTH HOUSE

People with Mercury in the eighth house can be a bit secretive or private. They have a deeply emotional way of processing ideas and information. These folks have the capacity to cut through many layers of information and static to get to the truth, but they run the risk of being obsessive and getting distracted by petty details. Closeness and intimacy are essential for them, and they need their partners to be their confidants for long-term compatibility.

MERCURY IN THE NINTH HOUSE

Quick, funny, and adventurous, people with this placement like to talk and share stories. They are highly philosophical and tend to have strong attitudes about higher education or religion, which is especially relevant for students or parents. Overall, they can be quite visionary and expansive in their cognitive processing. They may also be dismissive of things that bore them or don't match their worldviews.

MERCURY IN THE TENTH HOUSE

These folks are highly identified with their goals and plans, and they can be a bit demanding with their partners. They tend to be literal in their thinking and may need to practice refining the art of compromise. Partnership is an ongoing collaboration; these people have to be careful not to make life plans on their own and then try to plug other people into them.

MERCURY IN THE ELEVENTH HOUSE

Sharp, quick-witted, and intelligent, people with this placement tend to have a lot going on. They need a vibrant social life to be truly satisfied within their relationships. They're deeply concerned with issues of social justice and likely to find themselves in communities where people are exchanging ideas about the world. It's important to them that their partners share those interests.

MERCURY IN THE TWELFTH HOUSE

These folks don't always feel comfortable asserting their preferences or needs, in part because it can take them awhile to figure out what they think or want. This may lead them to come across as passive or passive-aggressive. It's important that they learn how to articulate their need to take space in order to figure things out. These people need to have some secrets, even if they're small. They do best with partners who are good at drawing them out.

VENUS ♀

Time it takes to traverse the zodiac: Approximately 1 year

Signs it rules: Taurus, Libra

Houses it governs: Second, seventh

LONG-TERM RELATIONSHIPS: VENUS

Venus rules the parts of our lives where we want connection, closeness, sensory expression, stability, security, and ease. It governs our sense of romance, sensuality, and tender connection; it affects how we flirt, make out, and touch one another. It governs the value we place on the relationships and people in our lives, the commitment we make to care for our partners, and the promises we make to create stability. Venus also governs our personal finances.

This planet is regarded as the "planet of love," but as this book details, there are myriad other facets of love and commitment. For that reason, it's important not to place all of our eggs in Venus's basket.

Venus is historically tied to women and the female gender. The glyph is conventionally used as the woman's symbol, but everyone has this planet in their chart. In recent years, there has been a loosening of the boundaries between femaleness and maleness, and people of all genders are increasingly able to experience and express their Venus in a way that is self-appropriate, even if it's outside conventional expectations of their gender assigned at birth.

ACCOMMODATION VERSUS AUTHENTICITY

Venus's placement in the chart can tell you where in your life you tend to be diplomatic and accommodating. All long-term relationships require a meaningful amount of compromise, and Venus is especially good at it. Where we run into trouble is when we make compromises that go against our values. Letting our partners know when we're compromising allows us to build up closeness and better understand and appreciate what our beloveds are doing for us—and they get to do the same.

TENDERNESS

This planet is also concerned with sexual intimacy—not so much with doin' it but with things such as holding hands, hooking up, and snuggling. Sensual intimacy is the foundation of long-term closeness; in many long-term relationships, that part of the connection can fade over the course of time, either because people get lazy or because it can be hard to be intimate with the same person year after year, especially when day-to-day life—dishes, health issues, co-parenting—takes over.

Venus plays an important a role in influencing your relationship with money and what you value. In a long-term relationship, this includes owning things together—not to mention potentially raising children or pets together. When people decide to merge financially, there needs to be some shared values around money. It's in our best interest be able to communicate honestly and diplomatically with our partners about the meaning and value money carries for us, and what that means in practical terms.

HOW TO WORK WITH THIS PLANET

If sex and intimacy aren't flowing, take a few months off from trying to have sex and instead commit to doing more snuggling, making out, and dancing together. The idea is to take a break from having outcome-oriented sexual encounters. In this way, you may be able to reconnect and rekindle your sensual connection.

VENUS THROUGH THE SIGNS

VENUS IN ARIES

The people with Venus in Aries are very demonstrative in relationships; they can be quite emphatic with their affection. They're not the most compromising, but they often have the directive energy to make things happen. They can forget to include their partners in decision making or asking questions; they do best in partnerships when they can remember to collaborate.

VENUS IN TAURUS

Fierce, loyal protectors of the relationships they're invested in, these people can be quite stubborn. Not fans of messiness, they run the risk of staying in a rut instead of upsetting the apple cart. That said, they are motivated to get their own way. They're happiest in relationships where their partners make time to give them gifts, good food, or a lot of touch.

VENUS IN GEMINI

Because they can see all angles of a situation, these people can end up changing their mind at the last minute or saying one thing and doing another. They are inclined to be generous and open-minded and genuinely interested in their partners. When they're in their happy place, they can be flirtatious, so it's important that their partners aren't too jealous or possessive.

VENUS IN CANCER

These people are so invested in their partners that they may need to be careful not to be too needy. There is a strong drive to attach and feel safe, but such drive can become problematic if a sense of home isn't felt within themselves first. Security is incredibly important to people with this placement. They are loyal and nurturing and tend to value time spent together as the best evidence of love.

VENUS IN LEO

People with this placement love to be spoiled and complimented; they really want their partners to think they're the center of the world. They care about social capital, and they like it when their partners either show up cute or make them feel cute. They're warm and enthusiastic and absolutely love giving and getting love. Being playful and going on dates are important parts of keeping romance alive for them.

VENUS IN VIRGO

Because they are quite particular about how they like to collaborate with their sweethearts, these folks may act in ways that seem selfish—but that's really not what they think they're doing. People with this placement require tangible equality in their relationships, so reciprocity is golden for them. Even in happy relationships, they need time to be left alone with their thoughts.

VENUS IN LIBRA

These people tend to be very diplomatic, and they do well in partnerships, even if they're not always the most forthcoming or decisive. They may find themselves in relationships in which they focus more on their partners' needs than their own. For this reason, they need to continue to develop their own lives and assert their needs and preferences.

VENUS IN SCORPIO

These folks can be quite possessive and secretive; it's important that they do their part to maintain honesty and transparency in long-term relationships. They have really deep sensual, emotional, and sexual feelings, so they need consistent quality time with their partners. Taking

space for themselves also helps them to show up for their partners.

VENUS IN SAGITTARIUS

Prone to restlessness or boredom, these people need to maintain a sense of playfulness in relationships. Having the sense that they're continuing to discover new things about their partners while co-creating a life around them is a big part of what makes them happy. They're naturally flirtatious and tend to have romantic, idealistic natures, which makes them good at keeping relationships alive.

VENUS IN CAPRICORN

Because they're not especially romantic, these folks tend to partner with those they can work well with. Venus in Capricorn people are willing to do the work that relationships require over the course of time. They can be directive and literal and hold their partners to high standards, so they need to remember to verbally communicate about problems before they become towering issues.

VENUS IN AQUARIUS

People with this placement can be quite aloof and may find themselves easily distracted—not just from their partners but from their relationships, too. It's important that they have a strong foundation of friendship in any long-term relationship because they need to fall back on a sense of comradery and equanimity. These people can be a bit odd and hard to predict and require a good deal of freedom and autonomy.

VENUS IN PISCES

Those with Venus in Pisces are romantic and sentimental. They are very sensitive and empathic and have the tendency to partner with people who have big personalities. Their capacity for love and romance is high, and they can be very supportive, but it's important that they remember to identify and protect their own needs, so that they don't feel taken advantage of.

VENUS THROUGH THE HOUSES

VENUS IN THE FIRST HOUSE

People with this placement tend to have great social skills, but those skills may sometimes get in the way of getting real or going deep with their partners. These folks can make decisions while getting others to think those decisions are their own ideas—that is, they're good at topping from the bottom. They can also be very focused on appearances, and they may have a hard time maintaining long-term romantic interest if their partners stop looking good to them.

VENUS IN THE SECOND HOUSE

Financial security is important to these people, but they may be a bit spendy, preferring creature comforts to a savings account. They enjoy physical comfort, and a big part of how they like to relate to their partners is through their senses. They tend to gauge their stability and security by how well they can get along with their partners—and that can make them pretty conflict-averse.

VENUS IN THE THIRD HOUSE

These people know how to communicate in a way that doesn't ruffle feathers, but they tend to be so talkative that they don't always restrain themselves. They like to stay busy and are often juggling many things, which can make them come across as a bit scattered. In efforts to keep the peace, they can say "yes" even when they know for a fact that the answer is "no"—a strategy that's likely to backfire on them.

VENUS IN THE FOURTH HOUSE

Home life and entertaining are both incredibly important to these people, and they want their spaces to look and feel lovely. The creative process of building homes with others fosters closeness in their relationships. They tend to be loyal and deeply invested in their partnerships and prioritize them in their lives.

VENUS IN THE FIFTH HOUSE

These people need to feel creatively attracted to their partner, and both romance and fun need to be consistent parts of their relationships if they're going to stay truly engaged over the long term. They have a strong desire to have their relationships feel generative—whether that means raising children, having fur babies, or even collaborating on projects.

VENUS IN THE SIXTH HOUSE

Compromising about day-to-day lifestyle choices comes relatively easy to these folks, and they enjoy showing their care for partners in habitual ways. They don't love upsets in their environments and prefer to have heavy conversations and interactions in private. They tend to have strong feelings about how things should be done, but they're usually willing to compromise for those they care about.

VENUS IN THE SEVENTH HOUSE

These people are very partnership-minded and tend to have especially compromising natures. They like having attentive partners who are invested in keeping things romantic, or they may find themselves letting go of that need in exchange for security. Inclined to be a little codependent, these folks need to keep an eye on their own autonomy.

VENUS IN THE EIGHTH HOUSE

Forging partnerships with people who can give them some sort of leg up—either socially or financially—is important to these folks. Sex and sensuality are essential parts of their natures and not things they can easily compromise. With feelings that run quite deep, they can be a little slow to process what they need from a partner or from a relationship dynamic more generally.

VENUS IN THE NINTH HOUSE

These people can be idealistic and tend to believe the best about their partners unless they have clear evidence to the contrary. They are adventurous and philosophical, and they can be incredibly reasonable when given due process in a relationship. This is not the most materialistic placement for Venus, but these folks may be impulse shoppers.

VENUS IN THE TENTH HOUSE

Once they've decided that someone is their person, folks with Venus in the tenth house are very loyal, but they also need to remember to include their partners in their life planning. They are used to being able to finesse situations professionally, so they can be caught off guard when things go sideways in their relationships. In other words, when charm isn't enough, they may struggle.

VENUS IN THE ELEVENTH HOUSE

These people need many vibrant relationships and connections in their lives to feel happy, so if their primary relationship blocks out others, they can feel stuck. They can end up being a bit rigid once they get attached to an idea, but they're very open-minded in general. If they place value on money, they have a knack for financial planning.

VENUS IN THE TWELFTH HOUSE

Resentments and upsets that build up over the years may incline these people to shut down on their partners if left unattended. It's imperative that they figure out how to have healthy boundaries, otherwise they may find themselves feeling unappreciated. People with this placement can be highly sensitive, romantic, and devotional in the ways they love.

MARS ♂

Time it takes to traverse the zodiac: Approximately 2 years

Sign it rules: Aries

House it governs: First

LONG-TERM RELATIONSHIPS: MARS

Mars is an essential planet to consider when it comes to long-term relationships. It governs fornicating and fighting, as well as the energy and the pace with which we approach our goals. This planet governs what we're passionate about, what we're willing to do about it, and how we do it. All of these elements are deeply essential to long-term compatibility and the viability of partnerships or marriages.

FORNICATING

When we partner with someone, we're essentially agreeing to hook up with them over the long term. Mars is a hunter not a gatherer (that's Venus), and when we're partnered, the hunt is off.

Once someone feels like part of your family, it can often be hard to sexualize them and get excited by them. That's where maintenance sex enters the picture.

There are three Martian keys to long-term sexual satisfaction with the same person on repeat. The first one is having a no-holds-barred private fantasy

landscape where we allow ourselves to think about sex, get excited, explore, and enjoy our bodies (separate from our partners). In this way, our sexuality is ours and not just something we share with our partners. The second key is being honest about what we do and don't like and expressing it in ways that involve more than just dropping hints. When we're in a long-term relationship, some sexual compromise is inevitable—and that varies from relationship to relationship. But when all we have is compromise, or our partners don't know that we're compromising, it's hard to stay sexually satisfied, and therefore active, over the course of years. Finally, keeping your Mars in the picture in a relationship also requires that you create unstructured downtime in bed—or whatever location makes sense for your relationship—where sexual connection can flow.

FIGHTING

Mars governs combat; it's about fighting and getting your way. It's the bully, the soldier, and the athlete. In relationships, it's important that we fight, fight fair, and fight about the right things. This requires introspection, impulse control, honesty, bravery, and clarity of intent.

Depending on your nature, you may often find yourself fighting about the surface things that bother you—instead of the reasons why. Or you may try to resist the urge to fight and avoid conflict even when something is actually wrong. Most of us err on one side or the other, and most relationships function in one way or the other.

Dissent—which is Mars's domain—needs to be expressed if you're going to lead a healthy life. It's important to be able to work with and embody the Mars energy in your chart in a way that gets results instead of drama. For instance, couples often fight about housework, but what we're really fighting about is whether we feel respected, whether there is equity when it comes to the boring tasks of life, whether we have the freedom to live the way we want to, and whether we have clear agreements. Fighting about the symptoms of the problem, instead of the problem itself, tends to lead to more fighting. So, what does it look like to fight in a healthy way?

Angry feelings and behavior are ruled by Mars. It shouldn't need to be said, but fighting with your fists is never okay. (I won't be getting into abusive relationships in this book, but physical violence, humiliation, gas-lighting, isolating, not respecting physical boundaries, controlling the household money, or threatening the other person are all behaviors that cross the line. They can generally be traced to functions of Mars and most of the outer planets.) Screaming is okay for some people and not for others—and so there needs to be an agreement within a relationship about what's effective when passions are flaring. It's not fair to hurl insults, demean our partners, or walk away during conflict, but all these things inevitably happen and they don't support the growth of a relationship. When we're

seeing red is the worst time to fight, but it's an important time to find a healthy visceral outlet for our feelings, so we can identify what's motivating those feelings.

If you're not willing or able to express agency in a relationship, you may find yourself choosing to be with someone who takes over the expression of your Mars for you—and it's probably a bad deal. In a healthy relationship, it's important that both parties have agency.

AMBITION

Having a sense of shared ambition—also ruled by Mars—can be very important when you're sharing your life with someone. Whether the issue is moving in together, relocating, changing careers, going back to school, or deciding whether to have children, major life-planning decisions require that each individual expresses agency as well as collaborates. If a choice requires your individual bravery, it may be hard to remember to consult your life partner. Conversely, you may lean on that person too much to help you make the decisions. This is where embodying your Mars consciously is invaluable to your relationship. This planet rules the pace with which you execute your goals, and your pace is likely to be different from your partner's. While you can adjust your behavior, your Mars is *your* Mars, and you can't become a new person. Relationship is a partnered dance that takes place over the course of time, and what matters most is that you can agree on the tempo.

HOW TO WORK WITH THIS PLANET

When arguing with your partner, practice figuring out what you're actually upset about, so that you can communicate it in a way the other person can hear. When you're mad about something, getting to a place where you have a clear ask will empower you and bring the fight to a more productive place. By investing in your own agency, you can meet your partner from a more embodied place, which is essential for both fighting fair and maintaining a hot sex life.

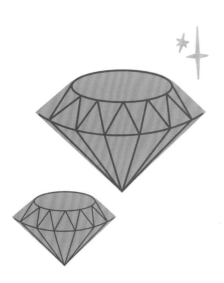

MARS THROUGH THE SIGNS

MARS IN ARIES

For these people, asking for forgiveness is preferable to asking for permission. They may feel as if their partner is trying to slow them down or keep them from moving forward. They tend to need to learn the value of compromise and collaboration within their partnerships. Good at what they do, they can be a bit entitled and may bulldoze over their partners without realizing it. They're motivated lovers, but easily bored and distracted.

MARS IN TAURUS

For folks with this placement, maintaining a sensual connection is really important for enjoying a long-term sexual partnership. They are quite stubborn but also intensely loyal. In their efforts to remain safe or right, they may sacrifice truly listening to their partners. If they can cultivate flexibility and greater resilience, it will serve them well in any long-term relationship.

MARS IN GEMINI

These people need to be interested in their partners' thoughts—about the world, about life, and so on—in order to maintain sustained sexual interest. They tend to have so much going on that their energies can become scattered, leading them to break promises and omit information. Their lives can become more streamlined and their behavior more reliable with their partners if they learn to pace themselves.

MARS IN CANCER

Sex is a form of intimacy for people with Mars in Cancer, so when genuine closeness isn't present in a long-term relationship, their sexual attraction to their partners can fade, too. They can be quite passive-aggressive when they're mad or when they feel that their plans have been thwarted. It's important for them to learn to manage their emotions so they can assert themselves in ways that their partners can actually hear.

MARS IN LEO

These people want to be valued for what they're doing, and attention and reinforcement from their partners is essential to them. They tend to really enjoy sex, but if they don't feel that they look how they're supposed to (or their partners aren't prioritizing their own looks), it can impact their sex drive. Leo isn't associated with humility, so these folks will benefit from learning to share the throne with their partners.

MARS IN VIRGO

People with Mars in Virgo can be especially habitual, so forming and maintaining healthy sexual habits and making time and space for intimacy to flourish is crucial to maintaining a long-term sex life. Because they're so methodical, these people can become fixated on what they're doing to the exclusion of romance or partnership. They need to be careful not to get in the habit of nagging or nitpicking, and instead communicate about the real problems lying beneath what irritates them.

MARS IN LIBRA

These people tend to be a little passive sexually. They may enjoy the process of connecting and exchanging desire more than the act of sex. They don't always feel comfortable talking about their needs, especially when they're angry, but learning to express those needs clearly will help get them met over time—in and out of the bedroom.

MARS IN SCORPIO

This is a deeply sexual placement for Mars, but that doesn't mean that these people want to have sex all the time. On the contrary, they may have control or safety issues when it comes to sex, and if the trust is in any way broken, their desire for their partners will wane. It's important that they maintain a private fantasy landscape, so that they can protect their sexual autonomy. When it comes to fighting, they tend to get upset in a very intense or compulsive way. They can also fight by projecting their dark feelings instead of communicating what's wrong. Self-care is an important tool to avoid becoming vindictive.

MARS IN SAGITTARIUS

These people love a good hunt, but they're not known for their stamina. They tend to have very sexual phases followed by phases during which they're less focused on their partners in pursuit of other passions. When it comes to fighting, they may act before they think and end up saying or doing things they really don't mean if they're not careful. These folks tend to make plans before talking about them with their partners; keeping an open line of communication is really important for their relationships.

MARS IN CAPRICORN

These are people with a great deal of stamina; they either are very sexual or tend not to prioritize sex in long-term relationships. And they have either vanilla or kinky tastes. This placement is not known for being the warmest or most affectionate, but it does give great discipline and self-control. If these folks aren't careful, they can develop rigidity and a bit of a papa-knows-best attitude toward their partners.

MARS IN AQUARIUS

Routine is the kiss of death for these people, who need some form of variety or surprise in order to maintain long-term interest in sexual intimacy. People with this placement can get so caught up in the genius of their own approach they can do a poor job of collaborating with their partners around major life decisions. When it comes to fighting, they often take a rational approach, which can make them come across as cold.

MARS IN PISCES

People with this placement vacillate between very sexual periods and phases where sex isn't relevant to them at all. It can be difficult for them to stay connected to their bodies. Making sure they are forthcoming about their needs and limits is essential to their long-term relationships; if that doesn't take shape, they may slip into unequal dynamics. Self-direction isn't always easy for them, and they may find themselves relying on their partners for too much direction at times.

MARS THROUGH THE HOUSES

MARS IN THE FIRST HOUSE

These people are passionate and pro-active, even if they're not compromising or subtle. They can come across as force-ful if they're not careful, and they must make a conscientious effort to slow down and meet their partners where they're at. They have a terrible time hiding their irritation, but, on the bright side, they're more likely to take responsibility for learning how to fight fair because of it.

MARS IN THE SECOND HOUSE

These people are willing to do the work that long-term relationships require. Financial security is important to them, although they may not always have a good plan for making or managing money. When they truly understand their partners' motives, they're more willing to compromise, but they are a bit obtuse in the face of subtle hints.

MARS IN THE THIRD HOUSE

This placement indicates that these people tend to be really busy. They need a sense of connection with their partners, even though they don't always remember to foster it. For these folks, flirting, text-ing, and staying in touch emotionally is an important part of keeping the chem-istry alive. They may be quite restless and can become distracted by occasional crushes—but as long as there's consent in their primary relationship, flirting can help them stay sexually present in their own bodies.

MARS IN THE FOURTH HOUSE

These folks are motivated to be in part-nerships and are willing to do the work involved in long-term relationships. That said, they can be stubborn about what they think needs to be happening. They crave stable, busy, and warm domestic lives. Hosting friends in their homes can be good for the longevity of their long-term partnerships.

MARS IN THE FIFTH HOUSE

This placement inclines people to be quite charming and motivating, and they love getting their way. Over the course of a relationship, however, they'll benefit from learning that sometimes the best way to get what they want is to collabo-rate. Having an active sex life is really important for their long-term happiness, and they will crave romance and play, even if they sometimes forget to prioritize it in their own actions. They can also be a little mean when they fight.

MARS IN THE SIXTH HOUSE

People with this placement tend to have a difficult time remembering to compro-mise or to bend to their partners' ways. They are driven to get things taken care of and will have a hard time maintain-ing interest or respect for partners who aren't doing the same. Solo sexual time is important for these people in order to stay connected to their partners physically.

MARS IN THE SEVENTH HOUSE

The seventh house is the place of compromise, and Mars is the planet of getting one's own way. Therefore, these people often find themselves in relationships wherein one person is directing the flow of the dynamic. Their relationships typically have a fair amount of tension, which can either be a source of passion and creativity or lead to constant agitation and bickering.

MARS IN THE EIGHTH HOUSE

People with Mars in the eighth house tend to need a fair amount of privacy and secrecy, even within their intimate partnerships. When it comes to fighting, they can hold on to upsets and insults for a very long time. They do best with partners who accept their need to recede into themselves. Ideally, they will have a sense of sanctuary with their long-term partners, with sexual connection being an important part of intimacy and closeness.

MARS IN THE NINTH HOUSE

This placement inclines people to want to enthusiastically convert others to their ways of seeing the world and doing things. They often try to rush or force their partners, but they're really fantastic at collaborating within long-term relationships when they take the time to listen. They can have wandering eyes or be quick to be offended (their passions can come on strong), but they honor their commitments and aren't given to grudges.

MARS IN THE TENTH HOUSE

These folks are very driven by what they want from their lives and tend to act like bosses wherever they are. They can be quite demanding, as they feel certain of their versions of right and wrong. Or, conversely, they may look to others to make judgment calls, which can be difficult in relationships. These folks can be quite moralistic and tend to hold themselves to the same standard they hold their partners to.

MARS IN THE ELEVENTH HOUSE

These people tend to be very active; they have a lot of pursuits and projects, and they need autonomy from their partners in order to pursue them. They like sex to be quick and to the point. They are quite motivated by being in groups of people but are not always fantastic at playing nicely with others. It's important for them to prioritize time and energy for their relationships.

MARS IN THE TWELFTH HOUSE

Maintaining their physical energy and presence in their own bodies can take a fair amount of intention for these people. They are very driven, both externally and internally, and the result may be that they get stuck from time to time or that they frequently outgrow relationship dynamics. It's also important that they don't become overly reliant on their partners for a sense of direction and may have to avoid attaching themselves to bullies.

JUPITER ♃

Time it takes to traverse the zodiac: Approximately 12 years

Sign it rules: Sagittarius

House it governs: Ninth

LONG-TERM RELATIONSHIPS: JUPITER

Jupiter will take the last piece of cake and enjoy it; it inspires us to be either selfish or very generous. This planet is about fun and adventure, and it rules the parts of us that need to feel free. This is the planet of expansion; it rules the philosophies and attitudes we adopt to facilitate growth and union in a relationship. A sense of shared aspirations and a sense of shared understanding are both necessary in order for long-term relationships to thrive.

COMMITMENT AND COLLABORATION

Jupiter gives us the sense of being on adventures with the people we can grow and explore life with. It is not a planet of compromise as it governs the parts of us that want to feel like we have options. Jupiter doesn't do well with limitations or rules. It's not necessarily associated with non-monogamous relationships (Uranus) or polyamory (Neptune), but it can be tied to infidelity. That's not to say that all people who have strong Jupiter

in their charts are destined to cheat on their partners—cheating happens for lots of reasons and from lots of places within the chart. But this planet governs our sense of entitlement. Those who have a strongly placed Jupiter can believe that what they're doing with other people has nothing to do with their partners.

This planet also rules our tendency to tell people what they want to hear. Its energies keep us focused on the big picture, not the details of getting along with others. Jupiter inclines us to think, "We're here, we're together, and I just want it to work." Where we have this planet in the chart, we tend to be optimistic, self-reliant, and resilient—but we also can be nagged by the persistent sense that there's something more. This tension can lead to dissatisfaction with life choices, feelings of depression, or over-reliance on our circumstances to bring adventure and growth into our lives. Where we have Jupiter in the chart is also where we need to take space so that we can fully process and transmute our limitations or problems into things that help us grow.

TRAVEL AND DRINKING

A big part of knowing others and being close to them emerges if you travel together. When we leave our comfort zone with someone else, we're in Jupiter's domain. This is the planet of escape and good times. It's also related to alcohol, a key to relaxation for many people, and one of the more accessible and socially acceptable modes of self-medication. And when it comes to long-term partnerships, it's important to consider the role that alcohol plays in our ability to socialize and relax, because, unlike wine, relationships built on drinking don't necessarily get better over time.

HOW TO WORK WITH THIS PLANET

Jupiter needs to feel a sense of growth and momentum; unless it's out of balance, it doesn't need a lot of our attention because it's resilient. This planet only causes trouble when there's too much of its influence in our lives—when we're gambling, being dishonest, or being flippant with the feelings or needs of others. So, this is a good place to instill the golden rule and do unto others as you would have them do unto you.

JUPITER THROUGH THE SIGNS

JUPITER IN ARIES

Assertive and forward thinking, these people have within them a sense of purpose and drive that can make them either inspiring to be around or a little cocky. They need to go their own ways, so learning what they will and will not compromise—and how to effectively communicate those boundaries—is important to those with this placement. Remembering to ask questions of their partners is key; even "How was your day?" or "How can I help?" can go a long way toward building a good relationship.

JUPITER IN TAURUS

These people have deeply felt values that will make them very happy—if they do genuinely live by them. They can be quite stubborn and risk-averse, but their ability to show tenderness and love is quite strong. Spending money and receiving gifts make them happy, but they should probably maintain their own bank accounts, at least for the fun stuff.

JUPITER IN GEMINI

Too many interests and the pursuit of too many different kinds of potential in their lives can make these people seem a bit scattered at times. They are quick-witted and dynamic, with good social skills, but they tend to be quite restless, which can create upsets in a partnership if things get too rote.

JUPITER IN CANCER

People with Jupiter in Cancer enjoy making other people feel cared for and tended to. They are nostalgic and can be quite doting when it comes to their partners. They like having a sense of spacious routine at home, such as reading the paper over coffee every morning. They have a strong drive to start a family, but what exactly that means is quite individualized.

JUPITER IN LEO

These people can be quite "extra." They love connection, play, and attention, and their enthusiasm is infectious. They may also be dramatic, gregarious, and deeply loyal, until they feel wronged, in which case their loyalties will quickly evaporate. When it comes to long-term

JUPITER IN VIRGO
People with this placement are good at handling the little things if they decide to fixate on them. They are attentive with their partners once they've had enough time to devote to their own self-care. It's important that they build relationships with those they feel they can talk to over the course of time. These folks must be careful about getting too deep in their own heads or disregarding the little things and succumbing to procrastination.

JUPITER IN LIBRA
The simple pleasure of spending time with others is what these folks enjoy most. This placement indicates diplomacy, likability, and the prioritization of partnership, although it can also mean laziness (and occasionally evading difficult conversations) once a partner is chosen. When things are unfair, it really upsets them. They're invested in what's real, and can soften the truth to avoid being the bad guy.

JUPITER IN SCORPIO
People with Jupiter in Scorpio love going deep and exploring the inner workings of a situation or relationship. They can be quite intense, but they're also tolerant and understanding with their partners. They need deep connections in order to feel satiated, and they enjoy sexual connection very much. They can be a bit indulgent, especially when it comes to good food, drink, and other luxuries.

JUPITER IN SAGITTARIUS
This is the natural placement for this planet. These folks are resilient, magnanimous, and optimistic. They can be inspiring and helpful to their partners. The only trouble comes when they don't listen before they speak—or try to push their best ideas onto their loved ones even if they're not receptive to it. They are broad-minded and tolerant, but this tendency can lead them to overlook warning signs in relationships if they're not careful.

JUPITER IN CAPRICORN
These people will rise to the occasion in the face of difficulty, in part because they have the vision needed to get there. They're honorable, think big picture, and are willing to do the work. They may vacillate between being willing to delay gratification and being intensely self-indulgent. They can be patient, but usually only if their partners have explained to them what the plans are ahead of time.

JUPITER IN AQUARIUS
Those with this placement have a great capacity for seeing symbolism in situations and reading between the lines. They're open-minded and tolerant and need to believe that their partners are doing good in the world. To exercise their restlessness and curiosity, or their broad-minded intellect, these folks need to have friendships and interests outside of their relationships; in this way, stepping away from a relationship can be a way of protecting and feeding the connection.

JUPITER IN PISCES

These people are very tolerant, compassionate, and empathetic, which makes them generous partners. They need time to recharge away from people. There's a risk that they'll get involved in dynamics wherein their generosity is taken advantage of. It's important that these folks develop a sense of their own boundaries and limits and see those limitations as opportunities for self-care.

JUPITER THROUGH THE HOUSES

JUPITER IN THE FIRST HOUSE

People with this placement have a lot of personality—they tend to be fun and inspiring to be around and a little loud. They take up a good amount of space, but they're generous and magnanimous with that space. Their big blind spots in long-term relationships are their inability to take no for an answer and their strong urges to have their partners agree with them, even when it may be healthier to maintain separate perspectives.

JUPITER IN THE SECOND HOUSE

These people can be financially quite generous or lucky, but they have a unique system for managing their resources, which can make it hard for them to collaborate. They have very tolerant attitudes toward differences in values or opinions—at least toward everything they're not stubborn about. These folks tend to have good social skills, but they can be quite different with the people they know well versus their acquaintances.

JUPITER IN THE THIRD HOUSE

These folks are great at talking and can be quite convincing. They have an innate sense of timing and the willingness and ability to stay interested in their partners, their shared life, and the immediate world around them. There is the risk, however, that they will be coercive in their enthusiasm and that they could take differences of opinion as personal slights.

JUPITER IN THE FOURTH HOUSE

Home and chosen family are incredibly important to these people, as they get a great deal of happiness from sharing space with people who care about them. They are warm, and will do what is needed to make the people in their families feel included. Spacious houses or nice views make them happy.

JUPITER IN THE FIFTH HOUSE

This house is often an indicator of fertility and virility in terms of procreation, and sex is very important to these people. They love flirting and play; when those parts of their relationships start to wane, they can get restless. These folks may want a big family, or they may opt to pursue creative projects instead of having kids.

JUPITER IN THE SIXTH HOUSE

These people have strong preferences around what does and doesn't work for them in terms of the day-to-day. That said, they're usually open and willing to compromise within relationships in an effort to keep those they care about happy. They are mentally resilient and can place their feelings and needs aside when needed.

JUPITER IN THE SEVENTH HOUSE

Partnership and marriage are incredibly important to these people. They're good at compromising when need be, and they tend to easily draw and attract people to them. Yet, when it comes down to it, they like to feel free and open. If they have the sense that they're trapped, these folks can get distracted or bored, which can be corrosive to their relationships.

JUPITER IN THE EIGHTH HOUSE

These people will often fall into money or have partners who share their resources. They like sex, and the frequency of hooking up can be quite important to them. They tend to hold on to grudges very tightly until they're able to let go of them completely. They find it hard to know when to call it quits in relationships, and they can obsess about intimacy issues for a long time.

JUPITER IN THE NINTH HOUSE

This placement can indicate a very tolerant nature, as well as an adventurous and endlessly curious one. There's a tendency here toward religion or being perpetual students. Those with this placement don't get bored, yet if their partners stop growing or being interested in the world, it may have serious implications for their relationships. These folks have to be careful about blurting things out without considering the consequences.

JUPITER IN THE TENTH HOUSE

These people are naturally good at self-presentation and self-preservation. They have big plans for their lives, want to be successful, and are willing to do the work to make it happen. They can be highly directive with their partners—not exactly controlling, but not compromising either. Learning to ask for feedback while planning will go a long way toward making their partners feel heard.

JUPITER IN THE ELEVENTH HOUSE

It's important for those with this placement to have many kinds of people in their lives. The more generous they are with their social energy, the more abundance they feel, which inevitably bleeds into their partnerships. Family is important to them, but their definition of family isn't likely to be terribly traditional.

JUPITER IN THE TWELFTH HOUSE

This placement gives people psychologically and spiritually resilient natures. Yet it requires that they remember to self-reflect, because the downside of that resiliency can be flying too close to the sun, burning themselves out, or being a bit of a Pollyanna. These people can be very generous and kind, or they may write others off without even realizing it. For them, one-on-one downtime with their partners is important for long-term closeness.

SATURN ♄

Time it takes to traverse the zodiac: Approximately 29.5 years

Sign it rules: Capricorn

House it governs: Tenth

LONG-TERM RELATIONSHIPS: SATURN

Saturn is not to be overlooked when it comes to the intimacy issues we bring to our long-term relationships. This planet rules what we believe is possible and real and the ways we are willing to take responsibility for ourselves. It also often articulates where we feel a sense of scarcity in our lives or a thread from childhood that we are forever pulling on.

DEDICATION

This planet governs time and commitment, making it essential for longevity in any relationship. Saturn is related to aging, and it can help us understand how to grow old with our partners. Saturn governs fear, scarcity, monogamy, and many issues that come up when we're committing to spend our lives with someone. Our life partnerships are often deeply impacted by our drive to feel secure, accompanied, and safe (economically, physically, and emotionally).

Saturn is the planet of adulting. It governs the responsibility we take for our own life choices, which is intricately woven into the fabric of any long-term partnership. It also rules the limitations that we face when grappling with responsibilities and the way those limitations tend to fall directly into the laps of our partners—and vice versa. This planet has real-life consequences, which can be felt over the course of time.

Likewise, our partners' Saturn may cause our lives to go in totally different directions than we have planned. Our paths are often directed by our partners, who model what is and isn't possible just by being themselves. Whether the goal or function of your relationship includes having kids, sharing a home, or merging your finances, choosing to partner with someone means that the way they take responsibility for orienting their lives— from now until you get old—is directly relevant to you both. If your relationship to Saturn in your own birth chart is not especially integrated, it can be hard to form partnerships in a healthy way around these themes.

SATURN AND DEPRESSION

Saturn is also related to cycles of depression or bouts of depression, which impacts relationships. If you have the fortune of being in a partnership over the course of a lifetime, it's inevitable that depressing circumstances or feelings will rear their heads at times. As an individual, you need to be able to take responsibility for your needs; sometimes that means asking for space and other times it means asking for help. Allowing your partner to support and care for you is as important as showing up and doing the same for them. We can build the most successful partnerships with those we can comfortably live alongside, and that structural compatibility has everything to do with Saturn.

HOW TO WORK WITH THIS PLANET

Where we have Saturn in the birth chart, we want to control things—or we feel out of control. Regardless of hardship or difficult circumstances, the key here is to own your part and to understand that your actions (or inaction) add up over the course of time. Strive to hit a balance between supporting your partners and allowing them to learn lessons in their own way, even if that means making mistakes.

SATURN THROUGH THE SIGNS

SATURN IN ARIES

The work for these people is to build a sense of self and an identity that is uniquely their own. The risk is that they are either codependent—in the hopes that their partners will answer life's big questions for them—or bull-headed and not great at cooperation. When they get angry, they may have a hard time not expressing themselves in a judgmental or conditional way. Learning how to fight fair is important for their long-term happiness.

SATURN IN TAURUS

These folks can be steadfast in partnerships, and once they set their minds on a person or goal within their relationships, they are pretty dogged until they get what they want. They don't always feel confident about the love in their lives, so they can be overly attached to other people's expressions of care. They are excellent at creating a sense of security within their relationships, even if they can also be stubborn about resisting change.

SATURN IN GEMINI

These people don't like being bored by their partners, but they themselves can get caught in ruts, which can be corrosive to relationships. They are rational but have lessons to learn around how to effectively communicate and listen. Folks with this placement can be so busy developing their counterpoint or playing devil's advocate that it can prevent them from staying truly present for an exchange of ideas with their loved ones. They need to understand that relationships don't develop on a point system.

SATURN IN CANCER

These people are not especially comfortable with showing their emotions, being vulnerable, or relying on others for support. They're motivated to create family with whomever they form partnerships, whether they're close with their family of origin or not. They're supportive of their partners and like to show their support and care through trackable actions. Even though they can be emotionally sensitive, they're not always the gentlest in how they voice their expectations of their partners.

SATURN IN LEO

Enjoying life is not the most organic thing for these people, even though they're loyal, hard-working, and charismatic. Their desire for children may be a driving one, but these folks have some heavy lessons to learn around having and caring for kids. They may want to be obeyed, which doesn't always go over well with their partners. They're not terribly resilient when it comes to upsets in relationships; they can hold grudges and have to be careful not to cut off their noses to spite their faces.

SATURN IN VIRGO

These people are highly discerning in ways that can come across as judgmental if they're not careful. They can get caught up in their routines and need to take stock to make sure that their relationships can hold space for the habits and the lifestyle they need. Compromise is a part of life, but when they don't feel it's possible or know how to ask for it, these folks can be quite controlling or micromanagerial.

SATURN IN LIBRA

The role of diplomacy is something these people really struggle with. They want to take matters into their own hands and be diplomatic in equal parts, so the rest of the chart will help decide which extreme they're likely to gravitate toward. Partnership is so important to them that there's a tendency to either rush in or put it off. The potential here is for maturity in

union, while the risk is to rely too heavily on roles within their relationships.

SATURN IN SCORPIO

Their relationship to sex and power is pivotally important for these people. Once their partner becomes part of their inner sanctuary, their loyalty and commitment know no bounds—but they are slow to trust and truly let people in. They can be possessive and have a hard time letting go and forgiving. People with this placement don't tend to like surprises, so their partners will do well to run plans by them as often as possible.

SATURN IN SAGITTARIUS

Those with Saturn in Sagittarius are willing to do the work of having their vision for their lives manifested. Having a global worldview, they are outspoken about matters of spirituality, justice, and science. When it comes to long-term relationships, they can be a bit rigid about their beliefs and their sense of right and wrong. This is an open-minded, progressive sign combined with a scarcity- and fear-oriented planet, so these folks can be quite directive in a way that leads to either successful life planning encompassing spiritual values—or just the opposite.

SATURN IN CAPRICORN

These people deeply care about being seen as effective, capable, and responsible. They can often fixate on what they think works most efficiently versus what actually works for them personally. Their need to build toward something lasting inclines them to take their partnerships very seriously. But then they tend to take everything seriously, and this attitude can make it difficult to achieve balance in their lives and relationships. They tend to put a great deal of focus on how their partnerships fit into their overall life plans, both spiritually and materially.

SATURN IN AQUARIUS

When these people are willing to go their own way, they can take an innovative approach to family and partnerships. If that doesn't work, they may isolate from others, which can incline them to deprioritize emotional intimacy. They're driven to be rational and reasonable but, of course, relationships are anything but. Learning to let their partners in—and letting them do things at their own pace—is essential for success in their long-term relationships.

SATURN IN PISCES

While this placement inclines people to be compassionate and empathetic, if they're not careful it can come at the expense of self-esteem or healthy boundaries. Learning how to say "no" is an essential part of being able to truly say "yes" for these people. They also need a fair amount of downtime for self-care, so that they can show up in their relationships in ways that are not too self-sacrificing or demanding.

SATURN THROUGH THE HOUSES

SATURN IN THE FIRST HOUSE

People with this placement are loyal, but can come across as quite hard or austere when they're feeling vulnerable or overwhelmed. Saturn in the first house, especially within seven degrees of the Ascendant from either the twelfth or the first house, is referred to as "the wooden mask," because these people are so hard to read. They can vacillate between hubris and humility. There's a rigidity to their nature, which can come across as entitlement if they're not careful. These folks will benefit from learning to share their process and ask their partners for help.

SATURN IN THE SECOND HOUSE

A sense of scarcity when it comes to resources makes these people a bit controlling about their possessions. They can be financially generous or tend toward stinginess. The work here is for them to act in ways that reflect their values, which is hard when they're being spurred on by fear or insecurity. Sharing their processes with their partner may help remediate the fear.

SATURN IN THE THIRD HOUSE

This placement can incline people toward being exacting with language or withholding communication from partners. In a healthy relationship, these folks can be constructive communicators, but when trust is broken down, they have a hard time being open. They need to learn how to ask questions and really listen to the answers even if they don't like them.

SATURN IN THE FOURTH HOUSE

Home and family are incredibly important to these people, and once they've let a person in, they loathe to see them leave. They tend to be very security-minded, which at times can lead them to make choices from a sense of scarcity and inflexibility. Once they've invested in their relationships, these folks are more likely to stick around and bear it than to break away—even if it's not healthy for them.

SATURN IN THE FIFTH HOUSE

People with this placement are not likely to be very spontaneous when it comes to sexual or creative expression. They tend to seek partners who are reliable and mature. While they can be very loyal, they can also shut down sexually when there's not a sense of safety and collaboration in their relationships.

SATURN IN THE SIXTH HOUSE

These people tend to have particular ways of doing things; they want their daily life to be reliable and consistent. As this is the house of habits, this placement makes people yearn for consistency from their partners, and they may be quite controlling in an effort to get it. At the very least, they want to know where their partners are at and crave regular communication.

SATURN IN THE SEVENTH HOUSE

Partnership is important to these people, but it's not always easy for them; there's a danger of codependency or controlling dynamics. They can also feel an urge to rush things to a place of stability before their relationships are ready. On the bright side, they're willing to do the work necessary to be in long-term partnerships, and as long as they can be honest about the difficult things, they make stable and hard-working partners.

SATURN IN THE EIGHTH HOUSE

These folks can have scarcity issues that complicate their ability to share finances with their partners, but working toward open communication around money may help. They can be either very sexual or quite sexually restrained and may need to explore role playing or kink with their partners in order to maintain long-term passion. Saturn in this placement can yield sexual rigidity and restraint or risqué experimentation.

SATURN IN THE NINTH HOUSE

Saturn in the ninth house tends to indicate a strict code of morality. If these folks can keep an air of openness about them, they will likely be able to have a collaborative relationship. If their morality errs on the side of judgment, however, they can become punishing or condemning. They need to learn the value of compromise when making big-picture life decisions within a partnership.

SATURN IN THE TENTH HOUSE

People with this placement have a sense of duty that inclines them to take on too much in the outside world and can lead them to neglect their personal responsibilities. When they can clarify what they want, they're really good at life planning. They run the risk of forgetting

to prioritize intimacy, which can happen at the expense of closeness with their partners and lead to loneliness.

SATURN IN THE ELEVENTH HOUSE

Being connected to the community at large is really important for these folks' sense of self, but they may forget to maintain their own friendships when in committed relationships. Even though they crave validation, they can find it a bit difficult to accept affection. They struggle with a sense of belonging and need to make sure they don't project that need onto their partners.

SATURN IN THE TWELFTH HOUSE

People with this placement make supportive and caring partners but are inclined to look outside themselves for guidance, answers, and structure; this may lead them to be in codependent or one-sided relationships. They need to cultivate backbone and responsibility, instead of defaulting to guilt. Learning to take the space and time they need for self-care is foundational to participating equitably in their partnerships.

URANUS ♅

**Time it takes to traverse the zodiac:
Approximately 84 years**

Sign it rules: Aquarius

House it governs: Eleventh

LONG-TERM RELATIONSHIPS: URANUS

Uranus rules individuality and autonomy, and it's the last planet to want closeness and intimacy, but it still plays an important role in long-term relationships. Where we find Uranus in our chart is where we need to feel a sense of freedom. It governs the part of us that wants to be left to make our own choices, at our own pace, without having to compromise or check in with our partners. When it comes to creating healthy partnerships, it's important to feel like we can be our own person, with our own sense of who we are. When we can achieve authenticity and freedom in our relationships, it's much easier to make compromises. Uranus's autonomy is also one of the forces at work behind the sense of mystery that exists in long-term relationships—the sense that you will never know everything about your partner, even if you want to.

INDIVIDUALITY AND INDEPENDENCE

Many of us turn down the volume on what we want, who we are, and even our freedom of movement for the sake of a marriage or partnership. And while that may at times be necessary, it shouldn't happen at the expense of our creativity, passion, or the truth of our own nature. Authenticity is very important; in order to be attentive partners, we have to be whole people. Yet, often we make our lives all about our partners, our family, or our kids, at the expense of our selves. When there's nothing left for us, our autonomy suffers and the more negative aspects of Uranus—restlessness, distraction, or detachment—will articulate themselves in our relationships.

Uranus governs obstinacy as well as stubbornness—the parts of us where we think we're being open-minded when, in reality, we're only open-minded about everything we're not totally fixed about. Uranus is also primarily concerned with the future; when your relationship is reliant on nostalgia, shared history, or outlived ideas, this planet tends to be displeased. In a relationship, we need to live in the present and to feel that we have a future that we're excited about.

This is also the planet of oddness and queerness, or what is unusual or out of the mainstream. We all have Uranus in our charts, but for many, Saturn and Jupiter—the planets that rule our ideas of what is "normal" or conventional—have more sway over how comfortable we are in showing our unique selves to the world. In this way, Uranus is also associated with non-monogamous relationships; a person who is strongly Uranian can feel the merit and value of having sexual agreements that encompass more than one person. But this planet's energies are less concerned with multiple intimacies and more with the freedom to flirt, hook up, or explore other options. It's also worth saying that just because some people have the sort of nature that allows them to feel capable of engaging in non-monogamous relationships in a healthy way doesn't necessarily mean that their cultural, familial upbringing, or life circumstances will support it.

TECHNOLOGY

How we relate to our devices and the time we spend online is a really big issue when it comes to modern relationships and intimacy. Uranus governs technology; building clear agreements about how much time you spend online is important—and depending on where you and your partner have Uranus in your charts, you're likely to feel differently about where the line should be. Disappearing into our devices and forming relationships that have no real-life component can be either Neptunian or Uranian (the former is escapist and the latter is distracted). When our thoughts are more interesting than whatever is around us, we can come across as pretty selfish. If we ignore the people who are sitting at the table with us, we're doing a disservice to ourselves and our partners.

HOW TO WORK WITH THIS PLANET

Take stock of your need for space, autonomy, and personal development, and don't forget to share it with your partners. Where you have Uranus in your chart will lead you to be future oriented, so learning to stay present and receptive is key. Remember to listen to your partner and invest in who they are in real time.

URANUS THROUGH THE SIGNS

See pages 68 and 144 for more information.

URANUS IN ARIES (1927–1934 AND 2010–2019)

When Uranus was in Aries early in the twentieth century, the United States experienced a massive stock market crash and the Great Depression began. The era required that people had to express more self-will, originality, and assertiveness in coping with survival.

The combination of Uranus and Aries can create a lot of originality, willfulness, and daring, but the energy is quite erratic and blunt. These two forces come together to create periods of time of agency and individuation, which can lead to me-first thinking and behavior or the kind of embodiment of self that allows for a greater sense of agency.

What this means for long-term relationships: These people need to make sure not to cut off their noses to spite their faces because this is not a terribly flexible placement. People born during this era might find themselves looking for something perfect and have difficulty compromising.

URANUS IN TAURUS (1934–1942 AND 2018–2026)

The previous time this placement occurred coincided with the years when the Great Depression really set in. Racism and xenophobia had a new global stage with the arrival of World War II. This was a period that forced individuals to take stands about who they were and what they prioritized. The collective push was a change in the global conversation about values. The same themes are coming up again and will play out until this cycle is completed.

What this means for long-term relationships: Folks with this placement experience tension between security and autonomy. They are likely to have either strong gender roles in their relationships or long-term relationships that shatter convention and include more flexible roles.

URANUS IN GEMINI (1941–1949 AND 2020–2025)

The last time Uranus was in Gemini was during a period when we saw advancements in both psychology and metaphysics. This generation grew up to become the radicals of the 1960s, and these people were able to make inventive use of the information they received about freedom, liberty, and independence.

What this means for long-term relationships: Uranus is the sign of revolution and Gemini is the sign of communications. Those in committed relationships are going to be caught up in their own

heads (on their phones all the time) or authentically curious about who their partners are and have a willingness to share the magic of their day-to-day lives.

URANUS IN CANCER (1949–1956; WILL HAPPEN AGAIN IN 2033–2039)

The last time we saw this placement was during the age of McCarthyism. A whole generation of artists and freethinkers were tamped down in the name of protectiveness and patriotism (several elements that are key to Cancer). There was the expansion of media and the arrival of television (and TV dinners, which were the beginning of processed food and provided people with more freedom without more quality). The key here is to find a way to balance self-protection with freedom without choosing one over the other.

What this means for long-term relationships: This placement can incline people to be deeply protective of their uniqueness and to have a heavy sense of nationalism. They may also radically redefine family and the emotional boundaries that happen within intimate relationships.

URANUS IN LEO (1956–1962; WILL HAPPEN AGAIN IN 2039–2046)

This was a time when entertainment became a much bigger part of Western society. The Vietnam War was in its infancy; Uranus in Leo is a time of forceful engagement. This is a generation of self-confident people who were very creative and also had a strong need for validation by external forces.

What this means for long-term relationships: When this placement happened last, it saw a lot of people exploring the meaning of their lives through having children. When it happens next, we may see more of the same or a cultural shift whereby people prioritize their autonomy over having children.

URANUS IN VIRGO (1962–1969; WILL HAPPEN AGAIN IN 2046–2053)

The last time Uranus was in Virgo, the draft for the war in Vietnam began in the United States, and people rose up in radical resistance. Many also dropped out of society. There was an emphasis on personal improvement as a route to social change. This was also when alternative health care began to play a larger role in Western culture. Virgo rules practical process, mundane reality, and day-to-day living. When combined with Uranus, Virgo also spurred second-wave feminism, which was very much about writing, speaking, and public analysis. Uranus in Virgo created a generation that experienced a newfound emphasis on personal agency and new access to lifestyle-improving techniques.

What this means for long-term relationships: These people need a sense of privacy and autonomy while also sharing their lives with their partners. This placement produces people with contemplative, self-reflective natures.

URANUS IN LIBRA (1968–1975; WILL HAPPEN AGAIN IN 2053–2059)

This generation was all about changes in social justice, diplomacy, and the arts. This was a time when alternative partnerships and roles in society became more eclectic and diverse, and women had more autonomy in their relationships. This was also a time when divorce really took a stronger role in society, and romantic partnerships were no longer seen as the only way forward in relationships.

What this means for long-term relationships: This placement puts an emphasis on fairness and freedom that can make relationships more well-rounded. But it can also create a lot of sensitivity, which can lead to a sense of walking on eggshells.

URANUS IN SCORPIO (1975–1981; WILL HAPPEN AGAIN IN 2059–2066)

This combination produced a brave but private generation. This period saw a generation that was reached by more corporations, advertising, and media than ever before. There was an increase in occultism and New Age culture during this time. Androgyny came to the fore with the rise of New Wave arts and music, and affirmative action made legal strides as more alternative voices stepped into the mainstream.

What this means for long-term relationships: Scorpio is a sign concerned with power, privacy, and intense experiences, while Uranus represents our eccentric, outsider, individualistic urges. People born during this time have strong desires to be recognized as individuals, even if they have a hard time valuing their partners' individuality.

URANUS IN SAGITTARIUS (1981–1988; WILL HAPPEN AGAIN IN 2066–2072)

The 1980s were the arms race years. This era saw an increase in humanitarian interest, as well as in fundamentalism. Kids were encouraged to have global pen pals, and individuals connecting to other individuals to create a global society was an important part of this phase.

What this means for long-term relationships: Sagittarius is about open-mindedness and expansion; it's also a cross-cultural sign. But the devil is in the details, and this placement inclines people to be averse to the little compromises that are necessary in any relationship.

URANUS IN CAPRICORN (1987–1996; LAST OCCURRED 1904–1912)

These were times when the roles of government and corporations took a stronger hold in society. It was a period when we could take our individual chaos and problems and come to a more systemic solution. Conversely, there could be great upsets to agreed-upon norms and the "right way of doing things." There was a major shift in the AIDS crisis during this time, as pharmaceutical companies stepped in to "protect us" from the epidemic. The systemic reach of the school-to-prison pipeline also grew significantly.

What this means for long-term relationships: These people can create a sense of autonomy and agency within old relationship structures. Or they may totally topple hetero-normative institutions and remake them in new ways.

URANUS IN AQUARIUS (1996–2003; LAST OCCURRED 1912–1920)

Aquarius is ruled by Uranus, and this is its natural sign. So, we have both the intensity of humanitarianism and a sense of interconnectedness and reliance on others. This was a time of great scientific and technological advancement. Google was incorporated in 1998, and this and other advances in data and information sharing were the mark of a mass, global shift. Computers made their way into classrooms, fostering a generation with regular access to people from around the world.

What this means for long-term relationships: With the expansion of gender roles and sexual liberation, there's the potential for greater equality or equanimity in long-term relationships. But along with that open-mindedness, these folks may have a hard time tolerating the emotional vulnerability inherent in human connection. They're also freethinking, open-minded, and willing to do things in new ways.

URANUS IN PISCES (2003–2011; LAST OCCURRED 1920–1928)

The earlier placement happened in the roaring 1920s, when there was a shift in morality and a greater emphasis on pleasure and disassociation. It happened again early in the twenty-first century during a rise in the role of pharmaceuticals and a growing dependence on them to manage our moods. Uranus governs that part of us that is easily distracted, and here we had an increase in sensitivity and an increase in the desire to feel pleasant. This generation is more woke than others that came before it but with stronger escapist tendencies at the same time.

What this means for long-term relationships: These people may struggle with compromising themselves within a union. They may try to mold themselves into what they think their partner wants, as a means of self-preservation. They need downtime in order to return to their lives and their partners whole.

URANUS THROUGH THE HOUSES

URANUS IN THE FIRST HOUSE
These people are impulsive and tend to be very focused on themselves, so making a concerted effort to involve their partners will serve their relationships in the long run. They can be quite abrupt, and they're not the greatest listeners in town. As they tend to have a lot going on, these folks may lose track of details and the agreements they make. Luckily, their innovative, creative natures help keep their partners entertained.

URANUS IN THE SECOND HOUSE
People with Uranus in the second house have their own unique sense of values and need to figure out for themselves how best to live their lives. They tend to have unreliable relationships with money in that their behaviors aren't always consistent, and their spending can be impulsive. These folks cherish the idea of relationships and partnerships but can easily feel pinned down when they're actually committed to others.

URANUS IN THE THIRD HOUSE
Boredom is the kiss of death for these people. They tend to be innovative thinkers, which can be great for interesting conversations and social interactions, but they may struggle with the routines involved in maintaining long-term partnerships. They'll benefit from remembering to ask questions and show interest in their partners, rather than assuming they have all the information or doing all the talking.

URANUS IN THE FOURTH HOUSE
Instability at home tends to be a common theme for these folks. It may manifest itself in frequent moves or a lot of activity and inconsistency in their home lives; these people will benefit from finding partners who can make peace with unpredictability. The key is for them to develop a sense of agency—and own the fact that they need unique living set-ups and more change than average—so that they'll feel less out of control.

URANUS IN THE FIFTH HOUSE
These people need variety in their sex lives in order to feel satiated in long-term relationships. Routines in the bedroom do not serve them well. Because of how much compromise children require, they are especially likely to need their partnerships to provide equality within co-parenting.

URANUS IN THE SIXTH HOUSE

These people tend to have high-strung nervous systems. They can be impatient, and they're likely to have a million things going on. While they tend to be more flexible than most partners, they have to be careful not to treat their relationships like afterthoughts. They need a great deal of surprise, intrigue, and variety in their lives, which will be expressed either at work or with some other daily preoccupation.

URANUS IN THE SEVENTH HOUSE

This placement indicates the need for alternative set-ups when it comes to relationships because it inclines people to be independent. If they're unwilling or unable to own their independence, they may choose relationships with people who are unavailable or unstable to passively get the space they need. They can have successful relationships, but it's unlikely if it's at the expense of their autonomy.

URANUS IN THE EIGHTH HOUSE

These individuals may have unusual or inconsistent sexual appetites. They are driven to change over the course of time, so they need their partnerships to be flexible and allow room for growth and difference. Humor, playfulness, and intrigue are essential for a long-term sense of connection. These folks may also need periods of solitude to recharge from their relationships and the world around them.

URANUS IN THE NINTH HOUSE

These people have eccentric worldviews, so they'll need to find relationships that have room for differences in opinions and approaches to life. Being adventurous, they may need to take vacations (alone or with friends) to different cultures from time to time as a way of making their lives feel more expansive.

URANUS IN THE TENTH HOUSE

These people may change course often and need to do so independent of their partnerships. When they don't have a sense of clarity about the direction of their lives, they may depend on their partners as a way to distract from needing greater freedom in their careers. These people can have a singular approach to their goals until they spontaneously change course.

URANUS IN THE ELEVENTH HOUSE

When these people have a strong sense of who they are outside of their relationships—especially when working to benefit humanity—it allows them to show up more completely inside their partnerships. Sex isn't necessarily associated with intimacy for them. For this reason, they may choose to be non-monogamous or benefit from having fantasy landscapes outside their primary commitment to stay sexually centered in themselves.

URANUS IN THE TWELFTH HOUSE

Learning to be true to themselves and to express their uniqueness within a relationship is one of the big life lessons for people with Uranus in the twelfth house. These people have a tendency to compromise too much or not at all. They typically struggle with whether it's appropriate to assert themselves, which can lead to defensiveness great for relationships.

NEPTUNE Ψ

Time it takes to traverse the zodiac: Approximately 165 years

Sign it rules: Pisces

House it governs: Twelfth

LONG-TERM RELATIONSHIPS: NEPTUNE

We all have times when we feel that we shouldn't have to spell things out for our partners—when they should just "get us" and instinctively know exactly where we're at. Those feelings are ruled by Neptune. This planet governs the parts of us that are preoccupied, romantic, and idealistic. Its effects are at once highly spiritual and deeply psychological. Where we find Neptune in the chart, we tend to be either spiritually present as our higher selves or quite disassociated through things such as television, video games, or drugs. When those activities are done in a balanced way, they might be absolutely fine; but when they're done to excess, they can be a way of shutting out our partners and checking out of our own lives.

STARS AND LIGHTS

Neptune rules our ideals, which are very different than our values. Ideals are like stars—they light up the night sky, but they're out of reach. Values are more like lampposts. They also light up the sky, but they burn out and have to be replaced from time to time (and while it's difficult to reach them, it's absolutely viable with some effort). When it comes to partnerships, Neptune challenges us to make sure that we maintain our values, so we don't rely too heavily on our ideals to light the way forward.

This planet governs the part of us that wants a soulmate—an idealized, perfect partner. But in actuality, all partnerships, marriages, and long-term relationships have mundane qualities. And while our ideas of perfect, imaginary partnerships might involve mind reading and serendipity, real life requires that we express our needs and pay attention when our partners express theirs. Neptune is really bad at both. This planet comes into play when we're not sure what we think or need. So rather than engage in conflict, we behave passively with our partners. We may feel that we're trying to be easy-going or compromising, but if there is unexpressed resentment or anger, we can come across as passive-aggressive. Similarly, when we attempt to compromise about issues we actually have very strong feelings about, we may end up misleading our partners unintentionally.

DEVOTION

Neptunian people tend to think a lot about other people's feelings and needs; they're deeply motivated by connection, devotion, and intimacy on many levels. Where Neptune falls in the birth chart, we have the tendency to want to be of service to others, to avoid being mean, and to live very much in our feelings and sensory impressions as opposed to our logical minds. This can incline us to get caught up in the clouds. Sometimes we may feel so entitled to our perspective that we shut others out without realizing that's what we're doing. It's hard to show up for or listen to our partners when we are too caught up in our own feelings.

People with strong Neptune in their charts march to the beat of their own drums; they don't always relate to linear time, so they can run the risk of flaking on their partners and putting strain on their relationships.

Neptune doesn't like binary lines, whether in relationship structures or otherwise, and people inclined toward polyamory often have this planet prominent in their chart; they don't want to limit their capacity to love. That said, unless one person in the dynamic has strong Saturn or Uranus in their chart to provide structure, polyamorous agreements can be made with fuzzy boundaries, which may disable one or more person's ability to fully consent to what's happening. Neptune doesn't like hard yeses or nos.

HOW TO WORK WITH THIS PLANET

Neptune asks you to acknowledge the potential you see in your partnership. Can you maintain a sense of romance while looking at the evidence of what actually exists between you and your partner? Ask yourself: What are you bringing to the table? Are you being honest and forthcoming about your feelings and behavior? Are you truly listening and making it clear to your partner where you're at emotionally?

NEPTUNE THROUGH THE SIGNS

You'll notice that some of the following years overlap. That's because all the outer planets retrograde (appear to move backward) in and out of each sign. That will often coincide with a planet being in two different signs in one calendar year.

Neptune takes 165 years to complete its cycle through the signs, and it spends 14 years in each sign. It marks the ideals, convictions, and spiritual ideals of a generation. For this reason, I have focused on the signs will most likely reflect my readers (and their parents).

NEPTUNE IN VIRGO (1928–1942)

These were Depression-era babies. Born into a period of scarcity, they needed to make do with less, and their spiritual values needed to guide them toward finding meaning when things felt dire. This was a generation in which people had to put self-care aside to deal with day-to-day survival. People born in this era needed to learn to take care of their bodies as a way to take care of their minds, and vice versa. This period was one where the world became larger with the advent of World War II—but there was a great deal of fear of what wasn't understood. There was a new boogeyman for this generation culturally.

What this means for long-term relationships: These people need to prioritize managing their relationship to worry, so that they don't create mountains out of molehills. They are likely to require space away from their partnerships from time to time in order to sift through their mountains of thoughts and feelings to get to the truth.

NEPTUNE IN LIBRA (1942–1956)

This phase coincides with the end of World War II, and it marks a period where ideals around love and a new global sense of connection emerged. (The United Nations was established during this time.) Nations came together with a Neptunian ideal of unity and a shared will to protect humanity. Children born at this time grew up to be the "make love, not war" generation. Libra is a relational sign—it's concerned with justice and fairness and expresses itself in a one-on-one context.

What this means for long-term relationships: Neptune in Libra is idealistic, glamorous, and spiritual. People in this generation—also known as the Baby Boomers—want to partner with others in highly romantic ways and strive to have more interpersonal empathy.

NEPTUNE IN SCORPIO (1956–1970)

The generation born during this time faced—and embodied—a great deal of intensity. Scorpio is all about letting go—and it's deeply concerned with death and sex for this reason. It is the sign that's associated with the underbelly of society, while Neptune governs universal connectedness. This generation expanded people's sense of community—it found new ways to commune and connect beyond school, the military, and church. The combination of Neptune and Scorpio can lend itself to addiction, escapism, and excesses in terms of sex and sexuality—and so many of the people born during this time grew up to deal with those things. Sex became freer but there were consequences. These children grew up in the AIDS crisis, and they were the first modern generation to suffer such dire health consequences of their sexuality.

What this means for long-term relationships: People in this generation were raised with organized religion and exchanged it for spirituality. Relationship dynamics changed as the women's rights movement empowered females to have more choice in lifestyle and partnership.

NEPTUNE IN SAGITTARIUS (1970–1984)

As children, this generation experienced greater connectivity than ever before. The world became much smaller as international travel became more common for the middle class. It was a time of global unity and connectedness. Western culture became less monotheistic in this time and alternative religion and spirituality were both normalized within this generation. Another cultural barrier was broken down during this era after *Loving v. Virginia*, the landmark civil rights case that invalidated laws prohibiting interracial marriage in 1967, making this the first generation to be born in legal interracial marriage in the United States. This generation is known as Gen X; they're very conscious about romance, social justice, and fairness and they really value liberty on a social scale.

What this means for long-term relationships: Gen Xers crave freedom through relationships. The broad interconnectedness and excess of options that came with the internet yielded more options for meeting people. These people expect love and romance and are willing to explore their options for longer than previous generations.

NEPTUNE IN CAPRICORN (1984–1998)

Neptune in Capricorn people are a generation prone to questioning the powers that be. But because of the omnipresence of TV, advertisements, movies, and games, this generation is also easily distracted. Capricorn is associated with capitalism, hierarchies, and structural power. The combination of Neptune and Capricorn refers to the idealized notion of authority—and the move into a nonbinary relationship to authority. The ideal here is a dissolving of old governments and national boundaries and transforming capitalism. This generation was the first one raised with pharmaceutical use as

a part of everyday life. These people were inundated by the presence of large corporations that had a huge hand in creating a culture that reinforced their product-driven objectives. This was a time when the environment and societal structure became a greater part of daily awareness.

What this means for long-term relationships: These people experience tension between the desire for stability and security and the desire to lose themselves in intimacy. They have a hard time identifying the healthy place of compromise between the two.

NEPTUNE IN AQUARIUS (1998–2012)

Neptune in Aquarius relates to connection and to collective consciousness. The intellectualization of ideals comes to fruition for this generation, which is one in which technology is deeply prominent. It has created a sense of interconnection that was unprecedented for any other generation. The children born during this time have had access to everyone around the world—there's a sense that everything is possible. The astrology of this generation was epitomized by the Black Lives Matter and anti-gun violence activism of the era—from Ferguson, Missouri, to Parkland, Florida. It was the first generation raised on social media, and they tend to feel a sense of shared ideals.

What this means for long-term relationships: This generation needs relationships that reflect their sense of autonomy and independence; there's a greater emphasis on collaboration and innovation than with prior generations. Learning to stay present is important to their success in long-term relationships.

NEPTUNE IN PISCES (2012–2026)

This is Neptune's natural placement, which makes it a particularly powerful place for the planet to be (its functions are strengthened in both good and bad ways). This generation is being born in a time of humanitarian and environmental crises. Neptune and Pisces combined are marked by significant feelings of uncertainty and confusion. Pisces is the sign of the unconscious, of what is hidden; these children are being raised at a time when things are being hidden from view and also emerging into the light. Again, we see pharmaceuticals and an overwhelming amount of media facilitate disassociation. (Pisces can be a very dissociative sign; under its influence, people can lose themselves in substance use, video games, and media in general.) This is also an age of art, as these children are born during a time of greater democracy of the arts, and people can self-publish and project their voices without the support of the traditional arts and entertainment industry.

What this means for long-term relationships: With this generation there is a movement further away from the institutional component of love and marriage, or the idealization of that institution. They are devotional and feel called to romance and unity.

NEPTUNE THROUGH THE HOUSES

NEPTUNE IN THE FIRST HOUSE

It's easy for others to project feelings and ideas onto these people; the way they appear is not always how they are. People with Neptune in the first house need to take pains to verbally share with their partners the truth of what's happening instead of dropping hints. They're romantic and idealistic, and even though they can be quite scattered or easily distracted, they'll do just about anything for the people they love.

NEPTUNE IN THE SECOND HOUSE

These people tend to have issues with money; they are typically a little bit spendy or disorganized, which can be a problem in a relationship where the resources are shared. They like to reserve their money for experiences and don't usually prioritize nice objects (as much as they like them). Easily swayed by their partners, these folks need to develop their own sense of self in order to be truly reliable for the people they're close to.

NEPTUNE IN THE THIRD HOUSE

These people need to space out at times; they need quiet times and they need to have confidence that what they say will be listened to. And while they can be very intuitive, those with Neptune in the third house can be quite anxious and tend to project ideas onto their partners. They need to remember to verbally communicate instead of making assumptions.

NEPTUNE IN THE FOURTH HOUSE

Home needs to be a sanctuary for these folks; it needs to offer a sense of escape from the big, bad world. This placement indicates a tendency to idealize family life, so these people are wise to confront the very real problems that may come up at home. It's also important that they don't rush into living with their partners before establishing healthy boundaries within the relationship.

NEPTUNE IN THE FIFTH HOUSE

Very romantic, these people may have a hard time with the mundane realities of a long-term relationship. They may have periods of time when sex is a powerful vehicle for connection and other periods when it just doesn't occur to them. Either way, flirtation is important for them, even in times where sex is less frequent. Having a creative life—or a fantasy life—outside of a partnership can help these people to feel alive and to bring more vibrancy into the dynamic.

NEPTUNE IN THE SIXTH HOUSE

This placement inclines people to have very sensitive minds and bodies. They have particular needs around self-care that require consistent maintenance or else it will detract from their ability to show up for their partners. They tend to let the physical objects in their lives pile up, so it's important that they're considerate about upkeep in the shared home.

NEPTUNE IN THE SEVENTH HOUSE

It can be hard for these people to accept their partners as they are, as they often prefer to focus on their potential instead. Those with this placement are very service-minded—and really want to be there for the people in their lives—but they can have a hard time focusing on more than one relationship at a time. This quality may distance them from their partnerships as much as bring them toward partners at various times.

NEPTUNE IN THE EIGHTH HOUSE

These folks go through cycles when sex is much more or much less desirable to them. Intuitive and sensitive, they need to feel that they can really trust their partners. Alternatively, they may assume that others are never trustworthy and choose partners they know they cannot trust as a self-fulfilling prophecy. If they can't be forthcoming about their boundaries, they may catch themselves being passive-aggressive with their partners.

NEPTUNE IN THE NINTH HOUSE

These are truth-seeking lovers of adventure who see partnership as a vehicle for creative growth. However, when the potential for conflict or growing apart arises, they may evade hard truths in the hopes that the issues will resolve on their own. These folks have to resist the desire to follow their partners' lead and instead must take responsibility for their own beliefs and choices.

NEPTUNE IN THE TENTH HOUSE

When it comes to life planning, these people can be very idealistic and demand too much of themselves, or they may wait around and expect their partners to figure things out for them. Either way, they need to cultivate clarity of intention. When these folks make life choices based on what they truly believe, instead of what they fear, things tend to get much easier. They are willing to sacrifice for the needs of their partners and will do best when they know how to ask for what they need in return.

NEPTUNE IN THE ELEVENTH HOUSE

For these people, socializing can be either a very distracting, anxiety-provoking experience or a source of inspiration. They must be careful that they don't rely too heavily on their partners to direct their social life and instead find the people and groups that allow them to explore different parts of themselves. Volunteering and other service-oriented opportunities can be quite good for these folks in a way that feeds their souls and their relationships.

NEPTUNE IN THE TWELFTH HOUSE

Neptune is in its natural placement here, and these people really need a lot of space and time to process their own feelings and experiences. They are highly sensitive and deeply impacted by the world, and their personal relationships can be a bit exhausting. Because of this, they may often find themselves in codependent dynamics. Developing a rich spiritual life and healthy boundaries will allow them to show up for their partners in more consistent ways and to articulate their needs directly.

PLUTO ♇

Time it takes to traverse the zodiac:
Approximately 248 years

Sign it rules: Scorpio

House it governs: Eighth

LONG-TERM RELATIONSHIPS: PLUTO

Pluto rules our ability to be our best or
worst selves; its energies are intensely
creative and powerfully destructive. This
planet governs shame, trauma, and abandonment issues, along with the capacity
for deep and transformational healing.

As an outer planet that takes 248 years to
orbit the Sun, Pluto's movement through
the signs can signify the compulsions,
challenges, gifts, and resources that pass
through an entire generation. For this
reason, it's less frequently looked to in
contemporary astrology for information
about individuals or relationships. But
when we look at Pluto through the houses,
we can learn about the healing work we
have to do as individuals—which has a
significant role to play in our relationships.

COMPULSION AND FEAR

The issues Pluto articulates and the
dynamics it provokes in us can be
especially difficult to navigate—and yet
they're important to get a handle on,
especially as we work to build healthy
partnerships. Most of us can hide our
compulsions, fears, and shame from
another person for a limited period of
time—but when we're in a long-term
relationship that becomes difficult or
nearly impossible, and eventually we'll
run up against one another's Pluto.

In chapter two, we talked about what
happens between two people when it's
still early enough to pretend like we have
it all together. Here, we're talking about
the phase that occurs when that's no
longer possible, when we have to show
up for ourselves and do the healthy emotional labor required to show up for our
partners.

Pluto governs our fear of allowing others
to truly see us. Where we have this planet
is where we tend to feel desperate for
support and validation, but simultaneously shameful about our real needs.
Pluto's energies are compulsive and
intense; it can inspire us to try to reflect
a neater, tidier set of feelings than the
complicated ones we actually have. And
when we try to change our behavior
without changing the underlying feelings, forging true intimacy becomes
much harder. Where we have Pluto in the
chart, we either repress and evade our
deep-seated issues or, conversely, over-
express them. But bearing witness to our
pain—by naming it, making eye contact
with it, and staying present with it—is an
essential first step. If we don't do that, the
relationship can end up reiterating whatever trauma we're trying to evade.

Intimate partnerships engage the most raw, unvarnished parts of us. So, it's inevitable that whatever trauma we've experienced, regardless of how deep or repressed it is, will play out within those relationships. Pluto on the angle—meaning when it's in the first, fourth, seventh, and tenth houses—often reflects childhood trauma that becomes pivotal to a person's psychology. That trauma may be anything from a major transition (like a move or divorce) to a death in the family to mistreatment or even abuse. Intense childhood experiences inevitably become triggered by whatever family we create—and long-term partners certainly fit in that category. For this reason, it's important to consider how those early developmental experiences have landed in our psyche and how best to support ourselves around them.

POWER STRUGGLES

Pluto governs power struggles, which can be corrosive in any long-term relationship, especially when there's not a clear agreement about what you're struggling over. When we feel incensed or defensive—Plutonian feelings—is when we are most likely to act out, shut down, and hide from our partners. In that way our actions can keep us from getting our needs met and from giving our partners a chance.

Pluto is also related to the parts of us that want to either let go or hold on for dear life. In long-term relationships—certainly in a life-long relationship—all parties must at various points let go of things their

partner does that are unfair or unkind. It's important to determine whether the act of letting go is healthy or an abandonment of self—and here's where self-care is crucial. Forgiveness can be a deeply Plutonian act when it's authentic and involves the regenerative process of holding a new truth in a different part of your psyche.

HOW TO WORK WITH THIS PLANET

When you can be present with your deep-seated thoughts, feelings, drives, and triggers without judgment or even an agenda, you are starting to truly work with Pluto. Learning to not abandon yourself—or your partner—is an important place to start, regardless of how Pluto impacts your relationship.

PLUTO THROUGH THE SIGNS
See pages 84 and 160 for more information.

PLUTO IN CANCER (1913–1939)
Pluto is associated with transformation and destruction and Cancer is associated with security, home, and nation. During this phase, we had World War I, the Great Depression and the beginning of World War II. This generation had a really rough go of it because they never felt safe, so they are prone to being highly protective or reactive. It was also a bit of a clannish or nationalistic generation (Jim Crow segregation laws were in effect during this period, and the KKK held a great deal of power). It was a real us-versus-them

world. The emphasis on family was really strong, as people were struggling through poverty and war.

What this means about long-term relationships: This generation spanned two world wars, so they dealt with fear and abandonment issues. This placement made people very attached to one another; they struggled to find their place within family versus finding family in their place. There was a deep reliance on family.

PLUTO IN LEO (1939–1957)

This generation lived through a period of oppressive dictators, including Benito Mussolini in Italy, Adolf Hitler in Germany, Kim Il Sung in North Korea, Ho Chi Min in Vietnam, Mao Ts-tung in China, Francisco Franco in Spain, Nikita Khrushchev in the Soviet Union, and many more. So, it only makes sense then that the people born during this period were shaken. The era also saw the explosion of the first atomic bombs in Hiroshima and Nagasaki. These folks were dealing with ferocious energy, so themes of control, success, and validation were all really strong. There was a great deal of racial segregation and xenophobia. The first Detroit race riots took pace during this period—in other words, people spoke out and were shut down violently. This was an era of anger expressed and repressed. Those born with Pluto in Leo were not responsible for these cultural shifts, but they were raised during these shifts— prompted by the generation before them.

What this means about long-term relationships: For this generation, gender roles within marriage had a more exaggerated presentation as television gained in popularity while they were growing up. Cooking became easier, housework was more modernized. This was the height of the nuclear family, which was tied to capitalism and a new class stratification.

PLUTO IN VIRGO (1957–1972)

This generation was raised by Pluto in Leo parents and were much more socially conscious than the immediate generations before them. We saw a lot of substantial changes to laws and shifts in medicine in this period. This Pluto generation may have abandonment issues. Pluto in Virgo has the compulsion to shift focus often, seeking the most perfect truth; but because there is no perfect truth, these folks can get caught up in routines and habits.

What this means about long-term relationships: The draft was in effect and the Vietnam War deeply impacted this generation. Many families struggled because of the emotional disconnect and trauma experienced by people coming back from afar.

PLUTO IN LIBRA (1971–1984)

After the Vietnam War ended in 1975, there was a return to prosperity and relative peace during this period. This generation didn't need to focus as much on practical survival as the generations immediately before it did, so there was more room for the arts and social justice issues to become a larger part of the culture. Friendships took on a much larger role. Generation X was very conscious about romance, social justice, and fairness. When there's injustice, they took it personally. There was also a spike in the number of latchkey kids during this period, and the concept of stranger danger took on weight and the cultural conversation became more about only trusting people you knew . . . as the world started to get much more connected. The Black Panthers started in Pluto in Virgo, but the bulk of the movement—the time it had the most power and when it was shut down by the government—took place in this phase. The rigidity of gender roles we saw with Pluto in Leo was softened by the time Pluto in Libra came around with the disco era and changes in the film industry.

What this meant for long-term relationships: People in this generation are deeply concerned with fairness, and this placement is related to a deepening and an expansion of how to connect to others in a meaningful way.

PLUTO IN SCORPIO (1984–1995)

This was the first generation to grow up with computers at home. Their sense of connectedness to the larger world can make them feel jaded or cynical. They've been exposed to all of it; nothing is taboo. We also see more androgyny—these kids were exposed to nuanced and complicated gender identities and sexualities through pop stars such as David Bowie and Annie Lennox. They had sexual images permeating the mainstream culture. They saw gay characters on TV and further expanded notions of gender and sexuality.

What this means about long-term relationships: Pluto is at home in the sign of Scorpio, marking this generation as passionate, intense, and wary of being hurt. These folks crave a depth of connection when it comes to partnership.

PLUTO IN SAGITTARIUS (1995–2008)

This placement also occurred between 1746 and 1762. People born during these periods were brought up with paradoxical understandings of the world. On the one hand, these were times of prosperity; on the other hand, political tensions were reaching breaking points. In the case of this most recent era, the oppressed and poor were becoming more and more impatient with the ruling class. There was an increased awareness of the need for change, and these people were prone to being interested in political change and revolution. These people were excellent at inspiring others with their charismatic energetic personalities. There was an expansion of gender roles and norms, and a burgeoning acceptance of different gender presentations. Social media and self-publishing became more available, making it possible for a whole range of formerly disenfranchised folks to bypass traditional gatekeepers and have their voices heard.

What this means about long-term relationships: While this placement intensified the need for personal freedom, it also deepened these people's capacity to share their lives. Amidst war and growing economic inequality, these people come together passionately.

PLUTO IN CAPRICORN (2008–2024)

The Boston Massacre, the Boston Tea Party, the American Revolution, and the signing of the Declaration of Independence all occurred during the prior Pluto in Capricorn phase (1762 to 1778). This current generation will undo a lot of the restrictions that were established during Pluto in Sagittarius—particularly as it relates to lack of privacy and corporate control. They will be highly committed to change, as well as sometimes cynical about the state of the world. They will approach the task of improving the world with grim determination. They will be serious, be dedicated to their causes, have rock-solid morals and ambitions, and use frameworks of oppression to their advantage. They will also embody power as opposed to preaching or lecturing about it. These people may place practical or external matters in higher esteem than personal ones. They will be very capable, but they may be ruthless.

What this means about long-term relationships: People in this generation will be capable of great emotional maturity. They will redefine family and are likely to choose to parent later in life.

PLUTO THROUGH THE HOUSES

PLUTO IN THE FIRST HOUSE

People with this placement tend to have an intense way of presenting themselves and are likely to try to control how others see them. And while they ultimately want to be seen and supported—they can't always tolerate either. They may be secretive or compulsively honest—or vacillate between those extremes. These folks often find themselves in very intense relationships, and that intensity can either alienate others or draw them in. They tend to be either very sexual or asexual. When shit gets real, their capacity to show up for others runs deep.

PLUTO IN THE SECOND HOUSE

These people are inclined to experience power struggles around their resources or to have an intense relationship to money and obligation. They equate cash with control and need to be careful not to develop resentment toward their partners on this topic. The more they can take responsibility for what they have, need, and believe, the greater sense of flow and collaboration they will have with their partners. If they place too much emphasis on money or on receiving and giving material gifts, they may feel like there are strings attached.

PLUTO IN THE THIRD HOUSE

When people have Pluto in the third house, they use communication as a means to power. They may find themselves omitting or withholding information or using past confidences against their partners when things go sideways. Their thinking can be deep and penetrating, which, when applied creatively, gives them tremendous insight for working through ideas and coming to authentic resolution. When applied negatively, their thinking runs the risk of being destructive, defensive, and mean.

PLUTO IN THE FOURTH HOUSE

People who have this placement often have abandonment issues—sometimes they even feel scared of being alone in their homes. Their drive toward creating families with others is really compelling, and they are inclined to hold on tight once they've determined that someone makes them feel secure. They can spoil the people they love as a way to compensate for resentments, but their willingness to stick around for their partners through difficult periods often allows them to transform pain into growth experiences.

PLUTO IN THE FIFTH HOUSE

These folks have very strong feelings about having biological children—either for or against. This is the house of creativity and the arts, so they may be driven to have a creative life wherein they birth projects, rather than babies. These folks need a great deal of attention, but not just any attention will do. If they're shown love in a way that doesn't feel like love to them, it can really hurt their feelings. Sex for them can be either the realm of power struggles or a way to build intimacy and trust; but having a sense of sexual agency is important if they're going to achieve long-term physical satisfaction with their partners.

PLUTO IN THE SIXTH HOUSE

These people can get so fixated on the responsibilities they hold in relationships that they may forget they have a choice—or forget how to check in as to whether it's working. Those with this placement need to have healthy personal boundaries so that they don't martyr themselves for their partners and then resent their partners for it. On the bright side, they're capable of moving mountains in their lives and know how to stick around for the long haul.

PLUTO IN THE SEVENTH HOUSE

Quite obsessive in their drive toward partnership, these folks can rush into commitments before the other person has been fully vetted. This can lead to relationships that don't have the strongest foundations. These people can be frightened of being alone, but they also need a great deal of time to themselves. They feel that transformation and growth are inherent to any long-term relationship, and that can either empower them to work through difficult cycles or incline them to stay in relationships where resentment and power struggles are disproportionately active.

PLUTO IN THE EIGHTH HOUSE

This is the natural placement for Pluto, so these people will often struggle with resentment and have a hard time talking about the roots of their problems, although that is exactly what they must learn to do. This is also the house of shared resources, and there's often an intensity around financial planning within partnerships. Sex is complicated for these folks; they're inclined to have periods when their relationships to their own bodies are either intensified or totally de-emphasized. When power struggles build up, or they feel disrespected, sex is the first thing to go. They often have strong feelings about dying and old age; it's important that they choose partners with whom they feel they can grow old and face death.

PLUTO IN THE NINTH HOUSE

Persistent about seeking truth, these folks are driven to get to the bottom of things. They can be quite dogmatic about their ideas of right and wrong, and they tend to have really strong feelings about religion, higher education, and other societal institutions. They have deep and penetrating minds, but they're not inclined to be great listeners, per se. It's important that these people cultivate greater flexibility when it comes to what their partners say and believe and take greater responsibility for their tone of voice when things get heated. Adventure and spontaneity are also quite intense for them.

PLUTO IN THE TENTH HOUSE

These people are incredibly ambitious and have a feeling that they're destined for something big. Because they see career as a measure of their self-worth, they can either self-sabotage or place a great amount of emphasis on it. Similarly, they may either hide behind their relationships or disproportionately prioritize ambition over partnership. People with this placement were generally raised by a parent who abandoned their own career to raise them—or abandoned them to pursue their careers. Either way, this can yield some defensiveness in how they prioritize their goals. Allowing their partners to help and support them is key.

PLUTO IN THE ELEVENTH HOUSE

These people crave a sense of belonging, and being a part of a community or a group of friends can be a source of great pain or healing. They may experience the type of power struggles with friends that are more frequently associated with partnerships. Therefore, it's important that their partners support them in being invested in their platonic relationships. That said, they may have intense reactions to their partners' friends and have a hard time showing up for their social connections. When they don't have friends or community, the risk is that they will place all of their needs upon their primary relationships.

PLUTO IN THE TWELFTH HOUSE

These folks tend to bottle up or hide away their most intense emotions, which can make them a bit passive-aggressive or manipulative in efforts to evade owning their drive to power. This can lead to self-destructive conduct or choosing partners who express intensity so that they don't have to. They need to learn to take greater responsibility for their choices and self-care. Their capacity to transform and grow is very great once they make the decision that they're going to do the work. They have a deep capacity for healing and for confronting their own psychology.

ACKNOWLEDGMENTS

We'd like to thank Kari Stuart at ICM for her support and belief in this project; our editors, Kaitlin Ketchum and Ashley Pierce, for their enthusiasm and dedication to making it shine; our graphic designer, Annie Marino, for patiently working through multiple iterations with us; and the whole team at Ten Speed Press for their work to get it out into the world. Thanks also to Joel Burden for adding color and life to this book, and Annabel Gat for her wisdom and support.

FROM JESSICA LANYADOO Thanks to my beloved forever fiancé, Anders; Nikki Sacchi for all of her support and mentorship over the years; and my astrology community both IRL and online for being fabulous heady weirdos down here on Earth with me. I also want to extend my deepest thanks to every person who has met with me for astrology consultations; you have trusted me with your heart and for that I am ever so grateful.

FROM T. GREENAWAY Big thanks to Justin, Marlow, and the rest of my family. And to everyone at the NOTTO for the invaluable companionship.

ABOUT THE AUTHORS

JESSICA LANYADOO has met with thousands of clients in the past two decades. She is an internationally respected astrologer and psychic medium, with fans and clients across the globe. Listen to her weekly show, *Ghost of a Podcast*, read her horoscopes, and use the free birth chart generator on her website at lovelanyadoo.com.

T. GREENAWAY is a journalist and editor whose work has appeared in the *New York Times*, NBC News, NPR.org, the *Guardian*, *Food & Wine*, and *Mother Jones*, among other places.

INDEX

Published in the United States by Ten Speed Press, an imprint
of Random House, a division of Penguin Random House LLC,
New York.
www.tenspeed.com

Ten Speed Press and the Ten Speed Press colophon are
registered trademarks of Penguin Random House LLC.

Library of Congress Cataloging-in-Publication Data is on file
with the publisher.

Trade Paperback ISBN: 978-1-9848-5624-1
eBook ISBN: 978-1-9848-5625-8

Printed in China

Design by Annie Marino

10 9 8 7 6 5 4 3

First Edition

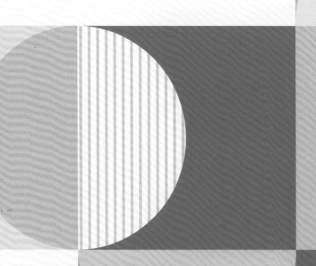